INSPIRATIONAL GUIDE
FOR THE
IMPLEMENTATION OF PRME:

Placing sustainability at the heart of management education

PRME Principles for Responsible Management Education

Routledge
Taylor & Francis Group

LONDON AND NEW YORK

Principles for Responsible
Management Education

Foundation for the
Global Compact

First publishing 2012 by GSE Research Limited

Published 2017 by Routledge
2 Park Square, Milton Park, Abingdon, Oxon OX14 4RN
711 Third Avenue, New York, NY 10017, USA

Routledge is an imprint of the Taylor & Francis Group, an informa business

Typeset in India by OKS Prepress Services, Chennai.

ISBN 978-1-909201-01-9 (pbk)

ACKNOWLEDGEMENTS

Co-editors:

Manuel Escudero (Chair)
Laura Albareda
Jose M. Alcaraz
Giselle Weybrecht
Merrill Csuri

Commissioned by the PRME Secretariat
Jonas Haertle (Head)

Schools that submitted case stories for the Inspirational Guide were invited based upon their submission of a PRME Sharing Information on Progress (SIP) report, active engagement in a PRME project or working group, or in their capacity as host of a regional PRME meeting. We would like to thank all contributors to the case stories included in this Guide, whose details are listed in Appendix 3.

PRME Principles for Responsible Management Education

ABOUT PRME

The Principles for Responsible Management Education (PRME) is a United Nations Global Compact sponsored initiative with the mission to inspire and champion responsible management education, research and thought leadership globally. The Six Principles of PRME are inspired by internationally accepted values, such as the Ten Principles of the United Nations Global Compact. They seek to establish a process of continuous improvement among institutions of management education in order to develop a new generation of business leaders capable of managing the complex challenges faced by business and society in the 21st century. Currently, over 450 signatories have joined PRME, representing approximately 80 countries. PRME's Steering Committee is comprised of global and specialised associations, including AACSB International (The Association to Advance Collegiate Schools of Business), the Graduate Management Admission Council (GMAC), the European Foundation for Management Development (EFMD), the Association of MBAs (AMBA), the Association of African Business Schools (AABS), the Association of Asia-Pacific Business Schools (AAPBS), CEEMAN (Central and East European Management Development Association), CLADEA (the Latin American Council of Management Schools), EABIS (The Academy of Business in Society), the Globally Responsible Leadership Initiative (GRLI), and Net Impact.
For more information, please visit www.unprme.org.

The *Inspirational Guide for the Implementation of PRME* was launched in June 2012 at the 3rd Global Forum for Responsible Management Education, the official platform for management-related Higher Education Institutions (HEIs) at the United Nations Conference on Sustainable Development (Rio+20) and the United Nations Global Compact Rio+20 Corporate Sustainability Forum. Marking the 20th anniversary of the 1992 United Nations Conference on Environment and Development (UNCED) in Rio de Janeiro, Brazil, the Rio+20 Earth Summit brought the world together in Rio once again to discuss and decide how to accelerate action for a healthier, more equitable and prosperous world for all; it provided a timely opportunity to plan for the future we want.

For more information, please visit: www.unprme.org/global-forum, www.compact4rio.org and www.uncsd2012.org.

TABLE OF CONTENTS

How to engage students with PRME

SECTION 6. MANAGING AND CONSOLIDATING PRME EFFORTS

How to translate PRME integration/adoption achievements into indicators and other measures for the purpose of evaluating progress

How to successfully report on PRME integration/adoption

Moving forward – What is the role of business in society?

APPENDICES

INTRODUCTION TO THE INSPIRATIONAL GUIDE

Since the inception of the United Nations Global Compact sponsored initiative Principles for Responsible Management Education (PRME) in 2007, there has been increased debate over how to adapt management education to best meet the demands of the 21st century business environment. While consensus has been reached by the majority of globally focused management education institutions that sustainability[1] must be incorporated into management education curricula, the relevant question is no longer why management education should change, but **how?**

PRME has grown to include over 400 signatories that represent a truly global spread of many of the most advanced and consolidated management schools and higher education institutions (HEIs). PRME offers a framework for change through adoption of the Principles, regular submission of Sharing Information on Progress (SIP) reports, engagement in PRME Working Groups and projects, and participation in regional and global meetings, such as the PRME Global Fora.

Although the PRME initiative is set to increase to 1,000 signatories by 2015, it is equally important for PRME to cultivate actively engaged participants. Therefore, the next step is for current participants to transition from a global learning community to an action community. For this purpose, the PRME Secretariat invited a small group of experts to coordinate an "Inspirational Guide for the Implementation of PRME" to be presented at the 3rd Global Forum for Responsible Management Education, the official platform for management-related Higher Education Institutions (HEIs) at both the Global Compact Rio+20 Corporate Sustainability Forum and the UN Conference on Sustainable Development – Rio+20 in June 2012 in Rio de Janeiro. The Guide intends to answer the most frequently asked

---

[1] Across the PRME community, different concepts are used; most frequently are corporate (social) responsibility, responsible leadership, and sustainable value for business and society.

questions concerning the implementation of PRME by highlighting real world examples from the most engaged signatories.

The exercise has proven successful, and this publication features 63 case stories from 47 institutions, representing 25 countries across Asia, Oceania, the Americas, Europe, the Middle East and Africa. They are the real actors in this effort, and their stories are truly inspirational. Their experiences are classified into six sections, which address the Six Principles of PRME (Purpose, Values, Method, Research, Partnership, and Dialogue) as well as important related aspects, such as how to get started, how to successfully report on PRME adoption, and so on.

The full richness of experiences set forth in this Guide is captured only by reading the wealth of innovative practices found in each case. Although each individual case presents a unique path of progress, several key strategic dimensions are found throughout. The introduction to each of the six sections provides a detailed synopsis of those relevant findings. Overall, progress in implementing PRME is evident across several distinctive areas:

- The adoption of PRME has served as the trigger for innovative organisational change within schools, and PRME is being implemented in a majority of cases with a systemic approach.
- Change in curricula is seen as a transformative effort with respect to content of different disciplines.
- Though not holistically implemented, this change in content encompasses two broad areas related to sustainability. On the one hand, ethics-related content has been incorporated into most subjects, and case studies with sustainability content are being widely developed and used. On the other hand, global sustainability issues (Millennium Development Goals, issues on poverty, human rights, anti-corruption, gender equality, labour standards, climate change, resource scarcity, etc.) have been included in a wide variety of courses.
- The process of embedding sustainability issues in the core of management education is leading to increased exploration of new learning methods and environments that are more suitable for teaching these complex issues, by addressing them not only in the classroom, but also through direct experience.
- There are multiple organisational efforts devoted to promoting research and publication of sustainability-related topics.

- Further, management schools that have started this transformation are also establishing a great variety of partnerships with stakeholders, including businesses, non-governmental organisations (NGOs), local communities, other management schools, and other schools and departments within their own universities. Most importantly, new co-creation processes are emerging as partnerships with students are becoming deeper and more dynamic.
- Finally, continuous improvement in reporting has resulted in greater transparency and accountability, and thus increased reputation.

While it is important to extract lessons from these case stories, it is equally important to reflect on the overall messages. The emerging picture highlights the important changes already taking place across management education today, the role of PRME in effecting such change, and also that additional progress is needed. The six following findings and recommendations elaborate on this wider narrative.

1. The implementation of sustainability values results in a holistic process of change

A consistent and comprehensive insertion of sustainability values at the core of management education results in a very dynamic process of change. It means a truly interrelated change on many fronts, as changes in one aspect bring forth changes in another. Thus, the decision to implement PRME leads to a gradual mobilisation of faculty, both in terms of curriculum innovation and interdisciplinary collaboration. The call to integrate sustainability at the core of the school impacts on the culture and behaviour of the school itself, through a number of projects of extracurricular transformations. This integration, in turn, implies the exploration of new learning outcomes and environments, particularly in experiential and service-learning. The result is closer, more collaborative partnership and dialogue with a wide array of stakeholders, primarily with the business community, but also with alumni, students, and other schools within the university, as well as with NGOs, public authorities and local communities.

2. The role of PRME as a catalyst for change in management education

PRME is proving to be an effective framework that fosters change at the school level and beyond. Several clear aspects can be distinguished according to the most frequent testimonies of the schools that have contributed to this publication, and are divided below into internal and external benefits.

Internally, adoption of PRME:

- Complements the mission of the school and/or reinforces existing values.
- Challenges the school to reframe conversations, thereby helping it to stay relevant and up to date.
- Provides a framework for systemic change and helps secure support and bolster coordination.

Externally, adoption of PRME:

- Increases visibility and lends credibility to the integration of sustainability issues into the strategy of the school.
- Provides access to a robust learning community that, through benchmarking, inspirational modelling and direct collaboration with other management schools, serves as a valuable support system.
- Facilitates dialogue and partnership with external stakeholders.

3. Curriculum change and the transformation of management education disciplines

There are many telling examples of how management schools and their faculty are integrating sustainability content into their courses, but in this area, the transformation is just starting. The task to achieve a substantial change in content adaptation of traditional business disciplines (e.g. business environment, strategy, accounting, finance, management control, marketing, human resources/HHRR, organisational behaviour, operations and logistics or information systems) is still in its first stages. For many, a pragmatic and realistic approach is to gradually introduce complementary sustainability-related topics and case studies as well as to introduce the practice of reviewing the curriculum on a temporal basis in order to create a process of continuous improvement.

Moreover, management schools "walking the path" of sustainability are, in practice, broadening the narrower concept of sustainability related to environmental, social and governance concerns of the company to one that includes the concerns of global sustainable development and potential solutions from social innovation and entrepreneurship. This has important implications for how to transform management education curricula, not only within the scope and content of existing disciplines, but also by incorporating new ones.

This challenge provides the opportunity for the PRME community, as a catalyst for change, to support the emergence of new platforms and projects that incentivise content transformation, both for existing and new issue areas and disciplines. The PRME Working Groups on Anti-Corruption, Poverty, and Gender Equality serve as humble beginnings for the broad work to be done.

4. The challenge of sustainability research

Another clear challenge emerging from the overall picture portrayed in this publication is related to sustainability research. In spite of the important progress made by many management schools, such research will remain a voluntaristic goal until top academic journals offer broader recognition to sustainability topics as a first category research subject. This is because research publication in A and B Journals is a crucial issue both for schools and their rankings, and for the career prospects of faculty members.

Beyond this, securing more institutional facilities (at the industry level) for the publication of quality sustainability research is the basis of persuading traditional business disciplines to adapt their content to the new paradigm of sustainability. The "theory of the firm" has to be revisited and reformulated, the "theory of the agency" has to be reviewed in the light of the current, dramatic excesses it has brought about and, in general, new management theories based on sustainability parameters need the space to emerge and gain academic legitimacy. None of this will be possible without a change in the importance given to this new brand of research by existing top-ranked academic journals.

PRME, as a community of not only individual management schools, but also a relevant share of the most important management-related international associations, should expand its role as a powerful advocate for this much needed change.

5. The challenge of experiential learning

The cases featured in this Guide demonstrate the evolution of management school learning environments towards a "new frontier" of experiential learning. While case studies, simulations and teamwork in the classroom remain important pillars of management education, responsible leadership implies a closer relationship with the business community.

In spite of the fact that many management schools are exploring these alternatives, experiential learning is very resource-intensive, demands an increasing array of partnerships, usually at an international scale, and therefore remains in its infancy.

PRME, as a learning community, could aid this process. The success of issue-specific work undertaken by existing PRME working groups and projects should encourage the establishment of new projects on teaching methodologies, such as "clearing house" platforms that support the development and potential assessment of international experiential learning. Additionally, the regional PRME meetings that took place in 2011 have laid the groundwork for the organisation of regional PRME chapters, which should be utilised to incentivise the consolidation of efforts and development of mutually beneficial relationships.

6. Moving from a learning community to a collective action platform

Making the Principles of PRME central to management education and academic activities may require management schools and faculty to invest (or divert) significant resources (time, money, etc.) in order to embed this new set of values (Principle 2), experiment with new and more impactful educational frameworks (Principle 3), undertake conceptual and empirical research (Principle 4), engage with and learn from managers (Principle 5), and establish a constant dialogue with stakeholders (Principle 6), that results in a sustainability-oriented business view that penetrates through to the broader society (Principle 1).

As the Guide shows, progressive and promising work is under way, and innovative solutions are already being implemented by individual PRME signatories. Since PRME, as an initiative, aims to be not only a learning community but a shaper of global management education, it is clear that, to have a truly transformative effect, a quantum leap is needed. As the case stories show, PRME signatories are now entering into the space of collective action, such as by hosting joint conferences and developing regional PRME chapters that foster growth and collaboration between schools. With the right incentives and enabling environments, this will, over time, change not only the paradigm of management education but also make significant and lasting contributions on the global sustainability agenda.

INTRODUCTION

The Principles for Responsible Management Education (PRME) initiative emerged at a time when management schools had started looking for new horizons and paradigms to adapt management education to meet the complex demands of the 21st century global economy.

The combination of two factors – the timely inception of PRME and the traction generated by the initiative itself – help to explain the most important evidence gathered in this Guide: Change is already happening, and many management schools are already "walking the talk" of sustainability. In fact, there are so many examples in this publication that the evidence should not be taken as merely anecdotal.

While this progress is robust, it takes many shapes and forms. Indeed, the variety of experiences is vast. However, patterns can be ascertained in the first "moment" of implementation. As featured in this section, when the decision to adopt sustainability as a core tenet of a management school is taken, it triggers changes at all levels of the organisation. The case stories herein demonstrate that the obstacles to embracing PRME are related not as much to the adoption of the Principles, but more to the integration of new ideas into the education process.

By the launch of PRME in 2007, corporate social responsibility and sustainability concerns, as growing international trends in the corporate world, had already won the battle of ideas, and many management schools were becoming acquainted with these values. In some instances, related values were already part of the mission of the school, while others had a long-standing tradition of employing a humanistic approach to education. These approaches were immediately transferable to the new global paradigm.

The problem was (and is), rather, **how to upgrade those values so that they become central drivers of the activities of the school**. The case stories in this section elaborate several inspiring practices, which are noted in the following paragraphs.

"Making the implicit explicit" is probably the most important element. A first lesson to be learnt from this section is that it is not enough to simply include the Principles, or similar aspirations, in the mission and vision of the school. This can be an initial advantage, but there is a long stretch between this "theoretical" recognition and the implementation of the Principles in a consistent way at all levels, including curriculum, research efforts, methodological approaches and organisational culture. Transforming the "implicit" values into "explicit" practices requires an altogether new emphasis – a refocusing of priorities, an effective buy in by all actors, and analysis of required organisational change.

The Principles of the PRME initiative are usually first accepted by a few actors, and there are some telling examples on how to transform that initial limited acceptance into an active consensus and approval of the Principles as drivers for action by all internal stakeholders: administrators, faculty and students. Here, the use of top-down and bottom-up approaches, through both formal and informal strategies, can be effective.

Very little progress is achieved without true conviction on the part of the leadership of the school, which has the crucial role of turning a theoretical acceptance of the Principles into a driver for organisational and educational change. This is because the adaptation of a management school to place sustainability at the core of its teaching, research, pedagogy and culture cannot be achieved without a systemic approach. And, therefore, the need for new structures, incentives and funding cannot be provided without decisions taken by leadership. Thus, a top-down strategy is of critical importance.

However, it is equally important to achieve active buy in from faculty, which is a complex undertaking. The overriding element, as shown in some cases, is to present and treat PRME as an inclusive and voluntary initiative and to establish a strategy of voluntary and incremental buy in by drawing on the capabilities and work of faculty leaders. One of the most inspiring strategies for this increased acceptance by faculty is to couple sustainability with related concepts and trends in management education that are already accepted, such as innovation or social entrepreneurship.

Students are another very important part of the equation. Provided that progress along the path of sustainability is based on a systemic approach, unleashing the potential of students is essential. There are many amazing examples, and several case stories in this section highlight students as the main initiators of very relevant transformative processes towards integration of sustainability in their schools.

According to the case stories, many schools are intent on achieving a specific mode of curriculum change. Although this is a gradual process, the overall approach to holistic curriculum change is not by "adding on" courses (e.g., the introduction of some isolated electives), but by embedding sustainability approaches in all disciplines.

Finally, a clear outcome of the cases featured in this section is that the implementation of PRME inspires not only curriculum change and new horizons for research, but also the transformation of the organisational culture, aligning the values and concepts that are taught and researched with the actions of the institution itself.

Among all the case stories, the effect of PRME on the strategy and activities of management schools can be seen in key strategic dimensions, such as:

1. Change towards sustainability in many management schools is already happening, and many schools are already walking the talk.
2. The obstacles to embrace PRME are not with accepting the Principles, but in implementing them.
3. Transforming the implicit values into explicit practices requires an altogether new emphasis – a refocusing of priorities, an effective buy in by all actors, and analysis of required organisational change.
4. Using top-down and bottom-up approaches, through both formal and informal strategies is important.
5. The role of the leadership of the school in turning a theoretical acceptance of the Principles into a driver for organisational and educational change is crucial.
6. It is important to achieve active buy in from faculty, which is a complex undertaking.
7. One strategy for increasing acceptance of sustainability concerns by faculty is to couple sustainability with related concepts and trends in management education that are already accepted, e.g., innovation or social entrepreneurship.
8. Students are a very important part of the equation; unleashing their potential is essential.
9. The overall approach to holistic curriculum change is by embedding sustainability approaches in all disciplines.
10. Implementation of PRME also inspires the transformation of the organisational culture of the institution itself.

THE BUYING IN ARGUMENT: HOW PRME CAN BE USED TO ENHANCE COMPETITIVE ADVANTAGE

Australian School of Business, University of New South Wales, Sydney, Australia

MAKING THE IMPLICIT EXPLICIT

Introduction

 Consistently ranked among the top business schools in Australia, the Australian School of Business (ASB) at the University of New South Wales is located in Sydney, Australia. Boasting over 57,000 alumni, the ASB is host to the Australian Graduate School of Management (AGSM) and 8 disciplinary schools (Accounting, Economics, Banking & Finance, Information Systems, Marketing, Management, Risk & Actuarial, and Taxation & Business Law), 12 research centres and institutions, 9 affiliated research centres, 13,948 students (undergraduate and postgraduate), 260 academics and researchers, and 177 professional and technical staff.

Challenges

As the title of this case study suggests, often the largest challenge of any institution is simply communicating its values effectively. The ASB seeks like-minded and strategic partnerships that provide opportunity for meaningful interaction, and the Principles for Responsible Management Education (PRME) initiative provides for such a partnership. We recognise that our ongoing challenge is to build on the momentum created by our PRME affiliation and constantly aim to apply principles of sustainability, ethics and social responsibility across all of ASB's learning and teaching responsibilities, thus making the implicit principles much more explicit.

> Increasingly, managers and future professionals are challenged to reconsider how value is created – both tangible value and intangible value, and how it can be valued by markets. The concept of risk management, including human capital risk management, has never been more important to corporations and to society. The Principles for Responsible Management Education are entirely consistent with the United Nations-supported Principles for Responsible Investment, both of which form a cornerstone of our teaching and learning. Together, they help us to frame our learning journey for our students, challenging them to reconsider questions about value, risk and sustainability, in order to give them the skills and confidence to challenge the status quo in their professional business lives.
>
> *Dr Loretta O'Donnell, Associate Dean (Education),*
> *Australian School of Business, University of New South Wales*

Actions taken

Beginning in January 2011, we held undergraduate student orientation workshops that highlighted PRME as part of the "first-year experience". Our PRME affiliation was directly linked to the ASB "graduate attribute" (i.e., qualities and skills we expect our students to develop by the end of their degree) of "social, ethical and global perspectives".

From 2012, ASB's PRME membership and engagement will be incorporated into our partnership listings as well as marketing materials for undergraduates and postgraduates. Our partners in educational programs include top tier universities in China, Korea, Japan, India with more to come. These partnership agreements will make explicit the fact that our curricula reflect the Principles espoused by the PRME initiative and so attract students who seek to develop the capability to implement these Principles, nationally and internationally.

The PRME logo has also been placed in additional marketing and promotional materials alongside other ASB strategic partnerships and affiliations such as Universitas 21, G08, and EQUIS. In doing so we seek to establish a clear narrative about the ASB's values, connectedness and position as educators and change agents. We view the implementation of

PRME in our curriculum as one key initiative in our journey to prepare our students to operate in a business environment that requires new solutions to new problems.

Results

We hosted the 1st Australia/New Zealand PRME Forum in July 2011, bringing together business leaders, academic leaders and faculty from 25 universities across Australia and New Zealand. This has accelerated opportunities for principles-based collaborative research, teaching and learning across our region.

New programmes, such as our Masters of International Business, and our revised Masters of Commerce, use PRME as a core design principle.

In April 2012, we hosted final year students from our local network schools in Sydney. The first theme they learned was that ASB stands for ethical, sustainable business practices. This is reinforced in our marketing material, in our curriculum design, and in our partnership arrangements.

Our Head of School of Finance, Associate Jerry Parwarda, illustrates the Principles in his observations on the obligations of the finance industry, which highlight the importance of ethical practices as a guiding force: http://www.youtube.com/watch?v=Nw2vcZrdwa8&feature=youtube_gdata_player

Why PRME is/was important

- The PRME initiative offers a tangible example of our ASB graduate attribute of social, ethical and global perspectives.
- The PRME initiative offers avenues for expanded research, increased student engagement, and expansion of like-minded networks around the world.
- It links with the United Nations-backed Principles for Responsible Investment (PRI) to provide a signpost for our students and staff to help develop creative responses to difficult business conditions.

Deusto Business School, University of Deusto, Madrid, Bilbao, San Sebastián, Spain

TURNING CORPORATE SUSTAINABILITY AND RESPONSIBILITY INTO A CORE COMPETITIVE ADVANTAGE

Introduction

Deusto Business School (DBS) was founded on a vision and a vocation to create one of the best business schools for management education in Spain and internationally. Its aim is to become a global reference, with the best international standards in all areas of management emphasising three key dimensions: sustainability, digital strategy, and innovation/entrepreneurship.

The school has a staff of nearly 200 professors and researchers and 270 visiting professors. Over 1,700 undergraduates are enrolled in its programmes and 1,000 students annually are studying for its master's degrees, open programmes and in-company programmes. With two campuses in Bilbao and San Sebastian and new facilities in Madrid, Deusto Business School focuses on innovation and staying abreast of the latest trends in management education and is firmly committed to meeting the demands of the world's changing social, environmental and economic needs in the 21st century. Our reputation is based on nearly 100 years of widely acclaimed quality education and teaching excellence, and on the achievements of thousands of successful business executives who have studied at the School.

Challenges

Four years ago, DBS launched a global project to adapt the School to the changing conditions in international business education. DBS's main commitment is to honour its promise to provide "business education to serve the world".

DBS has defined its strategic priorities in terms of three basic dimensions:

1. Sustainability
2. Digital strategy
3. Innovation and entrepreneurship.

In April 2010, the general director of DBS proposed to adopt the Principles for Responsible Management Education (PRME) as the framework for the introduction of its sustainability strategy. The proposal was approved by DBS's Faculty Executive Committee as a means to place the School in a leading position in the field of corporate sustainability.

PRME was, therefore, chosen as the strategic framework of DBS's new development, with sustainability as our core identity value, thus differentiating us from others both in the national and international arena.

Our adoption of PRME was based on a top-down and bottom-up policy. While the initial decision was proposed by the leadership of the School, faculty meetings were organised in June 2010 to engage all departments (finance and accounting, international business, marketing, strategy, organisational behaviour, and operations) in an internal debate. In addition, we invited international experts in responsible management education to take part in the discussion. As a result of the debate, the faculty committed itself to adopting PRME.

Thus, PRME lent clarity to the strategic vision of DBS to help businesses take account of it in long-term decision making, to encourage the engagement of, and dialogue with, stakeholders, and to introduce accountability policies and disclosure and transparency practices.

> We aim to attract participants and executives who want to be competent, committed, conscious and compassionate professionals and leaders.
> *Laura Albareda, Assistant Professor of Sustainability Strategy,*
> *Deusto Business School*

Actions taken

We have developed the three dimensions (sustainability, digital strategy, and innovation/entrepreneurship) in order to provide the School with a competitive advantage. They are now the pivotal elements in the design of the School's future, its purpose, its values and mission, programmes, teaching methodologies, educational guidelines and research centres.

How we implemented the strategy

1. We began by designing sustainability courses and introducing them into the majority of our programmes (e.g., the multinational MBA, the executive MBA, and the programme for leadership development). In order to initiate the new strategy, we invited visiting professors and leading practitioners in the area of sustainable business, corporate sustainability and responsibility, and directors of corporate social responsibility departments in global multinational companies to participate in the teaching of our sustainability modules.

2. Next, we adopted a faculty development programme on sustainability, with specialised seminars for faculty development in the area of sustainability in each of our departments. As a result, a good number of professors in different departments have begun to develop specific syllabi including corporate sustainability issues, specifically in relation to strategy, finance and accounting, marketing and human resources and operations.

3. The process has spilled over to our graduate and pre-experiential postgraduate programmes, with the introduction of an extensive, compulsory course on sustainability.

4. We have adopted a vigorous recruitment policy to hire international faculty members specialised in teaching and research in the field of corporate social responsibility and corporate sustainability. We have also inaugurated an ambitious programme of visiting professors.

5. We are currently building a global reference interdepartmental centre for sustainable business, employing a team of dedicated faculty members and researchers who are leading experts in their respective fields, as well as distinguished researchers, senior fellows and fellows.

6. We have created the DBS PRME Committee, composed of administrators, faculty members and students, and responsible for editing and publishing the DBS Sharing Information on Progress (SIP) report.

7. With these foundation stones in place, we are now progressing towards the next level: the complete integration of sustainability in the curriculum of our Deusto full-time MBA, introducing sustainability as an integral, transversal and multidisciplinary component. For this programme, to be launched next year, we have created a new educational framework, based on service learning of the participants as corporate conflict-solving officers, a project-based learning process and embedded workshops on critical thinking and reflective leadership, which will enhance the learning experiences for responsible leadership.

> Today the race to the top in business education is wide open. Those who have chosen sustainability as the cornerstone for training future leaders and managers hold a winning card and enjoy a clear innovative and competitive edge because they understand that sustainability is the most important component of the successful and competitive company in today's world
> *Manuel Escudero, Director General, Deusto Business School*

Results

Adopting sustainability as a competitive market advantage is already bearing fruit, and we have achieved significant results in this short period of implementation:

- The incorporation of global social responsibility values, strategies and tools in postgraduate and executive programmes taught by academic experts and global practitioners.
- In-company programmes and projects in sustainable business.

With our singular vision of the future of business education at the core of our master's, MBAs and open programmes, as well as our in-company programmes, our earlier expectations are being confirmed, and our strategic positioning is proving successful: companies and students alike are attracted to our distinguishing characteristic.

Why PRME is/was important

- It has been the motivating force for leading the entire faculty towards responsible management education and has provided a better understanding for the need of integrating triple bottom line issues in functional management areas.
- The PRME initiative has established the guidelines for our faculty recruitment policy.
- The initiative has provided inspiration and acted as a guide, serving as a reference for the design and implementation of the Deusto full-time MBA programme.
- The Principles of the initiative are an essential instrument for designing key performance indicators to monitor and evaluate our programmes and activities.

University of Applied Sciences HTW Chur, Chur, Switzerland

BUILDING A FORMAL INSTITUTIONAL SUPPORT BASE

Introduction

HTW Chur

Hochschule für Technik und Wirtschaft
University of Applied Sciences

Located at the heart of the Alpine region in the capital city of the canton Grisons, the University of Applied Sciences HTW Chur was accredited by the Swiss Federal authorities in 2000. Currently more than 1,600 students are enrolled in a variety of undergraduate and graduate programmes in management, tourism and hospitality, information sciences, ICT and civil engineering, and multimedia production, while 7 applied research institutes are engaged in knowledge and technology transfer.

Challenges

In its highly competitive market environment for higher education, Switzerland offers a wide range of world-level, as well as premium international and national, institutions. Initialised in the late 1990s, on the national level the universities of applied sciences have come of age and have defined their unique value propositions. Against this background, over the past decade HTW Chur has been constantly reframing its position along the topics of entrepreneurship, innovation and, more recently, sustainable development. In addition, its strategic objectives comprise a commitment to delivering superior quality in all its activities, as well as an emphasis on interdisciplinary collaboration.

Looking to the future, in order to ensure continued market penetration for its services, HTW Chur needs to further profile its idiosyncratic competencies. The relevance of responsible management education for achieving this goal has been repeatedly questioned by institutional stakeholders. As a matter of fact, from the beginning of our engagement with the Principles for Responsible Management Education (PRME) in 2009, it has been a great challenge to adequately inform the respective decision makers as well as convince our University's governing body to support this initiative.

Actions taken

From our experience, in the initial phase the Sharing Information on Progress (SIP) reporting exercise has been highly instrumental for gaining momentum in our efforts to implement PRME successfully. While critics would hold that the result is no more than another piece of paper, the process of developing a compact, concise and, at the same time, comprehensive report has been an important organisational learning experience. It outlines how a great variety of academic activities in the area of responsibility and sustainability across all of our faculties have been undertaken in the past. It has served as valuable means to illustrate the manifold initiatives and projects already in place and to demonstrate our University's engagement. As a result, it has become an indispensable document to communicate with our stakeholders about our future aspirations (http://bit.ly/e6zToL).

First-mover positioning along with a group of exclusive universities and business schools from our country is viewed as conducive to high profile learning from mutual exchange of experiences as well as enhancing agenda setting with regards to PRME-related issues. An emerging Swiss network of PRME signatories will be a platform for demonstrating the sincerity of our commitment.

While most of the initial efforts to become signatories of PRME came from a few academic staff, we have seen the continuing growth of an informal network to promote its philosophy in our University. This important pre-condition has helped to set the stage for a broader involvement of all University members and could only have been achieved by committed leadership and perseverance. A major successful step towards the serious implementation of a PRME process has been the installation of an open group of committed faculty and staff. Around 12 members represent all University departments in equal measure (management sciences, tourism and regional sciences, information and engineering sciences, and central services) have elected a steering committee consisting of 4 faculty members. In 2011, this "PRME initiative team HTW Chur" managed to gain formal appreciation from the University's board, including the necessary financial resources for the next three years to continue the roll-out of PRME activities. A mid-term "PRME roadmap for action" and an annual agenda will be concrete means to inform the University about our future activities.

At a different level, a number of public events such as our newly created Forum on Business Ethics are an ongoing platform for profiling our University as a pioneering institution in the area of responsible business and leadership education by highlighting our PRME-related achievements. At the same time, increasing visibility creates attention from the media and, in turn, from potential clients such as business executives, students, research partners, etc. Also, a recent inaugural event to introduce the "Vision 2050 – New Agenda for Business" (a mural based on a publication by the World Business Council for Sustainable Development in 2010) has geared media attention to our University.

> Activate informal networks to promote your case inside your institution and beyond. Always keep looking for potential followers.
>
> *Lutz E. Schlange, Professor of Entrepreneurial Marketing,*
> *University of Applied Sciences HTW Chur*

Results

There has been a continuous increase of academic initiatives dealing with a variety of responsibility and sustainability aspects. In particular, as an early adopter of PRME we have seen our research initiatives in the field of corruption prevention resonate strongly with potential partners from the United Nations Global Compact Network Switzerland. This has triggered a number of activities on University-, national- and international-levels and has since materialised to become a newly established field of research within our management department.

Just recently, a revised version of our code of conduct has reflected the PRME value base in three out of four central value statements for our University: "reflection and communication", "appreciation of partnerships", and "ethical responsibility". As a consequence, our commitment has helped us to shape a clearly defined ethical position and we have been experiencing our respective achievements as conducive to successful recruitment of prospective students.

This in turn helps to sensitise our University's governing body to the potential competitive benefits of our PRME membership.

Why PRME is/was important

- A top-level initiative, PRME has helped us significantly to convey our message as a responsible education institution.
- PRME represents a constant proof of our serious commitment.
- Our PRME initiative at HTW Chur has created a continuous flow of positive news and through this has raised media attention.

Seattle Pacific University School of Business and Economics, Seattle, Washington, United States

PRME ENHANCES COMPETITIVE ADVANTAGE

Introduction

Seattle Pacific University's AACSB (The Association to Advance Collegiate Schools of Business) accredited School of Business and Economics (SBE) offers three undergraduate majors: economics, accounting and business administration; and, three graduate degrees: MBA, master's in information systems management and a master's in social and sustainable business (www.spu.edu/depts/sbe/). SBE selectively admits 100 undergraduate students each year, and there are approximately 175 students enrolled in the master's programmes. SBE's vision of "another way of doing business" is fleshed out by 25 faculty members in the context of a 4,000 student, Christian university.

Challenges

SBE had a desire to develop a distinctive approach to business based on Seattle Pacific University's historic commitment to Christian faith and values. While SBE had always stressed personal integrity and ethics, it was less articulate about theological approaches to business, emerging organisational structures and institutional frameworks.

Actions taken

The key action step was to articulate a distinctive theological approach to doing business that was embedded in the Christian faith tradition with touch points linked to societal trends of rethinking business. In a nutshell, this approach is built on three foundational principles: service, sustainability and support. We understand that the role of business in society is to serve; in particular, business serves society by providing goods and services that enable human flourishing and by providing opportunities for individuals to express aspects of their identity in meaningful and creative work. Business must pursue these purposes subject to the limitations of sustainability. For us, "sustainability" is broadly construed and includes the need to sustain financial, social, communal, and environmental "capital". Finally, business operates alongside a host of other institutions including governments, non-governmental organisations (NGOs), educational institutions and other members of the civil society. Collectively these institutions are to work for the common good, and business must support and enhance the work of other institutions as it pursues its unique contribution to this joint endeavour.

> My advice in order to enhance your institution's competitive advantage is to take a serious look at the inspiration and legitimacy Principles for Responsible Management Education (PRME) can provide your university's curriculum. Issues of sustainability and responsibility in business are no longer nice, optional extras in business but critical factors to business success. PRME, with appropriate levels of support from the top of your organisation and faculty champions, can become a "Trojan horse" for positive change.
>
> *Ross Stewart, Professor of Accounting, Seattle Pacific University,*
> *School of Business and Economics*

Results

The result and benefit of this business philosophy has been the way it infuses SBE's teaching, research and writing. It enabled faculty buy in to occur with the Principles for Responsible Management Education (PRME) initiative and for the Principles in turn to influence SBE's emerging understanding of a richer role for business in society. The curriculum has been enhanced by changes at the graduate level, including the development of a standalone sustainability course and new international business courses focusing on business in the developing world.

At the undergraduate level, SBE has added a series of one-unit spirituality and business courses (many of which focus on creation care and steward-ship management), a new social enterprise concentration (including new courses in social venture, micro-finance and community development) and an entrepreneurship minor. Also, scholarship and research is an important part of SBE's distinctive approach to responsible business. In-house conferences addressing "another way of doing business" have been held to discuss faculty research. In the broader academy, research has been presented and published, and SBE has organised research colloquium with visiting academics engaged in responsible management research. Further, research grants and dedicated funding is available for faculty pursuing such research and for visiting academics to visit SBE and engage in collaborative research with SBE faculty.

Why PRME is/was important

- PRME complements and enhances SBE's existing mission and curriculum.
- The Principles confirm the role of business as a key player in providing solutions to the important issues of poverty, debt, sustainable development, health issues, and employment.
- PRME confirms the global nature and interconnectedness of the world of business.
- PRME confirm the importance of issues such as sustainability, community development, public-private partnerships, micro-finance and social enterprise as being front and centre in the business education agenda.

Cranfield School of Management, Cranfield University,
Bedford, England, United Kingdom

THE CRANFIELD EXPERIENCE

Introduction

Cranfield School of Management is one of five schools that comprise Cranfield University, based just north of London, England. Cranfield is the UK's only wholly postgraduate university. The Management School has been helping individuals and businesses to learn and succeed by transforming knowledge into action, for over 40 years. The School brings together a range of management disciplines through a significant portfolio of activities that includes research and consultancy, postgraduate master's and doctoral programmes, executive education, customised programmes and conferences.

Challenges

At Cranfield School of Management, we pride ourselves on educating the next generation of leaders, and creating thought leaders in academia and business. However, as the world becomes increasingly complex, so too must the skills and values of business and thought leaders. For us, a key challenge is how best to develop future leaders with the right values and skills, and underlying this, identifying what these attributes are. We need to encourage our students and staff to have deep insight into their attitudes and values, allow those to be tested on MBA and other management programmes, and internalise ethical behaviours.

We also recognise that for business schools that lead on such critical issues as sustainability and business ethics, we need to address issues of sustainability, and ethical behaviour, as a School, in our own operations as an employer, a customer, a provider of services and as a neighbour to our local community.

> Academic institutions (like all knowledge-intensive organisations that are highly dependent on autonomous and self-motivating knowledge workers), will have a plurality of interests and perspectives, and differing views. Academic institutions especially need to be careful to avoid any suggestion of the Principles for Responsible Management Education (PRME) initiative as an ideological crusade; but rather to present PRME as a principled response to a business imperative. Whilst the "cafetiere" i.e., top-down leadership and strategic framing/direction has a role, it is also critical to have the "percolator" i.e., the bottom-up, voluntary engagement and commitment of faculty and staff.
>
> *David Grayson, Director, The Doughty Centre for Corporate Responsibility, Cranfield School of Management, Cranfield University*

Actions taken

The Principles for Responsible Management Education (PRME) initiative is helping us to address these challenges, because it has created a vehicle for change, a springboard for action. Having become a PRME signatory, we established a PRME task force chaired by the director/dean of the School. This task force brings together senior faculty and staff including, for example, the directors of the MBA course, and the finance director who is in charge of the School's own sustainability plan, as well as the research director and the senior professor in charge of faculty continuous professional development. After reviewing PRME in a series of faculty meetings, the task force decided to prioritise the MBA programme, and the School's own sustainability practices. Several new electives have been introduced as well as a requirement for all core MBA courses to consider the implications of PRME for case-pack and course design – including an ethics elective to directly address developing future leaders with the skills for ethical decision making. The School is now undertaking a formal review of the Cranfield MBAs led by an interdisciplinary team of senior and junior faculty, and staff from different parts of the School.

Business schools can provide more opportunities for faculty to meet and share ideas and experiences, and for those that are interested, can create more opportunities for faculty collective learning and discussion. Some faculty might prefer to focus on their own subject discipline in a specialist, perhaps narrow way. This is not necessarily interpreted as opposition or hostility on their part, simply that of personal prioritisation. Positively, more opportunities for faculty collective discourse and holistic learning are provided, and deans must encourage individuals to engage in this.

David Grayson, Director, The Doughty Centre for Corporate Responsibility, Cranfield School of Management, Cranfield University

The task force has supported the formulation of the School's own sustainability plan. Specific initiatives include a book: *Cranfield on Corporate Sustainability* to which more than 30 faculty have contributed; the establishment of a school sustainability task force with four pillars (Environment, Workplace, Marketplace, Community) and a team on each pillar developing targets and measurements; the development of a corporate responsibility and sustainability management theme as part of the School's online Knowledge-Interchange for alumni and other users; and energy-reduction projects.

Results

In December 2011, the School executive reviewed the overall school strategy and formally made it one of our seven strategic priorities to "become a world leading centre for teaching, research and the practice of responsible management and ethics".

Why PRME is/was important

- These issues are likely to become more important in the future for accreditation bodies and potentially for rankings too.
- Our motivation for making the commitment to PRME is first and foremost because we clearly see the need for business, and management schools teaching managers, to have a responsible and sustainable impact on society, and because we want to fulfil our strategy – and preparing responsible managers and leaders is core to our strategy.

EGADE Business School, Tecnológico de Monterrey (ITESM), Monterrey and Mexico City, Mexico

THE FIVE DIMENSIONAL MODEL OF SUSTAINABILITY FOR FIRMS

Introduction

With locations in two world-class cities, Monterrey and Mexico City, the School has built a solid international reputation based on its innovative education model, its teaching and research achievements and the global character of its academic programmes.

Today, the EGADE Business School offers 19 postgraduate business programmes – MBAs, master's and doctoral programmes as well as specialist programmes and executive education for senior business leaders and family business owners.

Our 300-strong national and international faculty team teaches a student body composed of more than 30 nationalities, and our 12,000 alumni are building and transforming businesses and organisations in Mexico, Latin America and across the world.

Challenges

Small and medium-sized enterprises (SMEs) in Mexico face different problems that prevent them from achieving sustainability. The lifespan of an SME in Mexico is three years. In this regard, we find that a model socially, focusing on human and environmental care, makes it easier for SMEs to achieve sustainability. The Principles for Responsible Management Education (PRME) initiative fits properly to that kind of model.

Actions taken

We in EGADE believe that the Principles of PRME regard not just with ethical behaviour, but also with better performance for the firms. Thus our professors and students are encouraged to develop management models that reflect how an ethical behaviour affects in a positive way the performance of the firm. In this sense the humanism and management research chair has developed a model called "The five dimensional model of sustainability for firms" (with MOPSE as its Spanish acronym).

The MOPSE is based on a well-developed theoretical framework of the different approaches available that relate to the concept of entrepreneurial sustainability. In this sense we have developed a five-dimensional analytical diagram presented in systemic form that seeks to be simultaneously constructed from the interior and exterior of the company. These dimensions are seen with a focus on process. They start with the management of the company – defined as total management – and move on to competitiveness, analysis of the relationships and impact the company generates, both within and outside the company, and end with the transparency and communication the company presents to the different stakeholders, as well as to society at large. The model passes through a time variable that moves towards the hoped for entrepreneurial sustainability.

MOPSE takes into account not only the triple bottom line (economic, social and environmental), as the focus of responsible development of the company to society, it also takes into account the stakeholders' responsibility for transparency and accountability in their daily actions.

This model allows the student to review PRME transversely at different levels of the organisation: individual, group and organisational, and also to consider the effects that may be generated from their own actions.

> Our advice is to show both professors and students how responsible and ethical management can create value for business and can make them achieve sustainability. If you can achieve that, the students and the faculty will believe in the management principles, not just as an ethical behaviour, but as an enhancer for performance.
>
> *Consuelo García de la Torre, Professor of Management and Marketing,*
> *EGADE Business School, Tecnológico de Monterrey,*
> *Campus Monterrey Chair researcher "Humanismo y Gestión"*

Results

At this time, the team that developed the MOPSE is engaged in multi-regional research with several universities in Mexico (UNAM, U. Veracruzana, U. Baja California and EGADE), in Colombia, Peru, and also Trinidad and Tobago.

In 2009 we established within EGADE's curricular base a "current label", which is now mandatory for MBAs. This mandatory element sensitises students to the discussion of specific situations on ethics, corporate social responsibility (CSR) and sustainability. The case study methodology is supported by global, regional and local perspectives, where the ethical dilemma is central decision making. At the end of the course, students must develop a case based on real data and present the ethical dilemma, CSR or sustainability. The research by students and teachers supports the consolidation of the initiatives in this regard.

We also, in collaboration with a group of teachers from different countries of Latin America, developed a book to provide a regional perspective. Published in January 2012, we now use it as a compulsory course text.

In this sense, we encourage EGADE's research chairs to develop similar models and programmes around the ideas of business ethics, social responsibility and sustainability. We expect that in a short time, the professors and students involved in such activities can create sufficient enthusiasm throughout the School to engage others in such important themes.

Why PRME is/was important

- The model developed includes the values proposed by PRME.
- We encourage our teachers to develop research and new models based on the Principles of the PRME initiative.
- We interact with businesses managers to understand the dynamics of an organisation and to share best practices.

HOW TO GET STARTED? THE PROCESS OF DECISION MAKING RELATED TO PARTICIPATION IN PRME

Bentley University, Waltham, Massachusetts, United States

HOW TO GET STARTED: MANAGEMENT BY TALKING AROUND

Introduction

Bentley is a business university, combining an advanced business curriculum with a rich and diverse arts and sciences programme to prepare a new kind of business leader – one with the deep technical skills, broad global perspective, and high ethical standards required to make a difference in an ever-changing world.

Located 8 miles west of Boston, Massachusetts, Bentley enrols approximately 4,100 full-time undergraduate, 1,400 graduate (MBA and master's of science programmes), and 30-plus doctoral students, with over 290 full- and 180 part-time faculty. Bentley is accredited by the New England Association of Schools and Colleges, AACSB International and EQUIS.

Challenges

The challenge at Bentley, as with many colleges and universities embarking on any cross-institutional initiative, was to seek out and then build on the dedication and creativity of individual faculty members. The launch of Bentley's Alliance for Ethics and Social Responsibility and our institutional commitment to the Principles for Responsible Management Education (PRME) was based on a four-step process that involved a concerted effort to:

1. build on the research, teaching and institutional service interests of a core group of faculty members;
2. engage the campus community in a series of conversations about the significance of ethics and responsible management education;
3. draw on the capabilities and work of faculty leaders in this area; and
4. embed those practices into programmes and initiatives across campus.

> At the 1st PRME Global Forum I recall a conversation with a dean from a European business school, who was complaining about a finance professor at his institution who criticised the School's commitment to PRME. I laughed as I told him I thought I had the same colleague at Bentley. Instead of beginning with opponents, my experience is to start with those individuals who are already personally committed to PRME's ideals – preaching to the choir if you will – building on their energy and enthusiasm, providing support for their efforts, and linking them with like-minded colleagues in different departments. As a firm believer in the "tipping point", a small group of motivated individuals can generate pockets of commitment that can lead to large-scale institutional change.
>
> *Anthony F. Buono, Professor of Management and Sociology, Founding Director, Bentley Alliance for Ethics and Social Responsibility*

Actions taken

We began the process by **preaching to the choir**, starting with those faculty across the institution who were already committed to PRME's goals, leveraging institutional strengths, drawing on social capital, and creating small wins as a way of building communities of practice. Our Center for Business Ethics was launched in 1976 and Service-Learning Center began in the early 1990s. Drawing on the institutional visibility of these two programmes, we looked for ways to engage faculty members – through discussions of business ethics and civic engagement/leadership – to bring a sense of responsible management to life.

The basic strategy employed can be thought of as **management by "talking around"**, beginning with one-on-one conversations with key players across campus, and gradually building to one-on-two, one-on-three, two-on-two (and so forth) interactions. These discussions focused on understanding and honouring the past, conceptualising potential linkages across campus, and thinking about ways to engage key stakeholders both on and off campus. The underlying idea was to build on these smaller interactions to get to wider community conversations with the goal of, what organisation development guru Marvin Weisbord referred to as, "getting the whole system in the room".

The next phase – **providing context, creating content** – focused on ways to enhance individual learning as a foundation for organisational learning and envisioning new ways of thinking about responsible management. In terms of context, early on we determined that faculty would need support if they were going to meaningfully incorporate ethics into their discipline-based courses. As a way of facilitating this process, we created our Business Ethics Gadfly Workshop, with the intent of "seeding" every academic department on campus with "ethical gadflies" who would develop materials for their courses and encourage their colleagues to do the same.

Results

The goal of the "Gadfly" workshop was to assist faculty to feel more comfortable with ethics concepts, analysis and application so that they would be better able to work with our students in raising their ethical awareness and ability to make rational, ethical choices. In the workshop and accompanying readings, an attempt was made to balance exposure to ethical theory with hands-on practice in analysing cases and other teaching materials (such as films, simulations, role plays) from an ethical as well as discipline-based perspective. The mix of faculty from different departments and disciplines – sharing their ideas, experiences and concerns about these important issues – further contributed to an exciting and rewarding experience. Over time, with more than 160 Bentley faculty who have gone through the programme, it has enabled us to influence the ways in which ethics-related issues and topics are incorporated into courses across the curriculum, from accounting and finance to marketing, operations management, and human resource management, to organisational behaviour and strategy.

As an example of our approach to further support this contextual effort with content, we drew on the work of Bentley marketing professor Raj Sisodia and his 2007 book *Firms of Endearment* (Wharton Press). This work led to the development of "Conscious Capitalism", a new way of thinking about the role of business that emphasises commitment to a higher purpose (beyond profits per se) and a multi-stakeholder orientation, supported by conscious leadership and the development of a facilitative culture.

Finally, as a way of solidifying this effort, it was important to **make it real**, linking PRME-related goals with other structures, systems and processes on campus. As examples, this step included integration with Bentley's Academic Integrity System, institutional ethics policy and related ethics committee, Institutional Review Board (focusing on ethical issues in research with human subjects), students as colleagues initiative (engaging them in community projects, domestic and international service-learning, and research initiatives), and related institutional programmes, initiatives and experiences.

Why PRME is/was important

- PRME has provided a broader institutional framework that reinforces and helps to integrate many of the initiatives Bentley has been dedicated to and working on for over three decades.
- Completing the Sharing Information on Progress (SIP) report on a yearly basis has facilitated our ability to track our activities, capture and benchmark the breadth of initiatives across campus, and motivate faculty, staff and students to build on these experiences, encouraging them to take them to the "next level".

Copenhagen Business School, Copenhagen, Denmark

HOW TO GET STARTED? KICKING OFF THE PRME PROCESS

Introduction

**Copenhagen
Business School**

HANDELSHØJSKOLEN

Copenhagen Business School – where university means business

Founded in 1917, Copenhagen Business School (CBS) is one of the largest business schools in Europe with more than 18,000 students and 1,500 staff. CBS offers an innovative research environment to ensure value for society and a comprehensive range of degrees in various business disciplines. In 2011, the Aspen Institute ranked CBS ninth in Research in the Aspen Institute's global Beyond Grey Pinstripes review and ranking.

Challenges

A systematic approach to responsible management education

Scandinavian companies are disproportionately well-represented in the major corporate sustainability performance rankings and indexes, such as the Dow Jones Sustainability Index and the FTSE4Good. It is thus not surprising that issues of responsible management have traditionally been well embedded in Scandinavian business education. However, before signing onto the Principles for Responsible Management Education (PRME) initiative in August 2008, these topics were – to a large extent – addressed implicitly and unsystematically in the 17 study programmes taught at CBS.

Actions taken

Crucial factors in the success of taking up PRME at CBS

The process of signing up to PRME was initiated by the Centre for CSR, which started discussions on responsible management education (RME) with the support of 12-20 committed staff members. The discussion was then raised to 40 top managers, including heads of departments, where it was soon realised that RME already had a strong presence at CBS. As such, the decision to sign onto the PRME initiative became a way of streamlining this work through a formal anchor under the Office of the Dean of Education and making it visible as one of CBS's unique selling points.

> The management support has been important by making RME one of five unique selling points (USPs) for CBS and laying out a clear strategy and goals for where we want CBS to go in the future.
> *Kai Hockerts, Professor and Academic Director of Responsible Management Education, Copenhagen Business School*

Management support, which includes a highly visible endorsement of ambitious stretch goals, i.e., the Aspen Institute's Beyond Grey Pinstripes review and ranking, has been crucial in spreading out PRME in a systematic way throughout the organisation. Second, management support has been important in setting up a PRME office, creating positions for an administrative PRME manager and an academic director of PRME at CBS. Moreover, allocating a PRME budget has allowed us to kick-start transformation projects for internal staff and students.

Allocation of resources has allowed the PRME office to initiative the streamlining of RME throughout the organisation and to involve faculty more broadly. This process was started by offering 5 openings for 17 study programmes to review their curricula and be at the forefront of innovative programmes. This has since been offered to all programmes. Projects such as these have not only created awareness on RME, but also real change and new ways of teaching, i.e., Responsibility Day; the first day on campus for 2,700 BA students, where they are challenged with an RME case, and corporate speakers address some of the grand challenges of the 21st century. Finally, setting up future objectives publically in the CBS PRME report has been very instrumental in keeping CBS's commitment to being at the forefront of RME – constantly and systematically trying to improve the integration of PRME (see http://www.unprme.org/reports/CBS2010PRMEReportOnProgress.pdf).

Results

An obvious outcome of signing up to PRME has been a more explicit way of working with and thinking of RME. A clear result has been to achieve a research position among top ten in the world in the Aspen Institute's Beyond Grey Pinstripes review and ranking. Other examples include successful projects launched as a part of PRME, three examples of which are discussed below.

Curriculum change

As part of this initiative, the syllabus of each core course in a given study programme was analysed for RME content and meetings with the lead faculty were arranged. The initiative was launched in CBS with the full-time MBA during 2008/2009 and, at present, is currently being rolled out across 17 bachelor study programmes. The personal meetings have three aims:

1. Identify existing RME content and make it explicit in the syllabus and, where possible, in the learning objectives.
2. Offer support in identifying readings, cases and other material to increase the explicit RME content in the class.
3. Propose optional background readings to be included in the syllabi to allow interested students to study RME issues beyond the primary content of the class.

CBS Sustainability Alumni Network

The Network is creating vast opportunities for CBS to draw on the experiences of CBS alumni currently working within different areas of responsibility and sustainability. The Network is used for different purposes, i.e., the so-called "roundtable discussions", where corporations and academics get together to discuss issues around sustainability on an informal basis. The Network is also used for events and conferences as well as for providing interested faculty with guest lecturers from outside academia, taking the perspectives of NGOs, corporations, cooperatives, multi-stakeholder initiatives, etc. into the classroom and creating new ways of teaching. The latter is currently being turned into a book on practical CSR using the perspective of multiple stakeholders.

Establishment of a Green Office and a Green Ambassador Programme

This gives students and staff the opportunity to take an active part towards changing the mindset and culture through responsible and sustainable behaviour throughout the institution.

Why PRME is/was important

- Creating a unique contact for interested staff.
- Creating a way of benchmarking an effort to integrate RME by looking at other PRME schools.
- Through identifying potential areas and methods for improving the approach to RME.

DePaul University, Chicago, Illinois, United States

CONNECTING SUSTAINABILITY WITH THE UNIVERSITY'S MISSION AND VALUES

Introduction

DePaul University is one of the largest private universities in the United States and the largest Catholic University with 25,000 students enrolled and 9,000 in the Driehaus College of Business (formerly the College of Commerce).

Key facts

- **Enrolment:** 25,398 – including 16,384 undergraduates; 7,983 graduate students and 1,031 law students.
- **Founded:** 1898, by the Congregation of the Mission (Vincentian) religious community, which follows the teachings of 17th century French priest St. Vincent de Paul.
- **Named for:** St. Vincent de Paul (1581-1660.)
- **Motto:** "I will show you the way of wisdom" ("Viam sapientiae monstrabo tibi" – Proverbs, IV, 11).
- **Vincentian Organising Principle:** "... sent by his Father to preach the Gospel to the poor" ("*Pauperibus evangelizare misit me*" – Luke 4:18).

Challenges

The main challenge that DePaul faced was to bring together many diverse programmes, ideas and points of view to make the concept of sustainability visible and actionable at DePaul, building on the University's over 100 year history of serving the poor.

As opposed to the experience at many other schools that wrestled with just what sustainability might mean, at DePaul it was a relatively short conversation for people to connect concern for the condition of the poor, with a concern for the larger environment within which we all live. It builds on the initial response of Vincent de Paul to serve the poor in France.

The key question that emerged from a university-wide survey was: "In what ways does the focus on sustainability function to build DePaul's capacity to be an agent of social transformation?"

In sum, it was to make the short step to broaden the focus on justice and the poor to include the concern for nature: the environment and all forms of life.

Actions taken

Forming the Sustainability Initiatives Task Force (SITF) Ad Hoc Committee

Initially, three faculty members got together and convened a small group of faculty to discuss their interest in sustainability. From this initial meeting, and building on an initial paper on sustainable management developed for the Institute for Business and Professional Ethics, a white paper was written entitled: "What Must Be Done", which attempted to make the case for sustainability at DePaul, building on the mission and values of the University.

From Ad Hoc Committee to presidential level task force

We asked the president for formal recognition of the SITF, and he agreed, making it a presidential level committee, one of only two at the University (the other being the Fair Business Practices Committee (FBPC), which incidentally has used criteria from the United Nations Global Compact).

With the explicit endorsement of the President to pursue these tasks in a limited time frame, we were able to convene a broad, representative network of stakeholders. Through a decentralised, multi-stakeholder network of working groups with a specific set of tasks (audit, report, recommend) and specific time window, we were able to establish a baseline for ongoing improvement. Not only did this reveal strengths and weaknesses, it gave stakeholders implicit "permission" to do some blue sky thinking. After we had compiled our audit results and recommendations into a single report, the Committee had fulfilled its charge. Wanting to continue with a broad base of engagement and to empower units to begin pursuing some of the recommendations, we needed further endorsement from the President. He agreed that we should continue on as the DePaul Sustainability Network, with the general goal of enhancing campus sustainability, broadly considered.

Results

Lessons for leaders

- Many people care about sustainability and are very generous with their time, if they are given a venue to think big.
- Groups need "permission" and context to convene people (does this have support from the top?).
- Blue sky thinking, when grounded in an audit of current practices, is a powerful way for people to see campus sustainability as a commitment to ongoing improvement. There is no finish line, but there are milestones.
- Limited charge, specific time frame. We circumvented the common trap of speculating about the meaning of sustainability because we had a task (audit and recommend) and a limited time window.
- Most importantly, find ways to connect sustainability with the overall mission of the University. Otherwise, the effort may only focus on operations.

PRME – *towards a universal language of sustainability*

As we understand the term, sustainability is woven into the fabric of our institution and the Vincentian mission itself (St. Vincent de Paul, an inspirational and visionary leader, who was also a superb manager, said, "It is not enough to do good, it must be done well".). Seeing sustainability in this context allowed us to see it as a contemporary moment in a much longer story – a response to "what must be done". This is critical, as an organising story for DePaul. However, our mission is particular, if not unique, to DePaul. How can we engage peer institutions or other organisations if we frame sustainability exclusively in terms of our own mission? The Principles for Responsible Management Education (PRME) initiative helps us in two important ways:

1. It provides a common language that extends well beyond DePaul, Chicago, Illinois, and the United States – it is a global framework, like the United Nations Declaration on Human Rights.
2. It connects us to the UN, one of the few, if not the only, global fora for dialogue on such issues.

> PRME has served as a guiding framework for business schools all across the country and globally as well. At DePaul University, the Kellstadt Graduate School of Business was an early adopter. Now, DePaul is using it as an inspirational framework for sustainability initiatives throughout the whole University. We hope that PRME will be a model for other universities to adopt as they move forward in their own sustainability programmes that enlarge thinking to include academic programmes, economic viability, social responsibility, as well as environmental sustainability.
>
> *Patricia H. Werhane, Wicklander Chair of Business Ethics and Director, Institute for Business and Professional Ethics, DePaul University*

United Nations Global Compact – *language and principles for a vendor selection philosophy*

Here is a note sent to the FBPC http://mission.depaul.edu/Programs/fbpc/Pages/default.aspx: "We now have a selection philosophy for vendors and contractors on the procurement website: http://financialaffairs.depaul.edu/

procurement/prospectivevendors.htm. We have been working on this issue, in one form or another, for many years. With the language of the United Nations Global Compact, we now have a clear set of principles to refer to as we receive future complaints. The Ten Principles of the Global Compact are not unique to DePaul, so our vendors may already be familiar with them, may already be working to implement them, and now have a common point of reference.

Why PRME is/was important

- The Principles of PRME are not a new language or set of concepts for us. We have been working on these Principles, sometimes explicitly, sometimes inchoately.
- The Principles are a common language for teachers, students, and employers across the globe to articulate a commitment to a sustainable future. They should be a key element of sustainability literacy in the 21st century.

HOW CHANGE CAN BE INCENTIVISED FROM THE TOP (AND OTHER IMPORTANT ROLES OF LEADERSHIP)

Aarhus University, Business and Social Sciences, Aarhus, Denmark

SUSTAINABILITY AND PRME IN TIMES OF CHANGE

Introduction

 The School of Business and Social Sciences is a broad business school and one of the four main academic areas at Aarhus University. With approximately 14,000 full-time students, several thousand part-time students, almost 225 PhD students and more than 500 academic staff members, Business and Social Sciences ranks among the largest business schools in Europe. Furthermore, it is the largest business and social sciences unit in Denmark at university level with a broad academic base.

Challenges

Many universities reorganise, but how do you keep the focus on sustainability, with changing management, new strategies, organisational structures, etc.?

Creating a sustainable business school is a long and inspiring journey. Integrating the Principles for Responsible Management Education (PRME) is not something you do overnight. It takes patience, leadership and – most importantly – organisational understanding and flexibility.

Many universities and business schools struggle with changes in strategy, management, structures and systems. This poses both challenges and new opportunities for the PRME work.

This is the story of the PRME journey of Aarhus School of Business – now Aarhus University, Business and Social Sciences.

> Creating a sustainable business school based on PRME is a long and inspiring journey. Managers will come and go, strategies will change, organisations will be redesigned. This does not make PRME and the sustainable perspective less important. Be flexible, analyse the new strategic agenda, innovate and redesign your PRME activities to suit the new organisational framework.
>
> *Pernille Kallehave, Director of Development, Interdisciplinary Center for Organizational Architecture (ICOA), Special Advisor to the Dean (PRME and Sustainability), Aarhus University, Business and Social Sciences*

Actions taken

Step 1: Top down with local integration

Aarhus School of Business (ASB), Aarhus University was one of Denmark's largest business schools. ASB had approximately 8,000 students (bachelor, master, PhD, executive) and around 350 faculty and 350 administrative staff. ASB's annual revenue was 80 million EUR.

In 2008 the board decided on a new strategy for the business school. The basis for the new strategy was a thorough analysis of the future conditions for business and thus, the type of leaders and specialists that a business school should produce. This would of course influence the research priorities and the focus on old as well as new educational programmes. Thus, central to the strategy was the strategic focus on "sustainable growth through innovation", integrated in research, education, operations, relations and culture. In effect, ASB became signatory to PRME. Resources were assigned to support the new strategic theme, including new incentives as well as assigning a director to support the theme. The dean made a strong effort to support the theme both internally and externally. Particular efforts were made to engage some of the School's top faculty in supporting the theme and take ownership. The goal of the theme was that at the end of the strategic period the theme would be fully integrated into all activities of the School.

Several researchers from across the departments have participated with new research activities, ranging from sustainable supply chain, responsible investment, sustainable consumption to CSR, climate and energy law, leadership, green business models, etc. Through these activities it was confirmed that the research conducted at the School already had a sustainable focus.

A selection of new programmes have been introduced, such as the international full-time sustainable MBA, BScB in sustainability, BScB in ethics, master's in energy and environmental law, etc. In order to integrate the focus on sustainability across the School, a strong effort was made to include sustainable thinking in all existing programmes and courses. Students have initiated the "Aarhus Sustainability Network" and the School has placed focus on its own operations, and developed "a green campus strategy" for decreasing its own CO_2 footprint.

Step 2: Integrated sustainability

In 2010 Aarhus University started a major transformation in order to maintain its position as one of the world leading universities (among the top 100) of all significant rankings and move up further. Additionally, the University wanted to address the world's grand challenges through a cross-disciplinary approach, with respect to research as well as education. Nine faculties have been reduced to four. ASB merged with the Social Sciences faculty to become Aarhus University, Business and Social Sciences (BSS). With approximately 14,000 full-time students, several thousand part-time students, nearly 225 PhD students and more than 500 academic staff members, BSS ranks among the largest business schools in Europe and the largest in Denmark. BSS is created from the belief that a broader set of knowledge is required to address the business challenges today, which have been the general approach in business schools.

You could say that one of the major change factors of the University is **sustainability**. Global challenges in areas such as climate, energy, security, health and economy have both causes and effects that span different subject areas. They require interdisciplinary solutions created on a platform of excellent core competencies.

Results

A strategy for BSS was developed by the end of 2011. The strategy followed the idea that was set forth by the theme "sustainable growth through innovation" at ASB, by not making it a special theme, but assuming that it is integrated in all aspects of the BSS activities.

The PRME perspective is stated in the mission of BSS:

> As a broad business school, our mission is to add value to society by creating knowledge within and across the disciplines of business and social sciences and by educating our graduates to become innovative and **responsible individuals with a comprehensive understanding of the complexity of a global world**.

According to our dean, Professor Svend Hylleberg:

> Leaders in business and public organisations must have a broad set of competencies. The challenges facing leaders are very complex and global. Therefore, leaders today and in the future must have very broad skills in order to be able to act in this environment. They need to have deep skills, be able to work across disciplines and be innovative in order to solve problems, which they have not been faced before, e.g., climate change, hunger, poverty, lack of resources, etc.

The academic activities surrounding green economy, sustainable consumption, innovation, new business models, etc. are increasing in the departments.

The global competition PRME LEADERS + 20 – developed in close cooperation with the PRME office – is an important initiative for BSS and proves the continuous support to the sustainability perspective and the mission of PRME.

Step 3: new possibilities at university level

Global challenges call for cross-disciplinary solutions: A future perspective is to broaden the sustainability perspective to other parts of the

University: science, health and arts. This will enable the School to innovate even more and create future leaders with both a broad and international outlook and deep skills. A good example of this cross disciplinary perspective is the fact that both the dean of Science and Technology and representatives from Business and Social Sciences will be part of the Danish official delegation at the UN Rio + 20 conference, partnering with companies and political stakeholders.

Sustainable operations can also evolve better in this new context. The administrative part of BSS and Aarhus University has been centralised. Therefore, it is natural that the activities aimed at creating sustainable operations happen at University level as well. A recent step in this direction is that the experiences from "ASB Sustainable Campus" now form the backbone for a coming sustainability policy at the University.

Why PRME is/was important

- PRME demonstrates political and global commitment to the new role of management education.
- PRME's links to accreditation bodies, like EQUIS and AACSB, are important drivers for PRME implementation at school level.
- PRME provides for a global learning network and benchmarking opportunities.

University of Dubai, Dubai, United Arab Emirates

INCENTIVISING FACULTY MEMBERS THROUGH TEACHING ASSESSMENTS: A SUCCESS STORY

Introduction

The University of Dubai (UD) operates in the heart of Dubai City, catering to United Arab Emirates (UAE) nationals and expatriate students from 41 countries. It has two colleges. The College of Business Administration offers MBA and BBA programmes, which are internationally accredited by the AACSB and nationally by the Ministry of Higher Education and Scientific Research (MOHESR) of UAE. The College of Information Technology offers a bachelor degree programme, which is nationally accredited by MOHESR and internationally by the Computing Accreditation Commission (CAC), which is part of the Accreditation Board of Engineering and Technology (ABET).

Challenges

As the first signatory to the Principles for Responsible Management Education (PRME) from the Middle East region, UD encountered two challenges. The first one was to implement the Six Principles meaningfully. The second challenge was to get students and other stakeholders involved in the process, and make them take some practical steps towards implementing PRME.

Actions taken

Soon after becoming a member in November 2007, UD's top management initiated the actions by forming a committee to brainstorm different methods of implementation. Out of the several actions, which are reported through the SIPs, we found the most effective methods of implementation were curriculum changes and modification to the faculty teaching performance evaluation instrument.

Faculty members of all disciplines were asked to introduce case studies and chapters that cover topics related to corporate social responsibility, ethics, governance, human rights, and environmental issues. A course called Business and Society was also introduced as a core course of the BBA programme. The syllabus of the course includes the history of PRME, the Six Principles, and the activities by which UD is implementing them. Other components of the course are corporate social responsibility, implementation of CSR, business ethics, multinational corporations, globalisation, industrial pollution and environmental policy, methods of managing environmental quality, consumerism, and corporate governance.

Students' learning of the above topics is measured on the basis of course learning outcomes (CLO). Each faculty member prepares a spreadsheet at the end of each semester showing students' performance on the CLOs. Those CLOs that had grades below the benchmark of 65% are marked for action by the faculty member in the faculty development plan (FDP) for the year. Further, every semester UD students evaluate the faculty members teaching the above topics, including PRME.

In order to address the second challenge, UD first created awareness of PRME among the students and staff. Permanent posters with the Six Principles were placed in the reception lobby of both the campuses. Awareness campaigns conducted every semester also make the students aware of UD's affiliation with PRME. Guest speakers from industry often lecture students on CSR and related topics. Further, UD is a member of the steering committee of ENGAGE Dubai, a volunteering organisation. Currently more than 50 organisations take an active part in volunteering activities through ENGAGE Dubai. On different occasions students are taken on environmental field trips to locations within the UAE such as Masdar City, and overseas locations such as Kerala, India. They also attend events such as the Word Future Energy Conference. On a regular basis, UD students take an active part in the Clean up the World campaign organised by the United Nations Environment Programme (UNEP), the Earth Hour campaign to conserve energy, the Plant My Tree and recycling campaigns organised by Dubai Municipality, breast cancer awareness campaigns, and other such activities. In association with the Dubai Electricity and Water Authority (DEWA), UD conducted a workshop on conservation of water for students, faculty and staff.

As part of top management, President Omar Hefni has made strategic decisions to enhance the awareness of all UD stakeholders about their responsibilities towards society and the environment. He has attended the annual conferences of PRME in the past. Chief academic officer, Professor Ananth Rao directs the PRME activities at the University level, and takes an active part in PRME working groups. The dean of the College of Business Administration, Professor Mohammed Ibrahim, is instrumental in implementing the Six Principles in the University, and society at large. Assistant professor, Dr. Eappen Thiruvattal is active in the working groups, and coordinates the activities and reports them to the PRME Secretariat on a regular basis.

> In order to incentivise changes in the students' learning of their responsibilities towards the society, environment and governments, top management should implement curriculum changes periodically that reflect those interests. Each semester students' learning may be measured by their achievements of course learning outcomes. Gaps between the benchmarks and achievements may be addressed by the faculty member concerned. Teaching performance evaluations by students also may be linked to implementation of the Principles in class. Both these measures of faculty performance are reflected on the faculty development plan (FDP). Top management may review the FDPs while considering faculty promotions. Thus implementation of PRME becomes a good incentive for faculty members. I also recommend activities related to the Principles for the students, so that they get hands-on involvement with the Principles.
>
> *Eappen Thiruvattal, Assistant Professor, PRME Coordinator,*
> *College of Business Administration, University of Dubai*

Results

A specific variable included in the faculty evaluation instrument is: **"Instructor's role in developing students' course specific skills: Ethical**

and legal responsibilities in organisations and society"(Evaluation 1-5 Likert Scale). Faculty members not meeting the benchmark of 3.5 points out of 5 have to plan actions they will take to improve the ratings, and include them in the annual FDP for the review of the dean. A positive trend on these measures has been observed for the past five semesters. This trend indicates that faculty members are making more efforts to include PRME components in their lectures.

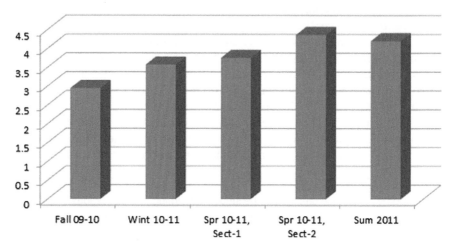

Figure 1. Students' evaluation of faculty teaching ethical and legal responsibilities in organisations and society, on 5-point Likert Scale. (Source: Student evaluation records, UD)

Why PRME is/was important

- As a UN-sponsored global organisation, the PRME initiative is important for UD, to focus our efforts and commit ourselves to the Principles.
- Business students, who are the future managers, must be aware of their responsibilities towards the society they live in, the organisation they work with and the government they are governed by. Implementation of the Six Principles acts as an effective learning tool for the students in this matter.
- Awareness of the Principles and their implementation gives the stakeholders insight into their responsibilities towards the organisation as well as society.

WHICH ARE THE BEST WAYS TO EMBED PRME IN THE INSTITUTION/PROGRAMME'S ORGANISATIONAL CULTURE?

Ashridge Business School, Berkhamsted, England, United Kingdom

APPLYING THE BEST OF CONTEMPORARY THINKING

Introduction

Based in England, Ashridge is consistently ranked as one of the world's leading business schools and works with over 100 organisations and 9,000 managers in over 40 countries every year.

It enables individuals and organisations from around the world to build management capability and to address individual and organisation development challenges. Clients span the private, public and not-for-profit sectors.

Its activities include open and customised executive education programmes, organisation consulting, MBA, MSc, doctoral and diploma qualifications, applied research and virtual learning. It is one of the very few schools worldwide to achieve triple accreditation from The Association of MBAs (AMBA), EQUIS and AACSB; the UK, European and American accreditation bodies for qualification programmes.

Challenges

While it is relatively straightforward to recruit sustainability specialists into the faculty to provide specialist courses and specialist modules within other courses, to really embed the Principles for Responsible Management Education (PRME) across an institution's culture is a far more ambitious challenge, which has required us at Ashridge to engage with the best of contemporary thinking on organisational change and try to apply it in our own institution.

My advice would be to seek to help and encourage faculty colleagues to see things differently, rather than trying to compel any kind of change. Rather than taking a scattergun approach of trying to influence everyone, focus on investing time in those members of faculty who are already expressing an interest. Generating small steps of change with these people, and creating success stories to influence others, will begin to build a critical mass one step at a time. Think about how organisational structures could be adapted to support and maintain new ways of doing things among those who've decided to try to do something new, rather than trying to use them to force change.

Matthew Gitsham, Director, Ashridge Centre for Business and Sustainability,
Ashridge Business School

Actions taken

We have attempted to combine informal and formal approaches to change with both top-down and bottom-up – a bit of everything! One of our first principles has been to not try to compel any uniform change, but to support innovators. We think that an inclusive process that tries to motivate people to engage in change, although perhaps slower and more patchy in the short term, is more meaningful and enduring in the longer term. To effectively research and teach anything you must be curious about it yourself.

Top-level commitment has been important, with a number of members of Ashridge's management team vocally making the case for why we should be thinking about sustainability in our work. In addition to the vocal support of our dean, our head of qualifications programmes, for example, has championed this during the redesign of the MBA programme, and the head of open programmes has championed this during a review of the open programmes portfolio. This vocal leadership has helped create the space for others in the organisation to take the risk to experiment and lead change.

Alongside support from the top there has been consistent effort to connect faculty and wider staff who are interested in sustainability into a relatively informal learning network. This includes guest speakers and sharing one another's experience of innovation. Sustainability specialists on the faculty are acting as coaches to others in disciplines such as marketing, strategy, innovation, and leadership, to help them learn and innovate in their own work.

Results

This informal work has only been possible with more structural change at the same time: there are now eight full-time sustainability specialists who have been recruited to our core faculty, and three of these individuals have had their roles designed to give them time to develop and coach others. The faculty performance management and appraisal system has been amended – a new individual balanced scorecard now recognises and rewards any innovation around sustainability. Formal internal quality assurance processes have also been amended – for example, programme review procedures now include a question on whether and how sustainability features within the curriculum. Ashridge's board of governors, which meets three times a year, reviews an organisational balanced scorecard, which now includes the School's carbon footprint as one of its key metrics. All of these structural changes have been made with the intention of supporting innovators to change and maintain that change, rather than to force compliance.

We have also taken a proactive approach towards ISO14001, which typically is restricted to an operational management system for environmental issues.

We have used this as a wider platform for our broader efforts at institutional change. For the past three years, as part of the ISO14001 process, we have been through an annual school-wide engagement process to review where we are on sustainability, where we want to be in the long term and what that means for the next year's activities. This has created a comprehensive set of around 100 objectives in specific areas ranging across curriculum change, energy usage, water usage, waste management, food and paper sourcing, and biodiversity management. Each of these actions have been volunteered and agreed by individual members of staff to pursue in the following year. In 2012 these have included actions ranging from conducting an in-depth review of the curriculum of three flagship open programmes to involving our staff in constructing biodiversity habitats for priority species in our gardens and grounds.

Why PRME is/was important

- PRME has been very helpful in this process because the fact that an institution as globally influential as the United Nations, and the UN Secretary General himself no less, are as interested as they are in what happens within business schools has been very useful in initially getting the interest of some members of faculty for whom this set of issues had not been on their radar before.
- The PRME also provides a unifying framework bringing together what a school does across the areas of teaching, research and campus management, and so in some instances provides a useful stimulus for making the case for structural changes.
- Finally, the international community brought together by the PRME provides an extremely useful and inspirational learning group for sharing ideas and experiences.

Sabanci University, Istanbul, Turkey

MBA ORIENTATION PROGRAMME

Introduction

Sabanci University (SU) and its School of Business were established in 1999 in Istanbul, the School of Business is accredited by the ACSSB. It offers MBA, EMBA, PhD in management and MSc in finance programmes. The University leadership, Business School faculty and students strive to be closely connected to all our stakeholders and to be engaged with the critical issues facing Turkey and the world.

As a signatory to the Principles for Responsible Management Education (PRME) and in compliance with our University's mission, our Business School is committed to embedding sustainability and corporate responsibility into our education. We have identified three means to accomplish this endeavour:

1. A mandatory course on ethics in business.
2. Incorporation of ethical issues and sustainability concerns relevant to each discipline into all of our core courses.
3. Practical learning through Company Action Projects (CAP)[1] during which students are required to analyse ethical dimensions and the social and environmental impacts of real life projects, and report to the company management.

---

[1] The emphasis of the second year of the Sabanci MBA is the Company Action Projects (CAP). CAP's distinctive feature is that these are real projects companies undertake. Our "client" companies participate in CAP not only to contribute to our educational mission, but also because they see real value in the work of our students.

Challenges

The Business and Ethics course is given during the last semester of the MBA programme, however, we wanted our students to have a general awareness of the ethical issues from the very beginning and be able to assess ethical issues related with their CAP projects before they took the Business and Ethics course.

Action taken

We have included an "Ethics and Sustainability Day" in our MBA orientation programme. The purpose of the Ethics and Sustainability Day is to create an awareness of the importance of ethics and sustainability in the practice of management and provide a framework to the students for assessing ethical and sustainability dimensions of business decisions and projects. By doing so the programme aims to:

- Help course instructors and students to focus on field/discipline specific aspects of ethics and sustainability in their coursework during the programme based on a common framework the students are familiar with.
- Provide students with basic knowledge and tools to identify ethical issues and assess environmental and social impacts of real life projects.

Preparation

- Students are required to read one or two articles reflecting on ethics and sustainability issues in business before the orientation week.
- The dean informs the students about SU's position as a signatory of Global Compact and PRME during the first day of the orientation. Copies of both the Ten Principles of the United Nations Global Compact and the Six Principles of PRME are distributed.

- Students watch two documentaries during the orientation week (*Darwin's Nightmare* and *Insider Job* were screened in the 2011-2012 fall semester).

Programme

Orientation is planned as full five days of lectures. Ethics and Sustainability Day is scheduled at the end of the programme, however the documentaries are screened in the evenings during the week. The objective of spreading the documentaries during the week is to "disrupt" the students' learning of classical tools and techniques, and prepare them for a reflective day on ethics and the role of business in society by encouraging critical thinking as "business as usual".

The six-hour lecture on the last day covers the following topics:

- PRME and Sabanci University's mission statement.
- Why ethics and sustainability have become key concerns for managers: A critical perspective of "business-" and "market-based" economic systems.
- Ethical theories and a framework for ethical analysis from a pluralist perspective.
- Importance of social and environmental impact analysis, tools and resources.

Simulation

Students play a simulation game to experience the ethical dilemmas faced by managers in the course of day-to-day decision making (Turning Gears from Darden was used in the 2011-2012 fall semester).

> My advice is not to be too concerned about appearing anti-"**business as usual**". Students receive critical perspectives positively and make sense of them as an exciting challenge that they have to deal with as future managers with creativity and intellect, and of course with responsibility...
> *Melsa Ararat, PRME Coordinator and Instructor for the MBA orientation programme, "Ethics and Sustainability Day"*

Results

Ethics and Sustainability Day was included in our MBA orientation programme for the first time in the fall semester of the 2011-2012 academic year. Students were very enthusiastic and participative in discussions on critical perspectives. As we move forward in the MBA programme, we expect our students to be more effective in recognising and addressing ethical issues in their CAP projects and other coursework. We also expect them to be vocal, with confidence in communicating their ethical concerns to the management of CAP project companies.

Why PRME is/was important

- PRME provided a solid framework to link SU's mission with the learning outcomes of our MBA programme as "our mission is to develop internationally competent and confident individuals, enriched with the ability to reflect critically and independently, combined with a strong sense of social responsibility; and, to contribute to the development of science and technology on a global level, as well as disseminating the knowledge created to the benefit of the community".
- In the process of reaching a consensus among the faculty on the importance of ethics and sustainability as essential themes that underpin our MBA programme, the Principles served as an invaluable instrument.

Babson College, Babson Park, Massachusetts, United States

FOCUSING ON PRME "FROM DAY ONE"

Introduction

Babson College is widely recognised as the educator, convener and thought leader for "Entrepreneurship of All Kinds". Located just outside Boston, Massachusetts, Babson has a strong global focus and is one of the few US schools to hold both AACSB and EQUIS accreditation. The College's innovative curriculum combines integrated and applied business and liberal arts programmes with unique, linked curricular and co-curricular learning experiences to prepare its 2,000 undergraduates and 1,300 graduate students to be entrepreneurial and responsible leaders.

Challenges

Babson was one of the first US adopters of the Principles for Responsible Management Education (PRME), signing onto the initiative in 2008, shortly after the Principles were developed in mid-2007. Adopting the Principles was a relatively easy task, since both the administration and the faculty recognised the consistency between the values within the Principles and Babson's recently revised mission statement: "To educate leaders who create great economic and social value – everywhere". Joint faculty and administrative leaders proposed to the faculty senate that Babson endorse PRME, and the vote to approve was unanimous.

Despite an easy endorsement of PRME, Babson faced a significant challenge in creating a culture on campus that consistently recognised the centrality of the Principles to what we do and how we do it. While the institution was clearly focused on creating a next generation of leaders prepared to address such important issues as sustainability and corporate social responsibility, this focus was not necessarily guided by the framework provided by PRME. While many changes occurred on campus that were consistent with PRME, they were usually driven by other forces and often ad hoc.

As is often the case, it is difficult to make something such as PRME central to the organisational culture by proclamation. Despite constant references to the faculty endorsement of PRME by key administrators, in practice the Principles initially served more as an external signal of our priorities rather than any kind of guiding light for internal activities. To truly embed PRME into Babson's culture, more members of the community needed to recognise its value as a unifying framework and develop programmes and activities that could be specifically mapped to the Principles.

> Based on our experiences at Babson, there is clear advice to offer to institutions who want to make PRME more central to their mission. First, leadership on these efforts has to come both from the top and from the grass roots – in our case, the faculty took the first steps to make an explicit link between our mission and the Principles. Second, if you want PRME to become embedded in the culture you must be unambiguous about how your activities relate to the Principles. Don't assume that, because something is related to PRME, others know this. If you want PRME to be a driving force, you must let others know exactly how your activities and programmes are linked to and shaped by the Principles.
>
> *Dennis Hanno, Dean of Babson's Undergraduate School*

Actions taken and results

Both faculty and administrative leaders at Babson realised that, if PRME was to become central to the activities on campus, it would require two main actions: the explicit recognition by key faculty leaders that PRME could and should drive change on campus, and an increased awareness across the entire campus community of the many Babson activities and programmes that were clearly linked to PRME.

To achieve the first objective, a broad-based faculty group was formed and initially charged with looking at how people, planet and profit issues could be more directly addressed across the College, both within our curriculum and in other activities. The group quickly moved towards a model that included concepts related to an idea they termed "SEERS" – social, environmental, and economic responsibility and sustainability. The link between SEERS and PRME was obvious, and in the document there was explicit reference to how PRME could serve as an organising theme for much of what Babson needed to do to improve curriculum and programmes. The report produced by this faculty group was endorsed by the faculty senate and has served as one of the guiding principles for a complete revision of both our undergraduate and graduate curriculum. Moreover, these same ideas served as the framework for a recently published book authored by several Babson faculty entitled, *The New Entrepreneurial Leader*. This book highlights SEERS throughout and demonstrates how these ideas drive what we do at Babson.

The second objective, increasing awareness on campus of PRME and how it relates to our activities, was achieved by creating a number of highly visible celebrations of what we are doing that is driven by the Principles. For example, an event was created to engage the community at the very beginning of the academic year in activities and discussions that demonstrated how anyone could create positive social change. This event, called "From Day One", invited all members of the community to engage in community service activities with a broad array of social action organisations. The day also included open dialogues on many topics related to PRME, such as sustainability and corporate social responsibility. This now annual event sets the tone from day one for the new members of our community, and from the first day of the new academic year by making it explicit that the Principles are an important part of what we do at Babson. An even more explicit focus on PRME was developed this year when "From Day One" was followed up with an event called "Thirty Days of PRME". A different Babson activity or programme that is directly related to PRME was highlighted across campus each day during the 30 days, with a culminating event entitled "Party for the Principles" that featured a keynote speaker and the unveiling of a significant community-wide art project related to PRME.

Why PRME is/was important

- PRME provides guidance on how we can achieve our goal of educating leaders to create great both economic and social value.
- PRME demonstrates that others also believe that our mission is an important one for the future of the world. While our community has fully embraced the ideals of PRME since the first day, it has taken events and activities such as From Day One and the Thirty Days of PRME to make the Principles a central part of Babson's culture.

PRACTICAL WAYS TO ESTABLISH A MULTIDISCIPLINARY (AND/OR MULTI-STAKEHOLDER) PRME TASK FORCE ACROSS THE CAMPUS

Bentley University, Waltham, Massachusetts, United States

THE BENTLEY ALLIANCE FOR ETHICS AND SOCIAL RESPONSIBILITY

Introduction

Bentley is a business university, combining an advanced business curriculum with a rich and diverse arts and sciences programme to prepare a new kind of business leader – one with the deep technical skills, broad global perspective, and high ethical standards required to make a difference in an ever-changing world. Located 8 miles west of Boston, Massachusetts, Bentley enrols approximately 4,100 full-time undergraduates, 1,400 graduate (MBA and master's of science programmes), and 30-plus doctoral students, with over 290 full- and 180 part-time faculty. Bentley is accredited by the New England Association of Schools and Colleges, AACSB International and EQUIS.

Challenges

Bentley Alliance for Ethics and Social Responsibility

As one of the original signatories of the Principles for Responsible Management Education (PRME) initiative, the main institutional mechanism for implementation and support of PRME is the Bentley Alliance for Ethics and Social Responsibility (BAESR), a collaborative effort dedicated to encourage and promote an institution-wide sense of ethics, social responsibility, sustainability, and civic engagement. Since the creation of its Center for Business Ethics in 1976, Bentley has continually promoted a sense of ethics and social responsibility through teaching, research, and corporate and community relations for over three decades. These efforts were given stronger emphasis based on the recommendations of a cross-university task force on ethics, service and social responsibility, convened by the College's provost and academic vice-president. The task force was charged to comprehensively scrutinise the College's status with regard to issues, programmes and accomplishments in the areas of ethics, social responsibility, sustainability and civic engagement. Following a semester-long assessment that engaged the campus community, the task force found that although many successful initiatives in these areas were under way, they were often isolated and would benefit collectively from further collaboration, coordination, and a clear, organising direction.

> As founding director of the Alliance, I fully realise the crucial role that top administration support plays in such cross-institutional endeavours. None of our efforts would have been successful without the unwavering support from our deans, provost, and president. However, for the goals of PRME to be truly embedded in an institution's activities, it must be seen as a faculty-led initiative, building on the interest, motivation, and passion of individual faculty members, and then amplifying and extending that work through an integrative structural intervention that links them together.
> *Anthony F. Buono, Professor of Management and Sociology, Founding Director, Bentley Alliance for Ethics and Social Responsibility*

Actions taken

One of the outcomes of this assessment was the Alliance, whose mission is to amplify and extend the work of the core centres and initiatives on campus that are focused on these issues, supporting and encouraging greater awareness of, respect for, and commitment to ethics, service, sustainability, and social responsibility in faculty research, curricula, and campus culture. A unique feature of the Alliance, which reflects the PRME initiative's commitment to inspire responsible management, is its integrative focus on these four core areas. In pursuit of its cross-campus mission, BAESR's efforts focus on:

- Supporting and encouraging collaborative and applied transdisciplinary **research** that has the potential to significantly affect current practice.
- Influencing **curriculum** development and pedagogical innovations intended to make students more ethically sensitive and socially aware.
- Ensuring a broader application of these principles and ideals in **campus life**.
- Attempting to foster lifelong **civic engagement** and a commitment to **responsive corporate citizenship** among students.
- Seeking to work closely with external organisations – **partnering** with academic and professional associations, corporations, and not-for-profit organisations in pursuit of these goals.

This Alliance is a collaborative effort that is dependent on the commitment of a broad range of stakeholders, including Bentley faculty, staff, students, and alumni, as well as business executives, corporate partners, relevant associations and other colleges and universities in an effort to enhance and disseminate these ideals across the institution.

The Alliance is currently built on four "core pillars" in the Bentley community that continue to operate as autonomous entities, but collaborate under its aegis:

1. **Center for Business Ethics:** Founded in 1976, the Center for Business Ethics is an internationally recognised centre that promotes ethical leadership, conduct and cultures as critical to an effective and legitimate role for business in society.
2. **Service-Learning Center:** Established in 1990, the Bentley Service-Learning Center), which has built an international reputation (recognised by *US News & World Report*), seeks to promote academic learning, to develop socially responsible working professionals, and to assist community partners in serving the human needs and interests of their constituencies.

3. **Center for Women and Business:** Building on the creation of the Women's Leadership Institute, which was created in 2003, the newly formed Center's mission focuses on the advancement of shared leadership among women and men throughout the business world and, in particular, the development and retention of women leaders at every stage of their lives.

4. **Valente Center for Arts & Sciences:** Created in 2007, the Center's mission is to help make the arts and sciences a vital, integral and challenging aspect of undergraduate and graduate education at Bentley.

Results

Combined with a series of programmes and activities across the institution, this initiative has led to a four-part approach that attempts to shape and influence a sense of ethics, service, sustainability, and responsibility throughout the classroom, campus life, the University's research agenda, and in outreach to the academic, corporate, and not-for-profit worlds. As part of the Alliance, for example, Bentley's Institutional Review Board (IRB) oversees the ethical treatment of human subjects in research, the Academic Integrity System sets and administers standards of academic integrity throughout the University, the Global Business Ethics Symposium sponsored by the State Street Foundation brings together international thought leaders from the academic, corporate, and NGO worlds for in-depth discussions of current practices and challenges in business ethics, corporate responsibility and sustainability, and the civic leadership programme, which serves as Bentley's chapter of the Graduation Pledge Alliance, seeks to enhance student civic leadership capabilities.

Why PRME is/was important

- PRME has helped to further solidify a clear, organizing direction for our efforts to capture the meaning of responsible management practices in our teaching, research, and campus life.
- The PRME has also facilitated our ability to network with like-minded associations, schools, and colleagues.

Thunderbird School of Global Management, Glendale, Arizona, United States

THE THUNDERBIRD EXPERIENCE

Introduction

Thunderbird School of Global Management (Glendale, AZ, US), is a globally oriented institution and therefore began implementing the Principles for Responsible Management Education (PRME) with a vision of the current state of global governance and the rising importance of business in world affairs. Global corporations have become a powerful structuring force in the global economy, a fact that implies new responsibilities for business leaders. The Principles provided useful guidance on how Thunderbird should prepare its graduates for these new responsibilities, but the question was how to foster a vision shared across the institution as a whole. While the School's president could unilaterally sign and endorse PRME, it was thought that a broader process of engagement with faculty, students and alumni could help integrate the Principles into the organisational culture.

Challenges

The starting point for the conversation would be the recognition of management as a true and honourable profession. As such, professions confer two important things to practitioners. The first is the knowledge and skills needed to perform the professional's duties, something business schools are very good at providing their graduates. But professions also recognise that those skills can be abused and cause harm to society. A doctor's skills can be used to cure or kill, for instance. In recognition of this, the professions like medicine and law provide a code of professional conduct to ensure that the profession serves society. Management has no code of professional conduct, yet the consequences of managerial decisions are often far-reaching as they are amplified by the power of corporations to leverage capital, labour and other resources globally. The process of debating and adopting the PRME became a vehicle for a larger discussion of professional management responsibilities and Thunderbird's role in imparting them to our graduates.

> Adopting PRME can be a transformative experience for a business school if it is treated as the basis for a dialogue about why we are training managers and their role in the world after they leave our School. Appropriately managed, PRME can foster an introspection that is uncommon in academia and strengthen not only curriculum, but also our institutional cultures.
> *Gregory Unruh, Director, The Lincoln Center for Ethics in Global Management, Thunderbird School of Global Management*

Actions taken

The discussion was kicked-off by a speech given by the School's president asking students and faculty to consider how we should train professional managers. This challenge fostered a broad debate among students and alumni, and then with the faculty. Student leaders from the Honor Council took the lead on facilitating a discussion. The Honor Council members met individually with each faculty member, seeking their feedback and input on managerial professionalism and PRME. When the time was ripe, the PRME proposal was presented for debate in the faculty senate, which ultimately voted unanimously to approve, thanks largely to the inclusive deliberative process that preceded the vote.

Results

With official approval, the next challenge was making the changes to the curriculum needed to live up to the Principles. Part of the challenge is finding space in an already crowded curriculum and addressing the concern that class time for PRME coverage would be allotted at the expense of the functional areas. But PRME again proved to be an important change vehicle because the Principles were in alignment with metrics that the Thunderbird accrediting body, the AACSB, was seeking. By linking the Principles with outcome assessments, PRME content has effectively become institutionalised in the curriculum through the inclusion of "Global Citizenship" as one of Thunderbird's core learning outcomes.

HOW TO ENCOURAGE AND/OR IMPLEMENT LOCAL COMMUNITY AND CAMPUS INITIATIVES

China Europe International Business School (CEIBS), Shanghai, China

PROJECT: MAKE YOUR BUSINESS SCHOOL CARBON NEUTRAL

Introduction

 The China Europe International Business School (CEIBS) has campuses in Shanghai and Beijing and offers unique management education and research from a position of "China depth, global breadth".

Each year, around 200 MBA and 750 EMBA students graduate from CEIBS with 10,000 students enrolling in executive education programmes every year. CEIBS's alumni network has a membership of 11,000.

Challenges

To calculate the CEIBS carbon footprint, then create a viable plan for reducing and offsetting the School's greenhouse gas emissions in order to minimise CEIBS's impact on climate change.

Students will eagerly help you build, if you encourage them. Point out entrepreneurial and leadership gains. Clear away barriers and offer access to your community resources. Student commitment grows gradually, so don't expect too much too soon: give them choice, and something for the CV.

Lydia Price, Associate Dean and MBA Academic Director, CEIBS

Actions taken

In alignment with the Principles for Responsible Management Education (PRME) initiative, CEIBS aims to "'walk the 'talk" of developing a sustainable campus at the same time we bring RME into the classroom. A key mechanism for us to blend teaching and campus development initiatives is the MBA Responsible Leadership Project (RLP) course, launched in 2009. RLP is the cornerstone of a process that links CEIBS students with corporate and non-profit partners to identify, research, and develop solutions to some of the most important issues that China faces by means of supervised student consulting projects. In 2010, one RLP team took on the challenge to accelerate the Green Campus project first started by students in 2007. The team called themselves The Decarbonators and aimed to execute the first stages of their project during 2011.

The first task facing the Decarbonators was to calculate the greenhouse gas (GHG) emissions from the Shanghai campus each year. The team drew from the expertise of four partner companies: carbon-auditing firm SGS, environmental protection organisation WWF, China-based solar panel producer Trina Solar and Chinese technology firm and air-conditioning experts DunAn. Using these resources, the students set out to measure GHG emissions from seven key sources: waste paper, food waste, non-food waste, steam, fuel, water and electricity usage. Gathering solid data required time-consuming input from all CEIBS departments. The final calculation was 4,500 tons of GHG emissions (or CO_2-equivalents) from the Shanghai campus each year. This is equal to the CO_2 emissions produced by a Boeing 737 travelling around the world more than 2.5 times.

How do we "neutralise" 4,500 tons of carbon?

The Decarbonators team realised that reducing GHG emissions would take time and so the most immediate task was to offset by planting trees and buying carbon credits. In April 2011, two members of the team, Robert Seiler and Eric Seidner, travelled to Kulun Qi in Inner Mongolia to start the "CEIBS Forest" by helping to plant the first 1,000 trees in partnership with international NGO, Roots & Shoots. The trees not only create a windbreak to reduce sandstorms, but also assist the local population to reclaim arable land. As poplar trees cease absorbing carbon efficiently when they reach maturity, they must be harvested and replaced with saplings. This cycle creates a sustainable timber industry and a new source of income for farmers while helping the environment.

The plan is that the new CEIBS Forest will be maintained by local farmers, and any tree that fails to grow will be replaced, guaranteeing that the CEIBS Forest always holds at least 1,000 trees. And, because each tree will absorb 250 kilograms of CO_2 during its 15 to 20-year life time, the new forest will allow CEIBS to offset 250,000 kilograms of greenhouse gas emissions. The offsetting capacity will expand yearly, as the CEIBS Forest expands.

Buying carbon credits was the most immediate solution to offset the residual emissions of the campus that could neither be reduced nor absorbed by the CEIBS Forest in the short term. The team presented the case for buying carbon credits to the CEIBS Management Committee who committed to pay for the first year of carbon credits. Through specialist advice from carbon broker, Evolution Markets, two projects emerged as worthy of a donation from CEIBS: a small hydropower project managed by Guizhou-based Liupanshiu Tuoyuan Group, and Xinjiang Dabancheng Sanchang Phase III Wind Power Project managed by Xinjian Tianfeng Wind Power Co. These projects not only support the local population in the rural areas of the Guizhou and Xinjiang provinces, but also make investments to educate local children on environmental protection and sustainable living.

> Faculty interest expands as student achievements mount, and jobs begin to emerge. Encourage learning and multidisciplinary approaches so that new-comers can join initiatives without making large up-front investments of their scarce time. Build resonance with your initiatives and gain corporate and community support. PRME conferences are a great way for faculty members to learn about the issues in an efficient and powerful format.
> *Mike Thompson, Professor of Management Practice, Director of the Centre for Leadership and Responsibility (ECCLAR), CEIBS*

Results

On 28 May 2011, CEIBS announced that it had become the first carbon neutral business school in Asia having implemented the first stage of a plan for carbon reductions. The CEIBS forest in Inner Mongolia had been started with 1,000 trees with the support of WWF and alumni donations and carbon credits had been purchased as a result of investments made in two hydropower. The Decarbonators RLP team has established a permanent internal management structure to continue the work of carbon reduction and annual offsetting, with the baton being passed to a new MBA2011 team and to successive MBA classes thereafter.

The concept of a carbon neutral campus will be incorporated in a five-year sustainability strategy, which will be developed by a team of MBA students in 2012. The strategy will set out how CEIBS plans to demonstrate its contribution to those internationally agreed standards of sustainability that are most relevant to the purpose, management and operation of a leading international business school. Within this strategy, the carbon neutral dimensions will include the launch of a new LEED certified campus, HVAC substitution, window and door substitution. A Green Behavioural Campaign will be launched with the aim of changing the behaviour of CEIBS students, faculty and staff to reduce and rethink environmental protection. To build enthusiasm, the MBA Energy and Environment Club plans to launch a series of energy-saving competitions during 2012. Each incoming class will be challenged to continue the work of carbon reduction such that the need for purchasing carbon credits will decline over time.

Why PRME is/was important

PRME offers a context for sharing ideas and practices, and for benchmarking with other schools. In attending a PRME conference in Copenhagen, we received great feedback and encouragement for the work that we were doing with the RLP programme. The conference also helped to deepen our understanding of the challenges to achieve environmental sustainability as we continually grow the global economy. As a result, support for student-led sustainability initiatives at CEIBS has grown continuously over time. Without the buy in of key decision makers within the school, student projects can quickly die or fail to reach their true potential. As a meeting place for sharing ideas and practices, PRME can help accelerate the work of building the critical top-down and bottom-up support needed to implement RME.

Euromed Management, Marseille, France

CSR OFFICERS – ESSENTIAL ACTORS IN CAMPUS SUSTAINABILITY

Introduction

Founded in 1872, Euromed Management is one of the largest and top ranked business schools in France. The main campus is located in the heart the Callanques National Park in Marseille, France with campuses and offices in Toulon, Avignon, Bastia (France), Marrakech (Morocco) and Suzhou (China). With over 5,700 students, the School offers an array of undergraduate, graduate and executive education programmes. Euromed Management is accredited by AACSB, AMBA and EQUIS.

Challenges

One of the main challenges every committed organisation faces, Euromed Management included, is how to disseminate CSR strategy and actions into every level of operations. At Euromed Management we chose to adopt a systemic and transversal approach to this challenge and in 2009 created a group of CSR officers that come from every department of the School.

If you are seeking a way to encourage and implement CSR-related activities on your campus you should look for a transversal approach. If a school can be compared to the human body, with various functions that work together in order to be operational, CSR is a "virus". You just need to find a way to spread it in your school, from the very heart to the extremities. The Principles for Responsible Management Education can provide the necessary framework for your CSR virus.

> I recommend that you take this framework and work with a representative from each service to build, reinforce, launch or create your CSR approach and activities. By adopting a con-constructive approach you can avoid many of the pitfalls and potentially stressful situations inspired by changes in curriculum and academic activities. Moreover, it is exceedingly important that you demonstrate that CSR can be used to achieve a person's, a department's and a school's objectives.
>
> *Tashina M. Giraud, Sustainable Development Manager, CSR Department,*
> *Euromed Management*

Actions taken

Currently, there are 25 CSR officers working in our French campuses, all of whom were nominated by their managers. In addition to their regular job duties, the CSR officers are mandated to serve as a link between the School's CSR strategy and the service they represent. This means that they are not only overseeing the "infusion" of CSR into their department, they also give feedback and bring to the table ideas and new projects. A few student representatives also attend the monthly CSR officer meetings.

Each CSR officer must:

- **Link:** transmit the CSR strategy of the School, make the connections between CSR and Euromed Management, serve as a link between the services and the strategy.
- **Think and reflect:** identify areas of improvement, gather good ideas that come from each service.
- **Inform:** raise awareness throughout the School on CSR and disseminate pertinent information.
- **Inspire:** promote actions/activities on CSR in the school, push CSR initiatives, motivate and achieve the sustainable development and CSR objectives of the school, contribute to the development of students' thoughts and knowledge on CSR.
- **Act:** incorporate CSR into each service's operations.

Finding time to develop ideas and projects through this group is not always easy. This systemic approach helps encourage campus initiatives as well as their implementation. Officers are encouraged to find a CSR project that interests them and to join, launch or coordinate it. In fact, last year, two new projects were launched and coordinated by CSR officers concerning dematerialisation and responsible purchasing. More recently, the officer from the human resources department used this network to brainstorm on ways to improve staff well-being.

The first major output of this group is the new "Wellness" service that was officially launched during the intake of fall 2011. Originating from a working group of CSR officers, this initiative seeks to improve the quality of life and health of our students, to be at the service of individual performance and to help prevent psycho-social risks. With a holistic and personalised approach, the group works on creating an environment conducive to the personal and intellectual development of each student.

Results

This project resulted in the creation of the Wellness Team composed of six members of the School's staff (Marseille and Toulon), who serve as an information relay between the students and the School's management. It also produced the Student Wellness Centre – situated in The HUB, the new Creativity and Innovation Centre, the Wellness Counselling Centre – a space reserved for students who would like a confidential meeting with the School's psychologist or with a member of the Wellness Team.

CSR officers from the programme department worked with the Wellness project team to launch a pedagogical workshop, taught by professors from the school of medicine, on stress, burn-out and addictive behaviours and substances. This "Wellness Workshop" was integrated into their personal development and programme requirements. More information can be found on the Wellness Website: http://wellness.euromed-management.com.

A second network of CSR officers was launched last year by Unis-Terre, a student association dedicated to sustainable development. As of this year, in order to receive school funding, each student association is required to nominate a CSR officer and report on CSR-related activities. This helps us promote CSR in all our extracurricular activities.

How does this correspond to PRME?

Euromed Management became signatory to the Principles for Responsible Management Education (PRME) in 2008. By accepting these Principles, the School's management made a number of commitments and PRME became a tool that the CSR department uses when working with different departments and programmes. The CSR officers are our response to Principle 2, our way of incorporating into our academic activities and curricula the values of global social responsibility as portrayed in international initiatives such as the United Nations Global Compact.

Why PRME is/was important

- A tool for institutional commitment.
- A legitimate basis for project construction.
- An internationally accepted set of principles that can be used by each CSR officer.
- A means to benchmark and learn from other management schools' best practices.

INTRODUCTION

Signatories of the Principles for Responsible Management Education (PRME) initiative have undertaken a wide array of efforts to embed sustainability-related content into their curricula, and to enable faculty to implement curriculum change. The challenges have been many, from dealing with faculty who are unfamiliar with these topics to courses and programmes that incorporate responsibility-related content in very unstructured and unsystematic ways, to dealing with courses that barely helped to develop complex decision-making skills or did not clearly include the teaching of global issues.

To confront these and other challenges, as shown by the case in this section, some signatories have undergone a thorough analysis of currently offered educational programmes to determine where sustainability-related content is already embedded and to identify those areas where it needs to be introduced by asking: "Where are we now, where can we start and where should we be heading in the near future?"

Some signatories have addressed this by creating new programme offerings in the form of courses, modules, certificates, etc. Many others have adopted bottom-up and/or top-down approaches and have added PRME-related topics onto existing courses (undergraduate, graduate and doctoral). A **horizontal approach** involving the introduction of corporate sustainability concepts within previously existing courses across diverse disciplines has been a frequent practice.

Frequent conversations have taken place among faculty in order to identify and align efforts on how to proceed with curriculum change. Among the initiatives undertaken, some schools have started with analysis of the syllabi of each core course in a given study programme to identify existing corporate sustainability-related concepts and then taken steps to "make them explicit". Frequently, the integration of PRME has taken place through incorporation, across the different academic disciplines, of multiple sustainability-related **case studies**, often based on professors' individual research and consultancy projects. The availability of multiple case studies centred on sustainability for the diverse academic disciplines has proven to be a very accessible practice.

Also, global sustainability issues – such as the Millennium Development Goals, poverty, human rights, gender equality, anti-corruption, labour standards, climate change, resource (e.g., water, food) scarcity, etc. – have been included across a wide variety of subject disciplines. Often these issues have been integrated into projects or seminars. For many schools, the ultimate goal has been that of teaching complex decision-making/problem-solving skills, or as one signatory put it, "to make sure that students can 'think systems'". To meet this goal, some schools have developed real world entrepreneurial experiences, such as innovative "labs" centred on service and action learning. Case stories that demonstrate the implementation of such experiential learning programmes are detailed in Section 3.

From the inspirational cases included in this section, it is clear that enabling faculty to implement PRME is a crucial task. Often, faculty have sought guidance from more experienced instructors on how to incorporate PRME and sustainability concepts into their teaching, seeking a deeper understanding of the relevance of other subjects to their discipline. Accordingly, several signatories have offered support to faculty in identifying readings, cases and other material. Some signatories have created specific pools of resources or a departmental "unit" with a supporting multidisciplinary faculty team. Other schools have been involved in the creation of regional management associations, explicitly aligned with PRME and sustainability – issues that have become central tenets of all their faculty development programmes.

Overall and, as portrayed by the cases in this section, PRME is seen as a coherent set of guiding principles that provide institutional legitimacy to curricula change. As some signatories' cases show, by aligning curricula with PRME, a clear message is sent to several key stakeholders about the strong institutional commitment to sustainability. The PRME initiative has also been seen as providing further impetus, support and legitimacy to **assurance of learning** and programme quality assurance processes (such as those frequently related to major academic accreditation agencies). That is, curriculum change is seen by different signatories as an opportunity to align and embed the principles of responsible management as a course learning outcome with the programme and course objectives of other disciplines, and concurrently, to assess student learning with regard to those learning outcomes.

Also, other signatories have used PRME as a guiding framework to achieve higher placement in the Aspen Institute's Beyond Grey Pinstripes review and rankings. Such endeavours have offered additional encouragement to most faculty members.

Readers of this section will find many useful ideas and tactics to start changing curricula and enabling faculty. Still, the task to undertake comprehensive curriculum/content adaptation within respective subjects (finance/accounting, marketing, human resources, international business, etc.) offers many challenges that require further efforts by PRME as a learning community. For some, the way ahead may consist of developing curricular initiatives that are practical and realistic, encouraging faculty members to review their curriculum now or on an annual basis, adding progressively updated sustainability-related content, using the PRME Sharing Information on Progress (SIP) report itself to monitor progress and raise awareness of sustainability integration, etc. As stated by some signatories here, the options are multiple but obtaining small wins in order to move forward becomes crucial.

In order to change curriculum and enable faculty to meet the needs of the sustainability agenda, PRME signatories have undertaken initiatives, such as:

1. Identifying, through analysis of current academic offerings (e.g., existing syllabi), relevant content already offered by the institution.
2. Incorporating sustainability and ethics-related content and case studies into most subjects.
3. Including global issues (Millennium Development Goals, human rights, poverty, anti-corruption, gender, labour standards, climate change, resource scarcity, etc.) in a wide variety of courses.
4. Designing new courses, modules, certificates, etc. on sustainability-related topics.
5. Developing experiential learning initiatives to teach systems-thinking skills.
6. Arranging for faculty members or departmental "units" (sometimes with a supporting multidisciplinary team) to coach and advise instructors with less experience in teaching sustainability.
7. Creating regional management associations with a key priority to train faculty in sustainability-related topics.
8. Establishing "review periods" (e.g., annually) to continually update curricula to incorporate sustainability themes and needs.
9. Using PRME to assist assurance of learning and programme quality assurance processes (such as those frequently related to AACSB and other academic accreditation agencies).
10. Using PRME as a framework to pursue higher placement in rankings, such as the Aspen Institute's Beyond Grey Pinstripes.

HOW TO STRATEGICALLY ADAPT A CURRICULUM TO THE PRME FRAMEWORK

Hanken School of Economics, Helsinki and Vaasa, Finland

PRME IMPLEMENTATION AND STRATEGIC CURRICULUM CHANGE: THE EXPERIENCE AT HANKEN SCHOOL OF ECONOMICS

Introduction

Hanken School of Economics is a leading, internationally accredited (EQUIS and AMBA) university in the field of economics and business administration. It has approximately 230 members of staff, including 120 members of faculty, operating in 5 departments: accounting and commercial law, economics, finance and statistics, management and organisation, and marketing. Hanken has about 1,900 students studying for BSc or MSc degrees and around 160 students studying for a PhD degree. The School offers seven international master's degree programmes in English. It has campuses in Helsinki and in Vaasa.

Challenges

Signing on to the Principles for Responsible Management Education (PRME) initiative by Hanken's former dean, Marianne Stenius, in 2008 helped to highlight the strategic importance of strengthening the integration of corporate responsibility (CR) in all activities at the business school. However, this does not mean that this strategic importance has been automatically recognised in all parts of the School. This is related to Hanken's governance system and its more bottom-up decision-making culture, which empowers active faculty members (initiatives are welcome), but also may constrain the strategic implications of their actions (an implementation in every discipline cannot be imposed or even strongly supported from the top). While the Hanken leadership is showing its

continued commitment to PRME, the level of strategic priority that has been given to CR issues at the School might not be as high as in more "top-down" schools. Thus, the faculty members who have been in charge of PRME implementation have used PRME itself as a lever to overcome these potential strategic barriers, in three main ways.

Actions taken

First, they have leveraged the fact that they are from different departments to articulate PRME curriculum change as a cross-disciplinary issue. By creating a CR study module incorporating courses from their respective subjects – supply chain management and corporate geography; and politics and business – and "horizontally" mobilising other faculty members potentially adhering to the Principles within subjects such as accounting, commercial law, management and organisation, and marketing, we have been able to develop a cross-disciplinary programme that has become the spine of PRME implementation and has shown that PRME should be integrated across all the different subjects in the School. The study module now integrates courses from almost all subjects, which means that students majoring in almost all subjects are increasingly exposed to courses integrating CR and ethical issues into their own major subjects.

Second, the writing-up and publication of PRME reports have been used to raise awareness of CR issues in the School, not only by giving opportunities to the deans to reflect on these issues when writing the prefaces, but also because the reports have been occasions for enhancing both internal and external communication on CR. In addition, the design and contents of Hanken's reports have received positive feedback from other schools involved in PRME, which has been noted by the deans and has contributed to raise PRME on their strategic agenda. This also means that the continuous improvement ethos (in terms of social responsibility) tied to PRME reporting is also increasingly accepted in the School. (See Hanken's case study "Beyond bureaucracy: Reporting as a strategic tool at Hanken" in Section 6 for more details and a discussion of Results.)

Third, the possible relation between PRME and further accreditation of the School has been used as a lever. Initially, PRME was marketed by the faculty members to the leadership of the School as a foresight that CR in the curriculum will become a more explicit issue in the accreditation processes in the future. In this case, the influencing tactics employed did not need to be very strong as the dean had picked up similar signals through formal and informal international networks, and was thus very keen on the idea. As Hanken is involved in several accreditation and re-accreditation processes, the School's leadership has allocated more explicit strategic importance to how CR and ethical issues are integrated in the curriculum. The faculty members in charge of PRME implementation have thus been invited to give our input on some of these strategic issues. In addition, the cooperation with another PRME signatory school (Audencia Nantes School of Management in France) has led to a joint session on the implementation of (and cooperation on) PRME at the AACSB conference in Paris during fall 2010; this has helped to put both schools more strongly on the map as role models in terms of PRME implementation, which in turn has helped raise the strategic nature of PRME internally. From the viewpoint of faculty members active within PRME, this has meant a feeling of more support for PRME initiatives both in course and programme developments and other PRME-related activities, such as the planned development of CR-related partnerships with companies and non-governmental organisations.

Since those faculty members who champion PRME are often not directly involved at a strategic level in the governance of their business school, they need to creatively find ways to make the most of the opportunities that PRME provides them for steering strategic curriculum change. My advice to faculty champions is to try and leverage the three above issues: (1) the notion that it is desirable for curriculum to be affected across the different subjects (not just one separate subject on ethics); (2) the reporting process as a way to raise the strategic profile of PRME at the School – through inviting school leadership reflections, using the finished report in internal and external communication – and place the School in a continuous improvement process; and (3) accreditation processes as opportunities to raise the strategic profile of PRME at the School and the international recognition of the School in terms of its contribution to responsible management education.

Martin Fougère, Assistant Professor in Politics and Business,
Hanken School of Economics

Why PRME is/was important

- Articulating the need for curriculum change across different subjects: creating a cross-disciplinary study module.
- Leading to enhanced internal and external communication on the CR-related work done at the School (through reporting as process and outcome) and its continuous improvement.
- Leveraging accreditation processes so as to both raise the strategic nature of CR issues internally and put Hanken on the international map when it comes to CR issues (both strengthening each other).

Queen's School of Business, Kingston, Ontario, Canada

STRATEGICALLY INFLUENCING A PROGRAMME CURRICULUM BY CREATING WIDESPREAD SUPPORT

Introduction

 Queen's School of Business (QSB is one of the world's premier business schools – renowned for exceptional programmes, outstanding faculty and research, and the quality of its graduates. Canadian executives regard Queen's School of Business as Canada's most innovative business school, offering students academic excellence and an exceptional overall experience.

Queen's School of Business – where Canada's first Commerce programme was launched in 1919 – is located at Queen's University in Kingston, Ontario. QSB offers nine academic degree programmes – an undergraduate commerce programme, three master's programmes (MSc in Management, Master of International Business, Master of Finance), four MBA programmes (full-time MBA, accelerated MBA for business graduates, executive MBA, and Cornell-Queen's Executive MBA) and a PhD in management. The School offers a portfolio of custom and open enrolment non-degree executive education programmes in Canada and in the MENA region (Middle East North Africa) that are considered among the best in the world. In 2011, the School had over 2,000 students and 81 full-time faculty.

Challenges

Queen's School of Business (QSB) is committed to the Principles for Responsible Management Education (PRME) and to ensuring that its curriculum supports the PRME framework. Curriculum development is a process of continuous improvement to ensure that content is current, innovative, and meets the demands employers, the expectations of accrediting bodies, and prepares students for success.

However, even when support for change comes from the highest level, curriculum change takes time, as it must balance a plethora of interests and

demands. Pressures faced include the need to deliver all of the required core content for the degree within a limited time frame, limited budget to fund the development of new courses, and the potential resistance to change from professors whose courses may be affected. Further, because responsible leadership covers all business principles, effectively addressing the Principles throughout programme curriculum requires a coordinated approach between many faculties and disciplines, which requires widespread buy in and support. Further, to ensure content is leading edge and innovative, it needs the leadership of top professors, which may require new professors to be recruited.

The common thread is that curriculum change needs to be supported from above, and the need to create buy in at all levels given limited resources. Through this case we share some of the actions taken by QSB to support the adaptation of the PRME framework into our programme curriculum by both adapting the existing curriculum and adding new curricular items. We hope it can be helpful to other PRME signatories.

> Getting the support and buy in of key individuals early in the process is critical when trying to move forward curriculum changes. Identify and involve key individuals throughout the process – use their expertise to advise on the development of the proposal itself, and to help identify the best process for how and when to move forward with the proposed changes.
>
> *Tina Dacin, Director, Centre for Responsible Leadership,*
> *Queen's School of Business*

Actions taken

Within QSB, support for the changes came from the Dean as Canada's first signatory to PRME and was supported by the actions of the School's Centre for Responsible Leadership. Acting as a central body whose mission is to educate students and foster research, outreach and advocacy on responsible leadership, the Centre for Responsible Leadership is able to support and influence change by engaging key individuals from across disciplines and programmes. Some of the actions taken, which we recommend as good strategies for other academic institutions to consider include:

Create buy in for change and identify champions within each programme

A curriculum review committee composed of faculty and administrative staff from across programmes and disciplines was formed to review existing responsible leadership programming and make recommendations for programme improvements. Key individuals were engaged and identified who have become strong supporters within each programme area.

The Centre also formed an external advisory board composed of leaders in industry and influential non-profit organisations to advise of emerging trends and on how to best deliver programme content to meet the needs of the future.

Adapt existing curriculum for immediate impact

QSB has engaged in many ways to expose students to new responsible leadership content using the existing curriculum. Examples include:

- Bringing in guest lecturers (business or community leaders) to speak in existing classes. Having students hear their perspectives/experiences/advice first hand can be very effective.
- Influencing the direction of individual assignments to have them address a responsible-leadership issue. For example, MBA students in the Certificate in Socially Responsible Leadership programme must have a responsible leadership focus on their final capstone essay, or management consulting projects.
- New cases have been developed (and are under development), which can be used in classes or case competitions.
- Hosting an annual Responsible Leadership Summit, bringing

together leading academics and practitioners to expose students to a variety of issues and topics in the responsible leadership space. This conference can be used to bring new content/ideas to students each year.

Develop new curriculum

The Centre leveraged its ability to influence curriculum change by strategically using the existing curriculum review process in the School. Champions from each programme were able to advise on the process, and help to create buy in from within each programme review committee. By focusing on benefits to both students and the programmes, solid cases for developing new responsible leadership themed courses were presented. New course ideas were also presented at a time when the School was looking for new electives to offer in response to increased enrolments. Further, feedback from students (both current students and new applicants, and input from a student advisory committee that was formed) was used to speak to the demand of students for programming in areas such as social entrepreneurship). Underlying the curriculum review process was the need to have this content integrated into core courses offered.

Launch pilot projects to try something new

As it can often be time-consuming and financially risky to develop and launch new programming, pilot projects are a great and safe way of quickly trying new ideas, getting feedback to improve the idea, and getting support for the initiative (or learning what is not worth pursuing). QSB launched several successful trials which that have led to additional programming including:

- Offering a design thinking and innovation workshop to first-year commerce students. This workshop was so well received that we are looking to launch a series of school-wide workshops, and looking at how we can integrate this content into core curriculum.
- Putting out a wide "call for expression of interest" for participating in working groups on new topics of interest (for example, addressing Aboriginal issues in Canada). This pulled together a very diverse group of people from across campus. A series of brown bag lunches

were held, to explore ideas and interests, how programming in this space could be developed, and it gave people the opportunity to explore and discuss their various research interests and potential areas for collaboration.

Results

By engaging key stakeholders, we are creating widespread buy in for curriculum changes to enhance and expand the responsible leadership content that our students are exposed to throughout their studies. The Centre is also establishing itself as a central spot within the School where faculty, staff and students can go to for assistance on course ideas and topics, or to share their ideas.

Some of the key outcomes from these collaborative efforts taken to date include:

- **The development of new courses:** Three new responsible leadership themed Commerce courses have been developed and are currently being offered (Strategies for Social Innovation, Sustainability, and Ethics). Two new course proposals are under development (an undergraduate capstone course on responsible leadership and MBA elective course on social innovation/social entrepreneurship).
- **Enhancement of existing curriculum:** A bank of responsible-leadership themed cases is being developed, which can be used by professors in their classes, or for case competitions. An increasing number of guest speakers are being identified and brought into the School to speak in classes, speakers series events, and conferences. Course assignments are being tailored to address responsible leadership issues.
- **New programme development:** The Centre has launched a new "Discovery Learning Workshop" series. These day long workshops are offered to faculty, staff and students from across the University. Two workshops offered in 2012 were in exploring Aboriginal issues in Canada, and social innovation/entrepreneurship. They offer a learning opportunity, as well as chance for faculty and researchers from across the University to discuss and collaborate on research.

Why PRME is/was important

- As a signatory to PRME, QSB's commitment to the principles of responsible leadership is very clear and very public. Having to report regularly against these external commitments is an additional driver for the implementation of curriculum change.
- Learning about innovative new ideas and approaches from other schools, and sharing ideas and best practices with other PRME signatories, is helpful as we develop new programming.

SUCCESSFUL STRATEGIES FOR CURRICULUM CHANGE

Copenhagen Business School, Copenhagen, Denmark

MAKING THE SCANDINAVIAN APPROACH TO RESPONSIBLE MANAGEMENT EDUCATION EXPLICIT

Introduction

Copenhagen Business School

HANDELSHØJSKOLEN

Copenhagen Business School – where university means business

Founded in 1917, Copenhagen Business School (CBS) is one of the largest business schools in Europe with more than 18,000 students and 1,500 staff. CBS offers an innovative research environment to ensure value for society and a comprehensive range of degrees in various business disciplines. In 2011 the Aspen Institute ranked CBS ninth in its global ranking of CSR research.

Challenges

When carrying out an initial survey of responsible management education (RME) content in CBS study programmes, the Principles for Responsible Management Education (PRME) team realised that RME content was included unsystematically and unevenly between the 17 study programmes taught at CBS.

> My advice is to have extensive talks with faculty and get internal backing for curriculum change (bottom up approach) and then go to the management, making them set clear targets for where they want this to go (top down approach). I believe that this dual approach is what got us where we are today.
> *Kai Hockerts, Professor and Academic Director of Responsible Management Education, Copenhagen Business School*

Actions taken

In order to streamline the RME activities at CBS and to make them more explicit, it was decided by the dean of education to launch an extensive curriculum-change initiative. As part of this initiative, the syllabus of each core course in a given study programme was analysed for RME content and meetings with the lead faculty were arranged. The initiative was launched in CBS with the full-time MBA during 2008/2009 and at present is currently being rolled out across 17 bachelor study programmes.

During the personal meetings the PRME team has three aims:

1. Identify existing RME content and make it explicit in the syllabus and where possible in the learning objectives.
2. Offer support in identifying readings, cases and other material to increase the explicit RME content in the class.
3. Propose optional background readings to be included in the syllabi to allow interested students to study RME issues beyond the primary content of the class.

Results

An obvious outcome of this process has been a more explicit way of working with and thinking of RME. A clear result from this is CBS's improved positioning in the Aspen Institute's Beyond Grey Pinstripes review and ranking where CBS placed 43rd on the global list, having leapt 20 places from the last ranking in 2009. Moreover, CBS holds the eighth place among the European institutions on the list.

Why PRME is/was important

- Creating management support, which sends a strong message throughout the institution.
- Creating the position of a PRME manager and PRME director who report directly to the dean of education, with the mandate to go out and incentivise these changes.
- Providing a clear international framework for working with RME.

Seattle Pacific University School of Business and Economics, Seattle, Washington, United States

STRATEGIES FOR PRME CURRICULUM ALIGNMENT

Introduction

Seattle Pacific University's AACSB accredited School of Business and Economics (SBE) offers three undergraduate majors: economics, accounting and business administration; and, three graduate degrees: MBA, master's in information systems management and a master's in social and sustainable business. SBE selectively admits 100 undergraduate students each year and there are approximately 175 students enrolled in the master's programmes. SBE's vision of "another way of doing business" is fleshed out by 25 faculty members in the context of a 4,000 student, Christian university.

Challenges

SBE was the first business school to adopt the Principles for Responsible Management Education (PRME) in the US Pacific Northwest. It was adopted because the Principles complemented the SBE's approach to business education, which understands the purpose of business as service. However the challenge for SBE was to align our curriculum with the Principles of PRME and encourage faculty to include the Principles in instructional design and delivery.

> My advice is to use the Principles of PRME to initiate curriculum and co-curricular innovation and change. Seattle Pacific University used a social venture competition as a catalyst for change in the curriculum such as undergraduate majors in social enterprise and global development and a graduate programme in social and sustainable business. PRME also provides one rationale for facilitating interaction between the practitioner and academic communities around issues such as business as a solution to alleviating poverty. Our students graduate with an understanding for how business can contribute to the common good.
>
> *Ross Stewart, Professor of Accounting, Seattle Pacific University*
> *School of Business and Economics*

Actions taken

The faculty took the action of developing curricular initiatives that were realistic and started with one undergraduate class on sustainability. This was coupled with the use of co-curricular strategies, such as starting a social venture competition or having teams from the business school participate in other University social venture competitions. This provided a "beach-head" for further curricular change and an affirmation that the Principles aligned well with the vision of how business can enhance human flourishing.

The social venture competition spawned a curriculum concentration in our business major on "sustainable enterprise", and this facilitated participation by non-business majors (such as global development majors) in business school classes. Social venture plans capture the interests and aspirations of students to make the world a better place, both locally and abroad. A local example is a social venture designed to employ ex-prisoners in a lawn-mowing business and to use the profits to provide job training skills and life skills support. A global example is an innovative engineering product, the Pure Pump system, which uses the power of running water (e.g., a river or stream) to move water to villages and towns while also powering a UV light system to clean the water of any contaminants. This kind of innovation and market creation initiatives influence curriculum development with courses created on social enterprise, micro-finance and global development, and programmes such as a master's degree in social and sustainable business.

Results

Such curriculum innovation and change provide concepts such as "business enhancing human flourishing" and "business contributing to the common good" with robust and engaging content.

Further benefits materialised around interdisciplinary initiatives. SBE organised conferences bringing together practitioners, students and academics around themes such as micro-finance or business as providing solutions to poverty. This spawned collaboration between the practitioner and academic communities. The conferences showcased PRME themes and SBE gained new appreciation of the dynamism of the practice community from diverse organisations such as Pioneer Human Services, the Gates Foundation, World Vision and Keva.

Why PRME is/was important

- PRME enhances and infuses SBE's existing curriculum.
- PRME aligns with SBE's aspirations for business as one of service to customers, employees and community within a context of sustainability.
- PRME provides a rationale for academic-practitioner conferences reaching out to the business community on key questions, such as business solutions to poverty.
- PRME provides institutional legitimacy to curriculum change and to business education being engaged with the key global issues.

HOW TO TEACH COMPLEX DECISION-MAKING/ PROBLEM-SOLVING SKILLS EFFECTIVELY

Griffith Business School, Brisbane, Queensland, Australia

INTRODUCING SYSTEMS THINKING AND SUSTAINABILITY AT GRIFFITH BUSINESS SCHOOL

Introduction

Griffith Business School seeks to excel as a provider of high quality, cross-disciplinary and internationally relevant business and public policy education and research, emphasising the relationship between business and society in promoting sustainable enterprises and communities. The School has approximately 9,700 students and 1,200 staff located on four campuses in South East Queensland at South Bank, Nathan, Logan and on the Gold Coast. Griffith was among the first signatories to the Principles for Responsible Management Education (PRME) and recently joined the United Nations Global Compact (UNGC), which sponsors the PRME initiative.

Challenges

With the world now facing severe and increasingly complex and inter-related economic, social and environmental risks, how should the manager manage today? Australia has experienced an economic boom for the last 20 years, based on the growth of its extractive industry sector and sale of fossil fuels and mineral to China, South Korea and Japan. On the other hand, it is also the world's largest per capita carbon emitter. These factors make the introduction of responsible management education an interesting concept: Will the market for local students understand that the world is changing while Australia booms?

One starting point is to see management not as a static problem-solving exercise, but as operating on different levels depending on the circumstance. So, sometimes management is an inspired thought, sometimes a small change or a nudge to an established way of doing things, sometimes it's a smile, sometimes it's exemplary behaviour. Some starting points are helpful:

- First, nobody knows everything, and everyone has a different mental model, even if they sometimes coincide – so, learn to listen.
- Second, not all problems have quick solutions – so learn to learn from mistakes.
- Third, everything is connected to everything and the discrete isolation of parts may be a chimera – so, start systems thinking.

Recent international research on the effectiveness of MBA programmes has identified that most programmes have a number of major gaps in graduate attributes (Datar *et al.*, 2010). These gaps include the following:

- Globalisation
- Leadership development
- Critical thinking
- Innovation and creativity
- Experiential/action learning

Datar *et al.* (2010) also found that there needs to be a re-balancing of the content of the MBA to reduce the emphasis on content or knowledge in favour of the development of key skills and students' self-awareness; particularly with respect to values, attitudes, and beliefs. These findings are supported by feedback from industry, alumni and current students, which suggested that the programme goals needed to be reviewed to include critical thinking, systems thinking, analytical skills, persuasive communication, cross-discipline integration and innovation.

There is no more urgent task for business and management schools than producing sustainability literate graduates ready to meet the demands of enlightened business practices in the 21st century. I strongly recommend adopting and implementing PRME as the foundation for tackling this responsibility. Becoming a signatory to PRME was a small but very useful step for Griffith Business School as it connected us with many other institutions from around the world that were on the same path. By explicitly making responsible leadership and sustainability core to what we do, actively engaging with others in this space, developing related course and programme specialisations and establishing an academic centre in sustainable enterprise, we've managed to achieve a great deal in the last five years. But the challenges before us demands nothing less than a complete re-evaluation of business and management education – so there is still much to be done

Malcolm McIntosh, Director, Asia Pacific Centre for Sustainable Enterprise, Griffith Business School

Actions taken

In recognition of the need for innovative decision makers, problem solvers and responsible leaders, from 2012 the School's newly redesigned MBA programme will feature a compulsory introductory course on systems thinking and sustainability. This course asks students to understand the connections between what may at first sight appear to be disparate parts of the MBA programme by linking strategy, ecology and economics, supply chain management and waste, financial and natural capital, people, planet and profits. In addition, an action learning or experiential approach (Datar *et al.*, 2010) will be a feature of the programme whereby all courses actively and intentionally draw on the life and work experiences of the students.

Results

The introduction of systems thinking and sustainability at the beginning of the MBA programme seeks to contextualise the focus on sustainable enterprise and help shape the way students see and experience the rest of the programme. Students will be immediately exposed to examples of successful businesses "doing well by doing good", which has become the mantra for many people in many businesses that are part of the emerging sustainable enterprise economy. The course will also highlight that good management requires a balance between synthesis and analysis, and our aim is to promote both rigorous analysis as well as ensuring our students can see whole systems – in other words that they can "think systems". Students will be equipped with the mental models and tools for integrating management, learning and business with the state of the planet and the state of humanity. They will recognise that issues such as climate change can only be substantively tackled when allied to social justice, and that sustainable enterprise is closely related to innovation, creativity and human rights.

Reference

Datar, S.M., Garvin, D.A. and Cullen, P., (2010), *Rethinking the MBA*, Harvard Business Press.

Why PRME is/was important

- PRME provided Griffith Business School with a guiding framework and a platform for exchanging best practice information and experiences on embedding corporate responsibility and sustainability into curricula, research and learning methods.
- Being the first Australian business school to become a signatory to PRME has provided institutional recognition and an instrument to benchmark our efforts as well as communicate and engage stakeholders on corporate responsibility and sustainability.

University of Cape Town Graduate School of Business,
Cape Town, South Africa

THE SOCIAL INNOVATION LAB: A CASE OF CURRICULUM INNOVATION WITH REAL LIFE IMPACT

Introduction

 Since its establishment in 1969, the Graduate School of Business (GSB) of the University of Cape Town has grown to become one of the premier business schools in Africa, with EQUIS and AMBA accreditation. The GSB offers post-experience, postgraduate degrees (such as MBAs), as well as executive education programmes. The GSB has around 2,500 students per year, and its 29 faculty members have a strong focus on emerging markets, social innovation, entrepreneurship, development finance, and values-based leadership.

Challenges

South Africa and the whole of Sub-Saharan Africa struggles with the paradox that, while the region is probably among the richest in the world in terms of its mineral resources, the population is on average very poor and unemployment is high. For example, South Africa has a population of over 47 million people, many of whom are living in poverty stricken regions and townships, and the current estimated unemployment rate – which has been greatly exacerbated by the global recession – is around 23% (Statistics South Africa, 2009, www.statssa.gov.za). Many citizens are battling for means of survival, and are wholeheartedly dependent on government grants, subsidies and charitable organisations.

It is for this reason that entrepreneurship, and in particular "social entrepreneurship", is well suited to the times. Although easily described, the most challenging part of entrepreneurship is skill, or skill development, and the need to educate new business owners to initiate ventures aimed at addressing the needs of society on a sustainable basis.

Our short-termist ways of thinking in business schools have clearly not contributed to much needed solutions. With the financial support of the Bertha Foundation, the GSB has, therefore, created the Bertha Centre for Social innovation and Entrepreneurship.

Some of the basic assumptions of the Centre and the GSB are as follows:

- There is a real need for another managerial paradigm based on holism, stakeholder interest and values-based leadership (see also the Allan Gray Centre for Values Based Leadership, recently established at the GSB with an Allan Gray endowment).
- From a business management perspective, we need to concentrate on entrepreneurial development and innovation.
- We should have an interest in social enterprise (of any kind and size), neither excluding social entrepreneurs nor focusing on them exclusively.
- We should have a focus on the contribution of business approaches to social innovation, in a (financially) sustainable way.

> My advice, to any school, would be to make sure that what you offer to students is relevant, applied in real circumstances, meaningful, and of use to a real community (of any kind). The key success factor is the degree to which the exercise, the experiment, the "teaching" is systemic.
> *Walter Baets, Director Graduate School of Business, University of Cape Town*

Actions taken

A holistic management interpretation

The GSB champions a holistic approach to management (see Baets and Oldenboom, 2009). Despite the fact that the prevailing, short-termist management approach has added insight and value to our understanding of the functioning of markets and companies, it champions too narrow a focus for what is now needed in business.

A more holistic, systemic approach that celebrates diversity is required to enrich the prevailing model. A holistic model demands that organisations satisfy the needs of more stakeholders than just its shareholders.

The conceptual design of the Social Innovation Lab

The Social Innovation Lab (SIL) is a one semester, integrated action learning project which students can choose after having completed the fundamentals in the first two terms of their MBA. The purpose of the SIL is for students to produce a financially sustainable business solution to a real social issue that they are very passionate about. They are given courses, methodologies and tutoring by a group of academics who co-teach/co-tutor this Lab. The issue worked on can either be brought in by the students themselves (provided there are real parties and communities involved in the proposal) or by any outside party (e.g., city council, company or angel investor).

Technically, the SIL replaces conceptually a number of current courses in our MBA, such as 30 credits of electives, the company analysis (20 credits) and the research project (60 credits), which currently constitute the second part of the MBA. Students work in teams of four, five days a week. The expected outcomes of the Lab are, for each group, to produce a business plan (possibly also a prototype) and a presentation, and individually a publishable case study and a learning log (all four of which are examination requirements).

Format

The requirement is that students must have finished the first part of the MBA year, covering the basics of business. From term 3 onwards, they move into another weekly schedule. Term 3 starts with a two-week session on the SIL itself, the expected outcomes, the working agreements, etc. During this period a 10 credit introductory course is also taught. After the starting period, the students have classes every Monday for the entire day. They work on their projects Tuesday to Thursday, and on Friday they have scheduled meetings with their tutors (in groups and, if needed, individually). A virtual learning community is put at the disposal of all students (and tutors) to enable them to share, communicate and learn from one another. At the end of term 4, the mandatory documents are delivered, and a formal group presentation is held in front of venture capitalists, social innovators and business people for students to put forward their group's business solution.

Curriculum

Other than the introduction to the SIL, the first two-week block contains a 10 credit course on systems thinking, complexity theory and action learning.

On the further Mondays of terms 3 and 4, five courses are scheduled:

1. **Social innovation and innovation methodologies** (including creativity, out of the box thinking, emerging enterprise consulting, sustainability).
2. **Social enterprise and entrepreneurship** (including social investment finance, social entrepreneurship, social franchising, the business plan).
3. **Design methodology** (including industrial design, design thinking, design strategies).
4. **Project management** (including scaling.)
5. Introduction to some **major sectors for social innovation** (mandatory, not crediting).

An important action learning project needs to be undertaken by groups of four students, working with real companies, NGOs, communities or local policymakers, on designing and testing a business solution to a real social issue. The outcome of this project should at least be a business plan and presentation, but could go as far as a prototype or even a first dry launch.

Results

Practically, the SIL replaces the 30 credits of electives and the 20 credits of company analysis by 50 credits of courses (the five courses mentioned above, each for 10 credits). The research project is replaced by an action learning research and field project (equally for 60 credits).

Thus far, roughly one third of the MBA class have chosen this option.

Faculty team

We have created a team of faculty members with complementary skills and a systems thinking/action learning background. The faculty team is responsible for the teaching and tutoring of the field work. The group needs to work as much as possible as an integrated task team, while also being a learning team.

Incubator

The last step in the process is the creation of an "incubator". Those successful projects that come out of the SIL can then be continued and nurtured in our own incubator.

Reference

Baets, W. and Oldenboom, E., *Rethinking Growth: Social Entrepreneurship for Sustainable Performance*, Palgrave, 2009.

Why PRME is/was important

- PRME has enabled us to provide an integrated approach of content innovation, pedagogical innovation and societal inclusion in order to come up with a systemic learning experience that has an impact on students.
- The Principles of PRME have helped us focus on adapting the pedagogical approach to PRME suggestions on pedagogical innovation.
- PRME has helped us to focus on societal impact and/or societal inclusion inviting thinking about experiments that involve immediate solutions for real social issues, involving communities, and focusing on inclusive development.

EGADE Business School, Tecnológico de Monterrey (ITESM), Monterrey and Mexico City, Mexico

FACILITATING DIALOGUE AMONG STUDENTS AND TEACHERS TO ENRICH THE LEARNING EXPERIENCE

Introduction

With locations in two world-class cities, Monterrey and Mexico City, EGADE Business School has built a solid international reputation based on its innovative education model, its teaching and research achievement and the global character of its academic programmes. The School was the first Mexican signatory to the Principles for Responsible Management Education (PRME), an initiative supported by the United Nations Global Compact.

Today the EGADE Business School offers 19 postgraduate business programmes – MBA, master's and doctoral programmes as well as specialist programmes and executive education for senior business leaders and family business owners.

Our 300-strong national and international faculty team teaches a student body composed of more than 30 nationalities, and our 12,000 alumni are building and transforming businesses and organisations in Mexico, Latin America and across the world.

Challenges

Teaching ethics in business programmes has always been a challenge for any teacher. In this sense, EGADE Business School has developed in the last two years a course in political, ethics and CSR business by developing case studies to induce students to think about the business and ethical implications of different decisions made in a company. In addition, the entire MBAs programmes' courses have an ethic transversal.

> Our main advice for those who are interested in teaching ethics, CSR and sustainability is to allow reflection, dialogue, and study cases as a teaching method. Encourage the students to question their beliefs and paradigms. Show them polemic cases, and encourage them to research about such cases in their environments. Moreover, we suggest establishing initial and final objectives; it does not matter if those objectives are in some way modest.
> *Consuelo García de la Torre, Profesora Titular de Administración y Marketing Directora de a Cátedra de Investigación "Humanismo y Gestión," EGADE Business School, Tecnológico de Monterrey, ITESM Campus Monterrey*

Actions taken

We have noticed that when the students face real problems in the form of study cases, complex constructs such as ethics become more understandable for them. In this sense, the global discussion among the participants in the class enriches in many ways the learning experience not only of the students, but of the teacher also.

Another great practice that gives value-added to the learning experience is the case study design. This activity consists of a contest where the students design, research and build case studies involving constructs such as business ethics, corporate social responsibility, social development, poverty alleviation programmes, and sustainability.

The cases discussed in class are national and international, regional and global. This gives the student an overview of what is happening in the business world and an understanding of how the taking of decisions can have consequences of high impact on the company, its stakeholders and society. In addition, the course curriculum includes sessions that review the different functional areas of the company and how decisions from any part of it can cause some people to benefit while simultaneously harming others.

Results

Students have developed a particular interest in participating in this course because from the beginning their thoughts about the traditional business model as related only to profits are questioned, and it also includes the dimension of how decisions impact on stakeholders. Over time this course has become one of the pillars of ethics education in our master's programmes.

In addition, students are assessed on the presentation of a case on an ethical dilemma to demonstrate that they have understood the key elements of learning in the classroom sessions. This has allowed us, over the past two years, to have a number of interesting casuistry from which we hope to create a casebook working with the chair of humanism and management, for which the students will be accredited.

Why PRME is/was important

The Principles have:

- given us some methods for teaching responsible management.
- given us the values associated with responsible management.
- facilitated dialogue among students and teachers regarding management principles.

HOW TO ENABLE FACULTY TO INTEGRATE SUSTAINABILITY/RESPONSIBLE MANAGEMENT TOPICS INTO COURSEWORK AND/OR RESEARCH

IEDC-Bled School of Management, Bled, Slovenia

SUSTAINABILITY AT THE CORE OF IEDC-BLED SCHOOL OF MANAGEMENT'S LEADERSHIP DEVELOPMENT

Introduction

IEDC-Bled School of Management is an award-winning international business school serving the needs of practising managers and experienced executives. Located on the Alpine lake, Bled (Slovenia), IEDC was established as the first business school in Central and Eastern Europe (CEE). Recognised for its innovative curriculum and global impact, the Bled School of Management's mission is developing professional and responsible leaders in CEE and beyond.

A School with a View

Challenges

As the pioneer in management development in CEE, and a change agent in the process of huge economic restructuring and social transformation, IEDC-Bled School of Management has always paid high attention to the subject of ethics and good governance in management education. Anticipating changes in the global business landscape and the emerging leadership challenges related to achieving and sustaining global competitiveness, while acting in environmentally friendly and socially responsible way, IEDC faced the challenge of introducing a total integration of the issues of business ethics, CSR and sustainable development into its curriculum, research, learning materials, faculty development and community service. The challenge got even greater as IEDC has become an internationally recognised innovator in leadership development for a better world, a school known for its consistent efforts to place issues of sustainability and sustainable development at the centre of it identity, operations, and outreach.

Actions taken

One of the first decisions made in response to the new sustainability challenge was the commitment to approaching sustainability in an integrated and systemic way. It was clear that social and environmental challenges should be discussed and addressed in a variety of courses and functional areas, and closely connected with the integrated areas of strategy and leadership. Faculty members teaching the different courses have been encouraged to review their curriculum on an annual basis, adding new sustainability-related content. The changes made to the curriculum throughout the functional, leadership, and strategy courses are also measured biannually as a part of IEDC's participation in and recognition by Aspen Institute's Beyond Grey Pinstripes review and rankings. Such measurement offers an additional encouragement to all faculty members.

To bring together the ideas discussed in different courses and offer an integrated framework, an extended compulsory sustainability course has been introduced, which is run in all IEDC's programmes. This course features a hands-on business project, whereby teams of managers must complete value chain analysis, re-envision business processes and products, and develop a clear business case for implementing the newly redesigned solutions. While a functional perspective allows for exploring specific social and environmental challenges and solutions in great detail, the strategic course on sustainability provides the "big picture" perspective at the level of a company, an industry, and the economy at large.

IEDC's curriculum efforts are supported by its own extensive research programme. Key concepts guiding the School's sustainability philosophy appear in numerous publications, cases and scientific articles, including the book on *Embedded Sustainability: The Next Big Competitive Advantage*, co-authored by Dr. Nadya Zhexembayeva, published in US, UK, and Brazil.

Faculty members are offered financial support for research-related expenses, with sustainability topics promoted with a special research fund.

The School also invests heavily in supporting the managers once they are ready to act on the newly acquired sustainability knowledge, as well as in contributing to the dialogue and partnerships with major learning partners. IEDC serves as a headquarters of UN Global Compact Slovenia, an association of business for sustainable development, and runs numerous initiatives that place sustainability at the centre of national competitiveness.

IEDC also headquarters CEEMAN, a global management development association of over 200 members from more than 50 countries, whose value platform and programme portfolio, including its International Quality Accreditation (IQA) accreditation scheme, highly resonates with the Principles for Responsible Management Education (PRME), of which CEEMAN serves on the Steering Committee. CEEMAN's International Management Teachers Academy (IMTA), aimed at developing a new generation of management educators for the new generation of business leaders, which places a special emphasis on social responsibility of faculty, is introducing in 2012 a new, PRME-related, disciplinary track. Since 2007, all new IEDC faculty members have been taking part in IMTA, making sustainability and responsibility themes required elements of IEDC's faculty development programme.

IEDC and CEEMAN also serve as the founding partners of a global sustainability think tank – Challenge:Future, which brings together over 25,000 young leaders committed to innovation and action for a better world. IEDC faculty has been involved in a wide range of Challenge:Future activities, which offer a unique resource for improving both research and teaching skills in the areas of social responsibility and environmental performance of business. The project also presents a new avenue for introducing the issues of sustainability and innovations into the business schools' curriculum and for encouraging the dialogue and strengthening collaboration between youth and educators.

When IEDC graduates, reporting on how their new capabilities have been appreciated and valued by their companies, also add that their own families recognised that they have become better human beings, I get reassured that there is a broader meaning of what IEDC stands for. And I also know that all

> this would not have been possible without a passionate commitment to and an absolute consistency with the philosophy of the Principles for Responsible Management Education (PRME).
>
> *Danica Purg, President, IEDC-Bled School of Management and President, CEEMAN*

Results

IEDC has made significant and systemic steps for embedding sustainability into its core curriculum, operations, and outreach. Sustainability has been recognised – next to ethics and aesthetics – as one of the three strategic pillars of IEDC's educational philosophy, as the basis for developing critical, transformational and inspirational leaders' mindsets.

This has been celebrated by the School's participants as a real value-added via course evaluation forms and regular alumni consultation requests. The IEDC's conferences and events in this sphere have created a truly public resonance, both nationally and internationally. For example, the 2008 conference on "Sustainable Development for National Competitiveness" was attended by HM Queen Elizabeth II and HRH the Duke of Edinburgh, and then UK Secretary of State for Foreign and Commonwealth Affairs, David Miliband, who delivered a keynote address.

IEDC's work has reached thousands of managers globally through articles in academic publications and practitioner outlets – for example, the 2011 *European Financial Review* article "Embedded sustainability: the strategy for market leaders" created a real resonance in the European financial community and resulted in numerous events and projects. In recognition of IEDC's leadership in the field of sustainability, The Coca-Cola Company has supported the establishment of the Coca-Cola Chair of Sustainable Development, led by Dr. Nadya Zhexembayeva since 2010. While contributing to the educational and research activities, the Chair creates also a fruitful platform for the School's many social and environmental initiatives.

All newly recruited faculty members have attended IMTA, joining the IMTA Alumni Association of more than 400 management educators from 34 countries around the globe, which has been very active in CEEMAN/PRME research and other efforts in fighting poverty through management education.

In all of IEDC's sustainability efforts, the Principles and initiatives of PRME have been very important as they represent a consistent philosophy to be followed by management educators, who realise that we have only one planet and thus, they have a responsibility to protect it through developing responsible business and responsible leaders.

Why PRME is/was important

- PRME, the formulation of which we actively contributed, highly resonates with IEDC's vision, mission and value platform.
- Through PRME, we have contributed to, and also benefitted from, a global legitimacy for the school's belief that responsible leadership requires responsible management education.
- PRME provides a platform for a broader exposure (i.e., sharing, benchmarking, and learning), as well as for a higher impact on business practices and management development approaches and innovation.
- PRME facilitates the internal and external integration and institutionalisation of our efforts, as was the case with the establishment of the Coca-Cola Sustainability Chair, the Global Compact Network Slovenia, Challenge:Future, and CEEMAN's membership in the PRME Steering Committee and leading role in the PRME Working Group on Poverty as a Challenge to Management Education.

HOW TO ADAPT CURRICULA/CONTENT WITHIN RESPECTIVE SUBJECTS

Asian Institute of Management, Makati, Philippines

A PURPOSE AND A JOURNEY

Introduction

Established in 1968 with the primary purpose of helping develop Asian societies through developing Asian managers, the Asian Institute of Management (AIM) is a standalone graduate school of management whose primary mission is to help develop Asian societies by developing Asian managers. AIM offers Asia's oldest MBA programme and has over 39,000 alumni in 70 countries. In addition to executive programmes, AIM offers five degree programmes in management including MBA, EMBA, and MDM (development management). AIM was the first school in Asia to receive AACSB accreditation. AIM decided to become signatory to PRME, because the Principles align with its own mission statement.

Challenges

For AIM, management education is a means, not the purpose. The lens through which every action is evaluated is not only whether students will become successful in their careers, it is whether they will be a factor in helping Asia progress. Historically, the MBA programme had specifically addressed concepts of responsibility in required subjects such as business responsibility and ethics. As the AIM MBA is heavily reliant on the case method, it was not difficult to include environment or stakeholder concerns in many case discussions.

In 2000, AIM launched the Ramon V. del Rosario, Sr. Center for Corporate Social Responsibility (RVR CSR centre). The Center's goal is to conduct research and training on the practice of CSR in Asia. The Center runs an annual Asian Forum on Corporate Social Responsibility (AFCSR) and administers the Asian CSR awards. However, social responsibility continued to be an implicit, rather than explicit, feature of the MBA curriculum.

Actions taken

Before the turn of the century, under the deanship of Jesus Gallegos, AIM revisited the School's mission with the School faculty. After long discussion, the faculty affirmed the heart of the mission statement: to help sustain the growth of Asian societies through developing professional, entrepreneurial, and socially responsible leaders and managers.

As part of the implementation of the mission statement, AIM reviewed not only the curricula, but also its own operations. This review resulted in many improvements including attainment of ISO 14001 certification in 2000; the very first awarded to a graduate school of management anywhere in the world.

In 2001, AIM was honoured with the first Beyond Grey Pinstripes Award for Business School Innovation in Social Impact Management. In 2006, a course on CSR in Asia was offered to all MBA students. This course continues to be offered as an elective of the MBA and the MDM programme.

In its 2009 mid-year conference, the AIM faculty asked the question of what makes the AIM MBA graduate different. The answer was that the AIM MBA explicitly identifies social responsibility as a critical descriptor for its graduates and societal development as a primary goal. In partnership with the RVR CSR Center, the MBA programme offered the Business Leadership and Responsibility (BLR) seminar: "The BLR seminar aims to bring together development (social consciousness) and enterprise (value creation) into the curriculum of all AIM students. The course objective focuses on centring leadership around self-knowledge, personal responsibility and global citizenship."

In the following batch, it was decided that the principles of responsible management and leadership would be embedded in the core functional subjects. Topics of business responsibility were explicitly tackled in the course on strategy management, and tackled as the situation or case allowed in other subjects. Topics of responsible leadership were tackled in Ethics and Human Behaviour in Organisations. All students were asked to work on a CSR project. Implementation of Assurance of Learning across all of the AIM degree programmes also resulted in embedding social responsibility within the curricula of all programmes.

> My advice is: First, that alignment is critical. Responsible management education begins with being responsible. Students evaluate the credibility of the School's principles against the authenticity of its leaders and faculty.
>
> Responsible management involves, not just knowing what is right but also the courage to do what is right. It is important to allow discussion of the grey zone and to provide opportunities to make real life choices. Finally, that an explicit mission statement as well as a disciplined method such as the Assurance of Learning can go a long way towards providing a framework for implementing responsible management education but true learning is about engagement.
>
> *Maria Elena (Maya) Baltazar Herrera, Program Research Director, RVR Center for Corporate Social Responsibility, Asian Institute of Management*

Results

Since it first received the Beyond Grey Pinstripes award, AIM has been a mainstay in the Global Top 100 of the Aspen Institute's Beyond Grey Pinstripes rankings. It continues to be the number one Asian school in the rankings.

AIM's reputation for responsible management education has helped it forge strong ties with global organisations.

With the emergence of social assets as a critical factor in business success, the principles of personal ethics and corporate citizenship have only become more valuable. This has been particularly important in light of the questions raised by recent events on the role of business in society and the role of managers in governing businesses, which require discussions framed by both principle and practicality, both passion and reason. AIM's strong relationships and long involvement in CSR and CSR research has allowed it to provide students with a rich knowledge base and community for understanding the role of business in society.

Perhaps the best gauge of the effect of AIM's efforts in responsible management education can be gleaned from its students. During the graduation of MBA 2011, the batch graduation speech was framed with a quote from W.B. Yeats: "Education is *not filling* a *bucket*, but *lighting* a *fire.*" *The* speech covered three key lessons learned in the programme: that relationships are the foundation of relevance; that integrity and honour must win over convenience and honest beginnings lead to great endings; and that dreaming the big dream is important, but requires the ability to combat failure with redemption.

Why PRME is/was important

In retrospect, the Principles for Responsible Management Education (PRME) provided the framework for:

- a clearly aligned mission,
- methods that allow students to argue, discuss, evaluate and make choices,
- projects that provide real life experiences,
- practical yet academically rigorous research implemented in partnership with business and development organisations, and
- a community that is devoted to constantly engaging and involving its stakeholders.

Australian School of Business, University of New South Wales, Sydney, Australia

SHARED ATTRIBUTES: HOW TO ADAPT CURRICULA AND CONTENT WITHIN RESPECTIVE BUSINESS SUBJECT AREAS

Introduction

 Australian School of Business

Consistently ranked among the top business schools in Australia, the Australian School of Business (ASB) at the University of New South Wales (UNSW) is located in Sydney, Australia. The ASB is host to 8 disciplinary schools (Accounting, Economics, Banking & Finance, Information Systems, Management, Marketing, Risk & Actuarial Studies, and Taxation & Business Law), the Australian Graduate School of Management (AGSM), 12 research centres and institutions, 9 affiliated research centres, 13,948 students (undergraduate and postgraduate), 260 academics and researchers, 177 professional and technical staff and boasts over 57,000 alumni.

Challenges

Current macro-economic conditions create a profound challenge to business schools globally to rethink our values, our principles and our contribution to society. Our students require a substantially more sophisticated learning experience to become leaders in these changing conditions. Our students want to develop the confidence to appropriately challenge the status quo, based on a deep understanding of current knowledge. Our students seek careers that will allow them to make genuine, long lasting contributions to their organisations, their families, their professional associations, their communities and their nations. This is entirely consistent with the Principles for Responsible

Management Education (PRME), which is why we are signatory to the initiative and actively seek to embed these Principles in all that we do.

> My advice to signatories to the Principles for Responsible Management Education is to embed these Principles, not only within the curriculum, but throughout all levels of their organisations. Our organisations and our business communities, nationally and internationally, require the insights implicit in these Principles to help a new generation of business leaders and graduates to create new solutions to complex business and social problems.
> *Gregory Whitwell, Professor and Deputy Dean, Students and Programs,*
> *Australian School of Business, University of New South Wales*

Actions taken

There are several actions under way in the ASB to adapt curricula to address the Principles of the PRME initiative:

- Embedding the Principles by linking them to our graduate attributes and programme learning goals (including critical thinking and ethics). The ASB is seeking to embed these Principles via the AACSB Assurance of Learning (AOL) process in all programmes.
- The cohesion, symmetry, and shared vision between the Principles and many of the ASB's own programme learning goals and graduate attributes offers a set of unique aspirations for which to be accountable. However, if these aspirations are not engaged or measured they will only remain aspirations, rather than realities.
- The ASB, via the AACSB accrediting process, is in the process of assuring its learning. Thus, by drawing on the ASB's own research and expertise, stakeholders, community partners, tier 1 alliances, and national and international partners, the Principles have been codified into the curricula and student experience.
- The Centre for Social Impact (CSI), housed at the ASB, has been designed to deliver sustainable management education, through seminars, dialogues with the broader business community and through the Graduate Certificate in Social Impact

- The CSI is a collaboration of four universities: UNSW, The University of Melbourne, Swinburne University of Technology and the University of Western Australia (UWA). The CSI helps students to lift their gaze and widen their vision about themes as diverse as: managing non-profit organisations, reporting on shared value and indigenous business education.

One of our AGSM programmes, Master of Business and Technology, offers a number of specific courses, as well as seminars on "wicked problems", which highlight and promote sustainable business. These courses include current debates and literature in the following disciplines:

- Business management for a sustainable environment
- Sustainable energy management
- Management of manufacturing systems
- Introduction to management.

As another example, ASB has created a compulsory core course, Business Communication and Ethics in Practice, for our Master of Commerce programme, following multi-stakeholder dialogue.

- We are using engaging case studies, simulations and problem-based activities, and guest speakers and seminars to debate the themes behind the Principles.
- Community-based projects to actively engage students in problem solving and leadership in the community, in for-profit and non-profit organisations.

Our colleagues Dr. Tracy Wilcox and Dr. Mehreen Faruqi have taken the lead, from a research perspective, and are conducting a scoping exercise on the content and impact of our current PRME-related learning and teaching practices. The first stage will explore all postgraduate programmes to document in detail how the Principles are being applied in our programmes. This will allow us to "capture the existing champions" of socially and environmentally responsible business practices in our course curricula and in teaching and learning, and serve as a gap analyses for future development in this area.

The ASB has also increased its partnerships and relationships with other PRME signatory institutions in order to benchmark its progress, through formal seminars and informal networking.

> Following multi-stakeholder dialogue the Master of Commerce has made the inclusion of COMM5001 Business Communication, Ethics and Practice a compulsory course focusing on embedding and integrating PRME principle of ethics and corporate responsibility course in our core work. From my perspective, as someone who has had a long-term interest in business ethics education and education for social responsibility, the fact that ASB has signed up to PRME is of enormous importance – as a legitimating device and as a means of demonstrating/asserting that socially – and environmentally – responsible management is not a nice-to-have or an add-on to "real" business education. This point has been well-researched by our colleagues both here in Australia and internationally.
>
> *Tracy Wilcox, Lecturer, School of Organisation & Management,*
> *Australian School of Business, University of New South Wales*

Results

As we move to systematically review all our academic programmes, at the postgraduate and undergraduate levels, the Principles will serve as a touchstone, to ensure we continue to create business leaders who act ethically and with sustainability principles as top of mind.

To illustrate the importance of the Principles of our curriculum design, we have reshaped one of our flagship programmes, the Masters of Commerce. In our new programme, we have one compulsory course for all students, which implicitly and explicitly incorporates the lessons learned from recent large scale corporate failures. The UNPRME are explicitly used as a framework for analysis. This is complementary to our existing course, Business Communication and Ethics in Practice, which allows students to develop a sophisticated ability to include ethical aspects in all their business decision making.

Why PRME is/was important

- PRME is a process that legitimates and prioritises the view that socially responsible management education is not optional, but is critical for the education of contemporary managers and professionals.

- PRME is important because it challenges us to provide a context for debates on sustainability in our fundamental approach to our teaching and learning.
- PRME provides further impetus, support and legitimacy to pro-gramme quality assurance processes being undertaken by the ASB (such as assurance of learning as a component of the AACSB accreditation process).
- Emerging national and international higher education quality and accreditation requirements are increasingly reflecting the Principles and values of the PRME initiative.

Graziadio School of Business and Management, Pepperdine University, Malibu, California, United States

THE SEER LENS: APPLICATION OF THE PRME INITIATIVE

Introduction

PEPPERDINE UNIVERSITY
Graziadio School of Business and Management

The Graziadio School of Business and Management, Pepperdine University located in Malibu, California, in fall 2010 launched a certificate in Socially, Environmentally and Ethically Responsible (SEER) business practice in the full-time MBA programme. Approximately 210 students comprise the enrolment in the programme, including both first and second year students.

Challenges

As MBA enrolment begins to decline along with a less than optimistic global economic projection, graduate business schools are facing recruiting challenges. In addition, as more schools worldwide earn AACSB accreditation, the competition for a declining market has become fierce. Clearly, attention to differentiation has never been as important as it is today. Graduate business schools in order to flourish will need to develop creative approaches to deal with the current problematic environment.

Actions taken

As a signatory to the Principles for Responsible Management Education (PRME) that is dedicated to a broad perspective of graduate business education, the Graziadio School has created a certificate programme to enhance its commitment to the Principles. The certificate in Socially, Environmentally, and Ethically Responsible (SEER) business practice not only describes our social-environmental focus, but also provides a unique programme that we believe will differentiate us in the MBA marketplace.

The underlying framework of the certificate programme is the SEER Lens, which integrates corporate citizenship, financial strength, product/ service quality and environmental stewardship. The concept is rooted in the macro-values model of Crooke (2008). The SEER Lens is aligned with the United Nations Global Compact strategic initiative that embodies human rights, labour, environment and anti-corruption while simultaneously supporting Principles 1, 2, and 3, purpose, values and method, associated with the PRME initiative. The design of the curriculum incorporated the following:

- Using the Beyond Grey Pinstripes (Aspen Institute) rankings measure as a template it was decided that courses in the SEER programme needed to contain at least 50% of either social- environmental and/or ethical content. (The Beyond Grey Pinstripes ranking assesses graduate business school curriculum, worldwide, based on the extent to which courses incorporate social and environmental issues.)
- To be consistent with the underlying framework, the programme needed to reflect the SEER Lens. Coursework and service activities were required to combine two or more of the dimensions of the framework: corporate citizenship, financial strength, product/service quality and environmental stewardship
- To construct an integrated programme that incorporates the SEER Lens, the curriculum would be composed of at least one course from each department. Each of the five departments at the Business School consists of two disciplines: accounting/finance, economics/ business law, strategy/information systems, organisational beha-viour/organisation theory, and marketing/decision sciences.
- The programme/courses needed to be aligned with the School's mission, specifically addressing values-centred leadership.

The certificate requires 8 units of coursework, 6 units of elective choices, and a required capstone course (Responsible Business Practice). In addition, students are required to complete a service requirement, which includes membership in Net Impact along with involvement in an event related to social-environmental activity. (Examples of the service responsibility include: coordinating a Net Impact project, being a member of the planning committee for Social Enterprise Week, assisting in the ethical case competition programme). All courses are two units, seven weeks in length. Classes meet four hours each week. The semester is divided into two, seven-week sessions. The split semester design in both fall and spring allows opportunities for students to take numerous electives.

As a commitment to Principle 6: Dialogue, we encourage student governance by bringing in the student voice in shaping the programme. It is our conviction that enhancement of leadership skills takes place both in and out of the classroom. It was the student voice that initially raised the interest in a certificate programme. Although GBS offered a number of courses related to social-environmental content, it was the students who came forth to recommend a structure that could be captured in a more formal manner. In support of Principle 5: Partnerships, we have engaged a number of business leaders from organisations committed to sustainability in the role of guest presenters in the classroom and symposia, and, in some cases, have taken an adjunct teaching position in the certificate programme.

Support for the programme in part is due to the Business School's mission statement, which provided a significant influence in securing approval for the SEER certificate. The faculty by an overwhelming margin (54 voted yes, 6 no) supported the proposal. The dean and associate dean also were in support, in fact, they were the primary drivers of the programme as a reflection of their commitment to the School's mission. The School's five-year Strategic Initiative identifies values-centred leadership and responsible business practice as primary goals. The Initiative reflects plans for continued development of programmes related to SEER as well as a fund-raising campaign for the purpose of building a centre for responsible business practice. As further evidence of administrative support, the dean currently holds a position on the AACSB Sustainability Conference Board.

My advice to those institutions considering a certificate or programme that incorporates CSR and environmental values into MBA curriculum is to make sure that these principles stand alongside great products and service. As business schools, it is our job to make sure that our students graduate with an understanding of how these values integrate into the real world. In the real world great product/service is paramount. Fortunately, understanding and applying these values into a going concern is now becoming a mainstream movement. Many Fortune 100 companies are now addressing CSR and their respective corporate environmental footprints in some way. As more companies begin to legitimately use this understanding to create a competitive advantage in their respective industry we, as educators, will be mandated to teach these principles as an integral aspect of the MBA education. Take some chances – we don't know it all. This movement is a freight train that is nowhere near slowing down. So, grab a hold, get a programme/certificate in place and lead, just lead.

Michael Crooke, Assistant Professor of Strategy, Coordinator, Certificate in Socially, Environmentally and Ethically Responsible (SEER) Business Practice Program, Graziadio School of Business and Management, Pepperdine University

Results

Our programme is only one year young thus far. The first year we granted 29 SEER certificates. We expect to come close to doubling that number in the coming academic year. In addition, we expect the number to increase once our information sessions begin in the coming fall semester. The graduating SEER class of 2011 has started a LinkedIn forum to maintain engagement with their fellow students. Their group topics include sustainability issues as well as mainstream business trends, which include a "SEER perspective". Feedback collected from students graduating with a SEER certificate was overwhelmingly positive and reinforced the mission of SEER; to train our MBA students to understand sustainability in a way that integrates the SEER values into the value chain – thus creating a sustainable competitive advantage, for them, their firms, and society at large.

To further the assessment process, the lead faculty in the programme have created a steering committee including a member of the first graduating class along with a senior executive from a southern California organisation whose company embraces social-environmental issues. Their function is to review strategy and curriculum and put forth needed improvements. Based on data gathered throughout the year, the committee made a number of curricular changes. Either due to lack of student demand (i.e., SEER electives that did not make it onto the programme based on low enrolment) and further review of the 50% criterion (i.e., SEER courses require at least 50% social-environmental content), the number of electives were reduced from 15 to 11. In addition, early in the initial semester of the programme, Net Impact officers along with lead faculty identified a group of three, first-year students to comprise the SEER committee. Working with faculty and administration they were able to bring in the student voice in advancing assessment of the programme.

Reference

Crooke, M. (2008), "A Mandala for organisations in the 21st century", Doctoral dissertation, UMI Dissertation Abstracts.

Why PRME is/was important

- Recognising the importance of graduate business education in embedding social and environmental content in creating strategic programme design.
- Realising the value of an integrated curriculum that address responsible business practice.
- Creating an environment at the Business School both inside and outside the classroom that incorporates opportunities to advance student development.
- Identifying organisations that are committed to social-environmental strategies that partner with the Business School to heighten student awareness.

IAE Business School, Universidad Austral, Pilar, Buenos Aires, Argentina

FROM CONTROL TO PREVENTION: INTRODUCING INTEGRITY COMPLIANCE INTO IAE BUSINESS SCHOOL'S CURRICULUM

Introduction

IAE Business School's mission is to contribute to the knowledge development and personal growth of business men and women, strengthening their managerial skills as well as the human virtues required for management. In pursuing this mission, IAE Business School actively looks for opportunities of collaboration with worldwide initiatives that share and promote its own values. As part of this ongoing commitment, on December 17, 2008, IAE became a signatory of the Principles for Responsible Management Education (PRME) and since then it has consistently aligned itself to the initiative's objectives and requirements.

Every year, over 6,000 professionals from around the world and the most dynamic industries join our programmes, effectively building a significant regional network for the leading multinational and domestic companies that entrust IAE with their organisations' training. IAE's faculty consists of over 50 professors with PhD degrees from renowned international business schools. Most are full-time professors who devote their time to teaching, research, management duties and business consulting. IAE's programmes include executive MBA, MBA, PAD (top management programme), PDD (management development programme), among others. IAE Business School is located in Pilar, Province of Buenos Aires, Argentina.

Challenges

Partially responding to the concerns of the local and regional business community, the academic community at IAE Business School giving instruction to future and current business leaders was in need of a more systematic approach in teaching how to deal with integrity problems. The

usual approach through internal control modules was both too formalistic and one-dimensional, that is, devoid of diversity in terms of scope of application (restricted as it was within the limits of finance courses). Attempts to introduce integrity issues through traditional CSR were also made, though also here the limitations of this approach were soon detected as the former was not able to grasp the complexities of regulations, norms and laws, "hard" and "soft", that integrity issues usually involve.

Actions taken

As a solution to offer a systematic approach through which to tackle business integrity problems with a focus on prevention/ex ante aspects, the Institution came up with the idea of adopting a complex approach to integrity compliance, the methodical study and examination of best practices that, while retaining some central tenets of traditional compliance goes beyond them, incorporating business ethics issues such as anti-corruption, environment, labour laws, human rights laws, and transparency.

> Embed the academic work in cooperation with business (companies, chambers of commerce, NGOs, etc.), e.g., mixed activities/workshops with compliance officers.
> *Matthias Kleinhempel, Professor of Business Policy, Academic Director of the Senior Executive Program for Latin America, Director of the Centre for Governance and Transparency, IAE Business School, Universidad Austral*

Results

IAE Business School has been able to start adapting curriculum to integrity compliance issues through three main actions. On the one hand, **a vertical strategy** consisting of self-contained, independent business ethics and corporate social responsibility modules/courses in all open programmes consisting of a conference/on-campus speaker, case sessions, and a senior manager discussing some real world dilemma situation. There are also focused programmes in line with this direct strategy: the most recent one is "Good Practices in Business and Compliance" whose goal has been to offer the most recent academic and business trends concerning good corporate governance, risk management and compliance, and to provide the indispensable tools to understand in all its complexity new approaches and different ways of implementing these trends. Among the aspects discussed in this programme are included general aspects of good corporate governance and the role of good business practices; the scope, impact and limitations compliance programmes in business firms; compliance strategies vs. integrity strategies; and key success factors of a good practices programme such as prevention, detection, and response.

On the other, **a horizontal approach** involving the introduction of business ethics aspects/dimensions within previously existing academic area courses. Integrating business ethics aspects in a coordinated way into existing courses constitutes a challenge: as modules and programmes cannot exceed allotted time, in order to fit in something new, something old has to leave. Occasionally modules are redesigned as new instructors bring in different approaches. Additionally, allowances should be made for all possibilities as efforts to coordinate the programme flow around academic areas such as business policy, strategy and finance. In this sense, it has proven helpful to build teaching cells in conjunction with the instructors of different areas.

In particular, attention has been paid to the incorporation of governance and strategy issues (including here stakeholder and trust theories) within the business policy courses and risk management topics within finance courses. The School offers a corporate risk management class in all the MBA and top management programmes. This course stresses the importance of doing a complete risk mapping process in which risks are identified, analysed and measured. The course explains in detail the importance of deciding which risks are going to be taken and which ones are to be transferred. The programme also analyses in some detail the alternative available hedging tools. This programme is becoming increasingly popular among firms that choose it for their in-company education programmes.

An additional third step has been given by way of the creation of a specialised Centre for Governance and Transparency focused on integrity compliance that not only fosters research and teaching in these topics, but also wants to be a point of reference by offering advice to companies, helping them create awareness on the topic through the design, development and implementation of tools to tackle integrity problems. A particularly interesting case has been the creation of a network of compliance officers and chief finance officers who are invited to discuss their problems in workshops. Former and current students are invited to become part of the Centre's activities, creating in that way a dynamic virtuous circle of teaching, research and business practice.

Why PRME is/was important

- The PRME initiative provides a comprehensive and coherent set of guiding Principles with which to strategically frame integrity and responsible management issues and problems and their elaboration.
- By aligning IAE Business School's curricula to the PRME initiative's Principles and values, a message is being sent about both the strong commitment the Institution has towards those values and the means through which those values are applied.
- Further participation in PRME's working groups and activities, allows IAE Business School to position itself as a reference point for these issues at a local and regional level, both for the rest of the business education community as well as the key actors in the private, public and civil society sectors that are already familiar with the Global Compact principles.
- IAE's Centre for Governance and Transparency involvement with PRME's Anti-Corruption Working Group as its co-chair has allowed for a closer interaction with the secretariat, including as latest results the hosting at IAE of two PRME meetings with experts from all around the world: the 2nd Anti-Corruption Working Group Workshop and the 1st PRME Latin America Regional Meeting (5–7 December 2011).

Robert H. Smith School, University of Maryland, College Park, Maryland, United States

CASE PRIMERS: A NEW INITIATIVE TO DRIVE CONTENT INTEGRATION

Introduction

The Robert H. Smith School of Business is an internationally recognised leader in management education and research offering undergraduate, full-time and part-time MBA, executive MBA, executive MS, PhD and executive education programmes. One of 12 colleges and schools at the University of Maryland, College Park, the Smith School has over 4,300 current students and 150 full-time faculty members. We are located inside the Capital Beltway, just eight miles from downtown Washington, DC.

Challenges

There is little doubt that the world is changing and, with it, business education. Resource scarcity, population growth, advances in technology, blurring of sectors, and consumer shifts are just a few of the challenges and opportunities framing our decade. We recognise that these challenges require a fresh approach, collaboration, and business leaders who are skilled in both qualitative and quantitative thinking. We aim to be at the forefront of problem solving, and are committed to preparing our students as leaders in a global economy that demands sustainable economic prosperity and transformative social change.

In order to prepare the next generation of global business leaders capable of shaping a sustainable economic, social, and environmental future we must incorporate cross-sector and entrepreneurial thinking in the education provided at our higher education institutions. To initiate curriculum change toward this new paradigm, my advice is twofold: first begin with faculty who self-identify, build an interest group and facilitate discussions/bring in colleagues from other institutions to share knowledge; then second, grow faculty engagement through hosting workshops to discuss application to each discipline and conducting mappings of cases/research similar to those primers created at the Smith School. Actively involve department chairs and tenured faculty in this process.

Melissa Carrier, Executive Director of the Centre for Social Value Creation, Robert H. Smith School of Business, University of Maryland

Actions taken

The Centre for Social Value Creation was created within the Smith School to inspire, educate, and enable individuals to use the power of business to build a more socially and environmentally sustainable world. With leadership from the Centre, the Smith School is rising to the challenge of integrating global social responsibility and social value creation as concepts into core courses and curriculum at both the undergraduate and MBA level. Working in a cross-disciplinary fashion, the Centre has engaged over 40 faculty from the departments of: Accounting; Decisions, Operations, and Information Technology; Finance; Logistics, Business and Public Policy; Management and Organisation; and Marketing in this effort.

In the early phases of our work, faculty sought guidance on how to incorporate concepts into their teaching and research while others were looking for a deeper understanding of relevancy to their discipline. Case Primers – department specific resources that assist in identifying ways to incorporate socially responsible/sustainable case studies into academic frameworks – were created and distributed to launch this initiative, and are seen as critical to driving content integration in core courses. Cases featured in the Primers were selected by benchmarking peer institutions such as Harvard Business School, University of Michigan, Georgetown, Berkeley, Duke and others. The Centre spoke directly to faculty teaching core courses at peer institutions and researched cases on premier case websites including ecch, SEKN and Harvard Business Publishing, and on other education websites such as the Aspen Institute's Caseplace and Beyond Grey Pinstripes.

> My advice is that organisations need to be sensitive to how technological and business process innovations transform local economies, impact local environments, affect political processes, and change the way we communicate around the world.
>
> *G. "Anand" Anandalingam, Dean, Robert H. Smith School of Business,*
> *University of Maryland*

Results

Following Case Primer distribution, two workshops were held in July and October 2010 by Melissa Carrier, Executive Director of the Centre for Social Value Creation, and Rachelle Sampson, Associate Professor of Logistics, Business and Public Policy at the Smith School in order to provide deeper level understanding and to help shape course content. Twenty-four faculty participated in the workshops, with representation from every department. Additionally, to supplement the case studies' integration, strategic electives were also developed to explore areas such as social marketing, social entrepreneurship, sustainable investing, enterprise in developing economies, green supply chain and strategic corporate social responsibility in greater depth.

In sum, as a result of the Case Primers and workshops, 48 MBA courses with specific sustainability and social value creation content now exist, along with 9 global studies courses. Content developed for the incoming MBA class of 2013 is required to have a minimum of 10% of content focused on sustainability and/or social value creation, with some courses already at 50%. Each new academic year sees more faculty involved and deeper integration in our curriculum. Newly created courses, like the graduate course Sustainability and Green Business and Undergraduate Social Innovation Fellows Practicum, act as a springboard for additional development.

Why PRME is/was important

- The PRME initiative's Six Principles align directly with the vision and mission of the Smith School, offering additional validation to the emphasis we place on social value and responsible leadership.
- The PRME initiative has helped give structure to our internal efforts in bringing diverse faculty together to achieve the School's mission.
- PRME provides an ongoing "checks and balances" platform to ensure Smith is transparent and accountable in developing global leaders as agents of change able to navigate a complex 21st century economy and world.

INCAE Business School, Alajuela, Costa Rica

INCAE BUSINESS SCHOOL: ADAPTING A BUSINESS SCHOOL CURRICULUM TO SUSTAINABLE PRINCIPLES

Introduction

INCAE Business School is a private, multinational, non-profit organisation dedicated to teaching and research in the field of business and economics. INCAE was founded in 1964 as a joint initiative between the governments and business communities in Central America. Since its inception, INCAE has had academic counselling from Harvard Business School. Fifty generations of MBAs have graduated from our campuses located in Costa Rica and Nicaragua and now lead world-class organisations, helping to improve the productivity levels and quality of life of the countries where they work. Currently, INCAE offers four different programmes – MBA, Master in Agribusiness Management, Global Real Estate Management and Global Executive MBA – and many options for executive education. INCAE signed on to the Principles for Responsible Management Education (PRME) initiative in 2008, using the Principles as points of reference for the continued improvement of INCAE's curriculum towards management programmes with strong components of sustainability.

Challenges

INCAE Business School has been characterised by its own strengths in management, particularly in its commitment to natural resources and sustainable development. The institution made sustainable development a major issue in its master's programme. During more than two decades, INCAE has adapted its curriculum by a gradual and flexible process. The specific needs of INCAE's stakeholders have been changing over time and the Institution has adapted to them.

INCAE uses the methodology of case studies for most subjects taught in our programmes. The way that INCAE has been adapting the curriculum starts from the research that the organisation does, which analyses and finds innovative experiences of programmes and projects that companies have implemented in the region. Experiences about CSR, sustainable management or ethics are documented in INCAE's study cases and later, taught to the students in the classrooms. All these experiences or initiatives are related with traditional subjects of business administration such as finance, marketing, human resources, etc.

> My advice in adapting a business school curriculum to sustainable principles is to pay careful attention to the needs of the stakeholders of the School to make adjustments in the programme that truly meet those requirements, so that changes in the programme serve to support the mission that follows the institution.
> *Jorge Vinicio Murillo, Project Manager, Latin American Center for Competitiveness and Sustainable Development (CLACDS), INCAE Business School*

Actions taken

In September 1996, INCAE established the Latin American Centre for Competitiveness and Sustainable Development (CLACDS, its Spanish acronym). Under the leadership of Dr. Michael E. Porter, competitiveness and sustainable development became the drivers behind research programmes. Since then, INCAE has developed research projects with companies, productive sectors, governments and institutional entities. All this research is an important source of study cases, knowledge and experience for INCAE's curriculum. Each programme or project of CLACDS is supervised from the beginning by a professor, who is in charge of the academic designing. The programmes and projects are developed thinking in a teaching component that will require the incorporation of the results and conclusions of the research in the classes. In this way, most of our projects contain some dissemination stage. Numerous seminars, workshops, and MBA classes are derived from projects developed by CLACDS. Also, from these projects we develop teaching materials such as case studies, articles and publications, which are used in the different academic programmes of INCAE.

The first requirement for this process to work is the commitment and conviction of our professors to sustainable development. They are essential not only for their knowledge to teach the classes, but also because they are responsible for the design of projects and programmes on these issues, culminating in the dissemination of knowledge in the classroom.

Additionally, the adapting process of INCAE's curriculum has required careful attention to the stakeholders' needs. Companies, governments and civil entities of the world increasingly require schools to form business leaders with a strong social consciousness, environmental commitment and expertise that allow them to perform successfully.

> My advice in adapting a business school curriculum to sustainable principles is to implement adjustments in the programme because there is a real belief in sustainable development and not for marketing purposes or following a trend. Adjustments should be comprehensive, covering the different components of sustainable development: economic, social and environmental.
>
> *Neil Camacho, Administrative Director of Master Programs*

Results

INCAE is committed to continued progress in the implementation of PRME. The initiatives carried out by INCAE, as part of this commitment, have been part of programmes that the Institution started decades ago. INCAE is committed to continuing those efforts that contribute to our mission to generate leadership for sustainable development for Latin America and for the world.

Why PRME is/was important

The Principles are:

- aligned with INCAE's mission to generate leadership for sustainable development for Latin America and for the world;
- consistent with many of the needs of INCAE's stakeholders;
- points of reference for the continued improvement of INCAE's curriculum towards management programmes with strong components of sustainability.

HOW TO INTRODUCE GLOBAL ISSUES

Griffith Business School, Brisbane, Queensland, Australia

HOW GRIFFITH BUSINESS SCHOOL INTRODUCED GLOBAL ISSUES INTO THE BUSINESS CURRICULA

Introduction

Griffith Business School seeks to excel as a provider of high quality, cross-disciplinary and internationally relevant business and public policy education and research, emphasising the relationship between business and society in promoting sustainable enterprises and communities. The School has approximately 9,700 students and 1,200 staff located on four campuses in South East Queensland at South Bank, Nathan, Logan and on the Gold Coast. Griffith was among the first signatories to the Principles for Responsible Management Education (PRME) and recently joined the United Nations Global Compact (UNGC), which sponsors the PRME initiative.

Challenges

Senior faculty at Griffith have been active in PRME, the UNGC, EABIS (The Academy of Business in Society), the Globally Responsible Leadership Initiative (GRLI) and other multi-stakeholder market-based initiatives for many years, and the School hopes to differentiate its products by teaching responsible leadership, sustainable enterprise and corporate responsibility. While the response from students has been almost universally positive, the faculty as a whole are not fully conversant with these initiatives or cognisant of the implications and adaptation of teaching content and styles has occurred more slowly.

Like the world economy, issues such as climate change, food security and poverty transcend national boundaries and are increasingly inter-related. These issues are accompanied by world power moving away from hundreds of years of US-European domination towards vast super-civilisations in Brazil, Russia, India, Japan and China. At the same time, faith-based fundamentalism all over the world challenges liberal democratic human rights-based social progress.

Despite the seismic shifts under way, recent international research has identified that global orientation is an undeveloped area in MBA graduate attributes (Datar *et al.*, 2010). It is critical business and management schools address this gap and ensure that they provide students with an enhanced understanding of the way the world works alongside being taught the core functional areas of business such as operations, supply chain management and strategy.

At the beginning of the 21st century we face the perfect storm of a burgeoning world population, climate change, global financial instability and resource depletion – potentially leading to whole systems collapse. It is certain that humanity faces a very different future. Business and management schools must ensure that the compelling immediacy of global issues are faced, and that the opportunities and challenges are fully understood, researched and articulated. Griffith Business School intends to be part of a global shift in education, promoted by initiatives like PRME, towards a positive approach to confronting this future by endeavouring to embody sustainability, ethics, corporate responsibility and sustainable enterprise in all we do – with all the paradoxes, surprises, ambiguities and learning that this change implies for us.
Malcolm McIntosh, Director, Asia Pacific Centre for Sustainable Enterprise (APCSE), Griffith Business School

Actions taken

Recognising that business and management education is at a crossroads, several years ago Griffith Business School redefined its purpose to be a provider of cross-disciplinary and internationally relevant business education and research that emphasises the relationship between business and society in promoting sustainable enterprises and communities. The School also articulated three core values that guide its activities, which include:

- **Responsible leadership.** Giving our students the knowledge, skills and values to encourage them to become responsible leaders in the future, with a concern for planet and people as well as profit.
- **Sustainable business practices.** Researching, developing and promoting social, financial and environmental approaches that lead to sustainable businesses and communities.
- **Global orientation.** Providing education and research that recognises we operate in a fast-changing global environment, and that prepares global citizens, with a special focus on the Asia Pacific region.

These values helped shape the recent redesign of Griffith Business School's flagship MBA programme. With its focus on systems thinking and sustainability, the first lecture in the first course of the programme now primes students on the state of the planet and humanity. It is made clear that business operates within and depends on the global ecosystem. Throughout the programme, students are exposed to various global issues, how these affect business and how business can respond to these issues in a positive, sustainable and meaningful way.

Results

Contextualising business and management education through an enhanced understanding of the state of the planet and the way in which business decisions are made, makes it easier for students to understand their chosen field, draw the links between various functional areas of business and appreciate how each area of business can and needs to be part of corporate sustainability. Having an understanding of the world is also paramount to enable students to see not only the challenges facing the world, but also the possibilities that exist for developing new business opportunities and their own careers.

Reference

Datar, S.M., Garvin, D.A. and Cullen, P., (2010), *Rethinking the MBA*, Harvard Business Press.

Why PRME is/was important

- The PRME initiative connected Griffith Business School with other leading business and management schools from around the world championing responsible management education, research and thought leadership.
- The Principles provided an internationally accepted framework for embedding corporate responsibility and sustainability into curricula, research and learning methods.

Aarhus University, Business and Social Sciences, Aarhus, Denmark

A COHERENT SUSTAINABILITY PROGRAMME

Introduction

 **AARHUS UNIVERSITY**

The School of Business and Social Sciences is a broad business school and one of the four main academic areas at Aarhus University, Denmark. With more than 16,000 students and 700 scientific staff members, Business and Social Sciences ranks among the largest business schools in Europe.

Challenges

In 2008, the board decided on a new strategy for the business school. The basis for the new strategy was a thorough analysis of the future conditions for business and thus, the type of leaders and specialists that a business school should produce. This would, of course, influence the research priorities and the focus on old as well as new educational programmes. Central to the strategy was the strategic focus on "sustainable growth through innovation", integrated in research, education, operations, relations and culture.

Actions taken

A first step in this strategy of integrating sustainability in research and teaching activities was to become signatory to the Principles for Responsible Management Education (PRME). In line with this initiative, a special teaching activity was introduced in relation to the bachelor programme Business Administration – Sustainability, focusing on various sustainability topics as integrated elements of the three-year education.

> The students are usually very engaged in the global issues. This gives you a unique opportunity to have inspiring discussions about the links between your course and issues like climate change, poverty, human rights, etc. By opening up for new and broad perspectives together with the students, you can create a new sense of meaning for them and get valuable input yourself. By inviting them to participate in the development of your course, you teach them to take responsibility of their own future and create a new kind of enthusiasm in class.
>
> This is the core of the global competition that we have set up together with PRME called PRME LEADERS + 20. We did a pilot based on my course "Cost benefit analysis" – and you can see the outcome at the video at www.prme-leaders20.au.dk.
>
> *Jan Bentzen, Professor, Department of Economics and Business,*
> *Aarhus University, Business and Social Sciences*

The programme contains the basic, traditional courses within business and economic disciplines accompanied by a set of newly designed courses dealing with sustainability topics. The latter are intended to form a coherent set of teaching activities with emphasis on sustainability with high relevance for an education in business administration.

Five courses, corresponding to approximately six months' full-time studies, are particularly devoted to these issues. It is the intention to secure that students who attend the programme are equipped with competencies fully comparable to business school BA programmes while at the same time relating the education to sustainability issues within the lines of business and economics.

The five courses focusing on sustainability

Environmental and Natural Resource Economics

Environmental economics is an important player in relation to managing natural resources and the environment. It plays a significant role in relation to environmental policies. The concepts and methodologies related to environmental economics can be applied in relation to evaluating environmental sustainability in order to deal efficiently with the environmental challenges, e.g., global warming, pollution, depletable resources, etc. The course focuses on classical topics from environmental economics, which are primarily related to microeconomics.

Sustainable Production and Consumption
This course touches on relevant topics within consumer behaviour with regard to sustainability and sustainable products (e.g., consumer trends, consumer decision-making processes, adoption of innovations, ethical consumerism, and environmental behaviours), the interaction between consumers and producers with regard to sustainability issues (via marketing measures and communication), governmental interventions into the latter (for example standards and labels) and producer-driven engagement (e.g., corporate social responsibility and leadership).

Sustainable Economics
Sustainable economics focuses on the economic aspects of sustainability and includes a wide range of topics concerning a long-run sustainable development of economies. The course will include topics related to both microeconomics and macroeconomics. Therefore, a basic knowledge of economics is a prerequisite for course attendance. Some of the main topics are: economic growth theory, sustainable growth, income distribution, climate, demographic topics, rich and poor countries, trade, protectionism, fair trade, and developing countries.

Project Evaluation and Sustainability
Project evaluation methodologies are very important in relation to economic and environmental sustainability in order to decide whether specific initiatives, for example environmental resource management, climate policies and energy or infrastructure projects, are helping to develop the economy in a more sustainable direction. The course in project evaluation – also known as cost-benefit analysis – will focus on sustainability topics and present basic economic evaluation methodologies in this context.

Seminar on Environmental Issues
The seminar paper – a short, written report – deals with empirical issues from the broad variety of descriptive economics. Issues are mainly chosen and based on a presentation based on statistical source material. The given issue is described, elaborated on and analysed using, for example, collected data, which is why a considerable part of the seminar activity is concentrated on how to select relevant information from national and international statistics.

Teaching sustainability courses and students' engagement

An efficient way of attracting attention to issues such as climate change and resource scarcity is to ask course participants about their own knowledge and attitudes towards such topics. A four-page survey covering a whole range of questions has been developed for the students attending the sustainability programme. The goal of the survey is to gain a better understanding of climate change related attitudes and beliefs of undergraduate students, but also to find out what motivates business students to minor in sustainability.

Results

When entering the sustainability programme, sustainability students are significantly more concerned that climate change will have a significant negative impact on standards of living. Of the sustainability students, 36% expect a significant effect on standards of living while only 8% of general programme students expect this to be the case.

We also asked students what they consider as the four biggest issues facing the world today. We found that overpopulation is the problem most frequently mentioned by sustainability students. It is considered by 72% of the students as one of the four biggest problems. Only 26% of the general programme students consider overpopulation as one of the four biggest problems. Their main concern is the global financial crisis (70%). Interestingly, the two student groups are very similar with respect to how frequently climate change is mentioned as one of the four biggest problems: 60% among sustainability students and 52% among general programme students.

Why PRME is/was important

- PRME demonstrates political and global commitment to the new role of management education.
- PRME's links to accreditation bodies, like EQUIS and AACSB, are important drivers for PRME implementation at school level.
- PRME provides for a global learning network and benchmarking opportunities.

SECTION 3. LEARNING ENVIRONMENTS CONDUCIVE TO RESPONSIBLE MANAGEMENT

INTRODUCTION

Signatories of the Principles for Responsible Management Education (PRME), as seen by the range of case stories presented in this section, are using a variety of methods to create new generations of responsible leaders and managers. They are doing so through the development of active learning environments that promote responsible management. These environments aim to link conceptual learning with application, to not only discuss these issues in the classroom, but to then have opportunities to experience and put them into practice in the real world.

Faculty at signatory schools are exploring a range of new teaching methods and courses that help their students to develop a range of not only hard skills and knowledge about these issues, but also the soft skills necessary to be a successful leader in an increasingly complex work environment. These include, but are not limited to, teaching students to think in a non-linear way, develop complex problem-solving capabilities, and effective collaboration skills.

For some signatories this is part of their underlying mission, the belief that societal values are best taught through experiential and immersion learning. For others this occurs following in-depth programme reviews and surveys with students and alumni. Each school approaches the topic in its own unique way. Some do so by embedding sustainability issues both in class and through out-of-classroom experiences and learning opportunities. Others do so by creating opportunities for students through degree and certificate programmes that are specifically focused on sustainability and responsible leadership.

Service learning is increasingly being incorporated into management curricula around the world. As seen in several of the case stories, faculty are finding that the issues around sustainability and responsible leadership are so complex and constantly changing that it is often most effective to learn about these issues directly in the environments in which they occur. Not only does such experience provide an excellent learning opportunity for students, but it also allows them to contribute in a direct and positive way.

The schools represented in this section demonstrate a wide variety of approaches. Some have projects occurring locally that pair students with local businesses, NGOs, organisations or even individuals to provide a service or advice. Others send students to work abroad in other countries and communities. Many start with an in class learning portion that prepares students with the necessary background and knowledge to both learn from this experience and be able to give back.

Despite its popularity with students and its growing success as a mechanism to learn about responsible leadership, schools have experienced a range of challenges with this approach, as can be seen in the following case stories. These types of learning experiences are time- and resource-intensive for both faculty and staff. Introduction of new modules is often met with conflict about finding space within the curriculum. Although schools are finding that most faculty are broadly supportive of their attempts to incorporate principles of responsible management into learning programmes, some faculty are less so, often because they see no additional incentive in regards to their career progression. Some schools find innovative ways around this challenge, such as asking students to develop their own hands-on projects that show how business can contribute positively to solving social and environmental problems. These innovations are important as all signatories involved in this project agree that professor engagement and leadership in teaching is key to ensuring the success and effectiveness of such programmes.

Signatories are also entering into a range of innovative partnerships in order to further research and teaching in sustainability and responsible leadership topics. These partnerships involve not only business, but also NGOs, community groups, the media and other stakeholders. Schools are finding that the response is quite enthusiastic from partners, sometimes having more partners interested than their programmes can accommodate. Extensive work is being done in increasing communication with stake-holders and exploring ways to ensure genuine participation. As one contributor put it, "Instead of separating 'we-academics' from 'they-practitioners' working to bring both groups together in practical learning and sharing".

Several schools are facilitating this discussion with students and stakeholders through increasingly elaborate virtual platforms online. Here learners become contributors rather than passive recipients, each contributing his/her own experiences and solutions to different global problems. These are spaces where faculty can create and share teaching materials that can be customised to the different needs of their students.

In order to foster learning environments that cultivate responsible leadership, a range of partnerships are emerging across and within universities themselves. Schools are finding ways to partner with other schools to work on research and teaching projects together. Innovative electives are being developed that not only incorporate elements such as service learning, but also bring together a range of different departments within management schools, and other schools across campus, such as public policy and law. Some schools are also using co-teaching, pairing faculty from different departments to teach these complex concepts more holistically.

Included in the mechanisms being further developed to foster responsible leaders are case studies specifically focused on topics around sustainability and responsible leadership. This includes case studies around the topics explored by the United Nations Global Compact and also increasing local case studies that explore issues dealt with by business in specific regions of the world where management schools are located.

In order to foster learning environments to meet the needs of the sustainability agenda, PRME signatories have undertaken initiatives, such as:

1. Exploring ways to not only discuss these issues in the classroom, but to experience and put them into practice in the business world.
2. Developing both hard skills and knowledge and soft skills, such as problem solving and stakeholder engagement, which are increasingly crucial for responsible leadership.
3. Providing students with the opportunity, through service and experience learning, to participate in hands on-projects both locally and internationally.
4. Ensuring that faculty are active and on board and that incentives are aligned to enable their involvement.
5. Reviewing missions and curricula to find opportunities to add and embed these experiences within the programme.
6. Developing partnerships with a range of stakeholders, including business, media, NGOs, government and community groups.
7. Developing partnerships within and across universities, including between the management school and other schools, such as law and public policy.
8. Creating virtual learning platforms that facilitate learning and discussion about responsible leadership between stakeholders, students and faculty.
9. Exploring and testing of a range of innovative teaching methods including new electives.
10. Developing international, national, regional and local case studies around the topic of responsible leadership.

HOW TO DEVELOP EFFECTIVE EXPERIENTIAL/ SERVICE LEARNING TO SUPPORT THE PRINCIPLES

Albers School of Business and Economics, Seattle University, Seattle, Washington, United States

TRANSLATING CONCEPTS AND PRINCIPLES TO BUSINESS THROUGH THE SUSTAINABILITY PRACTICUM

Introduction

The Albers School of Business and Economics at Seattle University is home to over 1,700 graduate and undergraduate business students. In addition to our MBA for working professionals, we also offer master's degrees in finance, international business, and accounting, as well as leadership and health leadership executive MBAs. An Albers education is values-centred and prepares students for ethical and socially responsible leadership. Participating in the Principles for Responsible Management Education (PRME) initiative signals the importance of sustainability to Albers, as well as an opportunity to share our experiences and learn from others working in this area.

Challenges

Albers takes pride in linking conceptual learning with application. Our goal in the MBA sustainable business specialisation is to produce students who are capable of working immediately in positions of sustainability management. To assure the ability to translate concepts and principles to business, the required capstone course in the specialisation is a Sustainability Practicum in which students work in groups with a partner business firm to solve the partner firm's sustainable business problem.

Actions taken

The Sustainability Practicum is a one-quarter course that meets weekly. Principles of Sustainable Business is a prerequisite course. The first session presents the general framework for doing consulting projects (expectations for professional conduct, typical responsibilities of the partner firms, non-disclosure agreements, etc.), schedule of work, and expected deliverables, which include a formal proposal, work agreement contract, presentation to the client and professor and written report. The first session also includes short presentations by partner firm candidates, usually six to eight firms. By the second session, students have voted for their preferred partners and the instructor has formed groups based on those votes and selected the partners. The course target is 15-18 students and 5-6 partner firms. Students spend the remainder of the quarter working on their projects, meeting with partner firms outside of class, using class time to get group feedback from the professor. At the end of the quarter, groups present their findings to key leaders of the firm.

> The Sustainability Practicum is successful because it embodies the feature elements of an Albers' degree – the intersection of organisational and personal values with academic excellence and experiential learning. All for the good of people, communities and the planet.
>
> *Greg Magnan, Professor of Operations and MBA Director,*
> *Albers School of Business and Economics, Seattle University*

Results

We have taught the course twice. Partner firms have been identified through individual faculty connections, and also by a staff member who finds projects for all courses that involve service learning, including the Sustainability Practicum. We mention the sustainability specialisation and the partnering opportunity in many of our conversations with businesses in our community. Responses are generally enthusiastic. We have more potential partners than we can accommodate. Firms are sensitive to sustainability challenges and impressed with our general commitment to ethics and community service.

The touchstone for the Sustainability Practicum course is the University's commitment to service learning. All programmes in the University have at least one course available to students that includes a term-long, service-learning component. Sustainability challenges lend themselves to service learning because they tend to involve dimensions of social justice, community improvement, and, often, assistance to non-profit or entrepreneurial enterprises.

In the 2 iterations of this course so far, students did 10 projects. Among the partner firms have been Boeing, Vulcan Industries, Seattle's Children's Hospital, and the city of Twisp, WA. Projects have addressed such issues as a conversion to sustainable electricity, a sustainable neighbourhood growth strategy, an employee commuting plan, and a feasibility plan for an organic waste composting business. All partner firms have expressed delight with the results. To date, only a few students have completed their degrees, but at least two have taken positions in sustainability management.

Why PRME is/was important

The course addresses many of the Principles of PRME by:

- developing the capabilities of students to be future generators of value and to work for a more sustainable global economy (Principles 1 and 2);
- using an educational framework grounded in the University's commitment to service learning (Principle 3); and
- engaging both students and faculty in partnership with businesses and community organisations (Principle 5).

Fordham University Schools of Business, New York, New York, United States

SOLVING PRME CHALLENGES: THE SUSTAINABILITY IN BUSINESS INTERDISCIPLINARY MINOR AND THE INTERNATIONAL SERVICE LEARNING PROGRAMME

Introduction

 Founded in 1841, Fordham is the Jesuit University of New York with programmes in liberal arts, business, and professional education. The Gabelli School of Business has 2,000 undergraduate students. The Graduate School of Business Administration has 1,500 students. The business schools are jointly served by 110 faculty.

Engaging students to understand core values is a primary mission of Jesuit education at Fordham University. Underlying this philosophy is the belief that societal values are best taught through experiential and immersion learning, including service programmes in local or global communities. This approach to education is based on carefully chosen experiences supported by reflection, critical analysis and synthesis. In particular, students are encouraged to take the initiative and make decisions. It is a very active mode for learning.

Challenges

There are many challenges confronting schools steeped in traditional business curriculum as they seek to integrate the Principles for Responsible Management Education (PRME) or sustainability frameworks. Below are some that are being addressed at Fordham Business Schools:

- Many faculty are already teaching concepts relevant to PRME from within their disciplinary perspectives. The PRME challenge is to create opportunities and channels for these faculty to diffuse their knowledge across disciplinary "silos" and to inspire those within their own disciplines to entertain new approaches.

- Helping students engage in PRME values through service and experiential learning is very time and resource intensive for both faculty and students. It requires partnering and coordinating with experts and organisations outside the classroom. Students may also need faculty support as they learn to dialogue with people in settings quite different from those encountered in academic learning environments.
- While business students quickly appreciate courses oriented towards practical skill building, it can be more challenging to help them "see" some of the less tangible, but more lasting values that come from contextual appreciation associated with PRME/sustainability-oriented service and experiential learning. It requires faculty with enthusiasm and special talent to instil these principles in a way that enhances critical thinking on the issues while also focusing on those competencies needed to address concrete job challenges.
- Building a curriculum relevant to PRME is an emergent process and may require innovative use of materials and courses already in place. At Fordham, one approach has been to allow undergraduate students into graduate courses, with the permission of the instructor. This vertical integration of students is better suited for some students than for others, however. Greater oversight and mentoring by advisers is needed for this to be successful, but it can raise the bar for undergraduate students and, in turn, it can provide mentoring opportunities and leadership challenges for the graduate students.

Fordham has found its place in the PRME community through a confluence of efforts. It has both "top-down" commitment from the administration and "bottom-up" passion from faculty and students. Our advice is to start by looking closely within your own walls through the Sharing in Progress (SIP) PRME report process. Identify the key administrators, faculty and students within your school that already embody these values. Engage them in the PRME process, and then build towards institutionalising their passion and energies by creating programmes like those illustrated at Fordham and at other PRME participants in this Inspirational Guide. Essential teaching

> elements must include not only transmittal of factual information, but interdisciplinary, immersion, experiential, and service learning experiences that will foster ownership of the PRME message.
> *Donna Rapaccioli, University Professor, Dean of Business Faculty and Dean of the College of Business Administration, Fordham University*

Actions taken

Gabelli students have two opportunities to engage in PRME-related service learning/experiential courses. The newest programme, an interdisciplinary Sustainability in Business Minor, was launched in partnership with Fordham's College of Liberal Arts in September 2011 and was created in response to student demand. The foundation course for this programme encourages participants to use an interdisciplinary framework to assess positive and negative impacts of traditional economic approaches to business, and encourages triple bottom line thinking (economics, environment and social equity). Ultimately, students are challenged to develop their own hands-on projects that show how business can contribute positively to solving social and environmental problems. In the first group of students, fall 2011, business plans were created on projects ranging from building a vertical garden at Fordham University to developing ways to purify water in developing nations. Immersion projects and sustainability internships are available for students within the minor track.

The development of the undergraduate Sustainability in Business Minor is an evolving process that has drawn on the talents and expertise of many faculty. One particular spark has been the ongoing success of the undergraduate International Service Learning (ISL) programme at the Gabelli School of Business. The ISL programme especially has "primed the pump", so to speak, for students and faculty. At its heart is the Fair Trade and Microfinance Consulting Project, a year-long experiential learning course that counts as six academic credits. Through the consulting project, students gain experience in micro-finance by "doing business" with the local people in a developing country such as Kenya. A long-term trade relationship with a handful of developing world artisans has grown out of the ISL programme. Imported wares from these organisations are sold on campus, with profits returned in the form of micro-finance loans to ambitious artists that the students have met on their trips.

Results

The results and benefits are best described by the Gabelli School of Business students themselves:

> Between the smell of sewage and the sight of a woman suffering from AIDs holding a sick baby, I was hit, all-out by poverty [in Kenya]. When I entered college, my original intentions were to major in finance, get good grades, intern and graduate with a great salary. Now, not a week goes by when I don't reflect on Kenya and on how I can build a career with some social impact.
> *Sean O'Connor, an ISL student*
>
> Employers are looking for business school graduates who understand the bigger picture, and sustainability is a key factor in that picture. Many of the companies we will be applying to for jobs have sustainability concerns embedded in their operations and in their shareholder responsibilities. No one wants to be investing in a company that is not sustainable in the future. The Sustainability in Business Minor is educating us about those concerns and we will be better able to present ourselves for employment with this broader understanding of the economic, social and environmental challenges that society is facing.
> *Michele Calabrese, a Sustainability in Business foundations course student*
>
> The triple bottom line approach makes more sense to me. Increasing shareholder wealth at the expense of society, just doesn't work. It is the stakeholder model that is more viable and adaptable to long term growth. It is exciting that Fordham is now teaching us to think in these terms.
> *Dhurata Osmani, a Sustainability in Business foundations course student*

Why PRME is/was important

- The PRME process has played a vital role in capturing and focusing both "top-down" commitment from the administration and "bottom-up" passion from faculty and students.
- Joining PRME initially created the impetus for self-reflection, and that was the starting point for drawing Fordham Business Schools down the path towards greater expression and embodiment of the Principles in curricular, extracurricular, and research activities.

- Active engagement with PRME – including participation in webinars, the opportunity to contribute to this Inspirational Guide, attendance at PRME meetings and conferences, and the interactions shared between PRME participants – helps to keep the Fordham administration and faculty engaged and focused on furthering these Principles.
- From advice to stimulation of new ideas, the enormous body of information and experiences being tabulated and shared by the responsible management education community is invaluable.

Mendoza College of Business, University of Notre Dame, Notre Dame, Indiana, United States

ADDRESSING THE DIVIDE BETWEEN THEORY AND PRACTICE

Introduction

Mendoza College of Business at University of Notre Dame in Notre Dame, Indiana is a premier Catholic business school that seeks to foster academic excellence, professional effectiveness, and personal accountability in a context that strives to be faithful to the ideals of community, human development, and individual integrity. Mendoza, home to 2,535 students and 155 faculty members, offers programmes including: undergraduate studies, MBA, executive MBA, executive education, MS in Accountancy, Master of Nonprofit Administration, non-profit professional development, and associated programmes, such as ESTEEM, joint MBA/JD, joint BS/MA, and joint BS in Engineering/MBA.

Under the leadership of former Mendoza College of Business Dean, Carolyn Woo, Mendoza began its long history as an advocate of the United Nations (UN) Global Compact. In 2007, Mendoza advanced the Global Compact cause further when Carolyn Woo represented AACSB to engage an international task force of 60 deans, university presidents and official representatives of leading business schools to develop the Principles for Responsible Management Education (PRME), which was officially launched in July 2007.

In January 2008, Mendoza College of Business became signatory to PRME. In doing so, Mendoza joined business schools and academic associations worldwide in committing to align its mission and strategy, as well as its core competencies – education, research and thought leadership – with UN values embodied by the Six Principles of PRME.

Challenges

As part of the University of Notre Dame community, where approximately 80% of students are active in social service each year, and as a signatory to the PRME initiative, Mendoza recognised the need to develop meaningful and practical service-learning experiences to address the divide between discussing corporate social responsibility in the classroom and putting it into practice in the business world. Under the leadership and guidance of Dean Carolyn Woo, Mendoza responded to this challenge by building on its available resources to create new initiatives. Working with partner organisations (**both** on-campus and external) to identify service needs, as well as with faculty, students and alumni to address the changing business landscape, Mendoza developed unique service-learning offerings that give students the opportunity to deepen their academic experience while also engaging hands-on in responding to community needs.

Actions taken and results

Course highlight: Business on the Frontlines

Introduced in 2008, Business on the Frontlines is an innovative course that takes experiential learning to another level, giving students the opportunity to examine directly the impact of business in war-torn countries. Through a cross-campus alliance between Mendoza College of Business, The Law School, and the Kroc Institute for International Peace Studies, students engage in a course that integrates developmental economics, international relations, politics, and philosophy together with two weeks of hands-on work in the field.

Service learning requires investments, which include explicit staff time and faculty load for design, implementation and evaluation; budget for staff travel and planning; travel support and living stipends for students. As such, it is important to treat service learning as part of the core curriculum (rather than supplemental or extra-curricular) so as to commit proper resources as we would do for classroom instruction.

Successful and rigorous service learning experiences must be preceded by and integrated with solid academic preparation. The Business on the Frontlines and international social entrepreneurship courses require seven weeks of in-class preparation before students go into the field. The Tax Assistance Programme requires students to have been trained in workshops first.

Clear objectives and deliverables are important so that the service-learning project does not just become a feel-good experience. These objectives include understanding the multiple dimensions of a problem, their structural causes as well as possible strategies for intervention. In the process, we encourage personal reflections and journaling by students to develop empathy, solidarity with people in need, and a sense of how they could as individuals and professionals make things better.

Carolyn Woo, former Dean, Mendoza College of Business,
University of Notre Dame

The concept for Business on the Frontlines stemmed from Dean Woo's relationship with Catholic Relief Services (CRS) as a member of its Board of Directors. CRS, a humanitarian agency, serves as an integral partner in the course, identifying the business- and peace-related projects that students work on while in the country, and providing the necessary operational support and relational connection to war-torn communities. Through this interactive and introspective experience, students are challenged to probe deeper into their beliefs as to what should be the role of business in society and what should be their own role in business and society.

Since its inception, Business on the Frontlines students have made significant contributions to the war-torn communities. Examples include:

- In Bosnia, students worked with CRS staff to determine the capabilities and resources necessary to build a small business incubator, which has now been implemented in the ground floor in 17 locations of the social housing CRS builds for internally displaced people from the Bosnian war to return to their home regions.
- In the Philippines, students designed a supply chain for the farming, producing, and selling of the Arabica coffee bean, assisting CRS in building small business cooperatives for struggling Muslim and Catholic farmers.

- In Rwanda and Kenya, students expanded on CRS's existing agricultural programmes by integrating a business component, helping small farmers move towards building larger businesses by making an investment in their marketing and accounting skill sets.
- In Uganda, students' contributions to a water resource project to maintain local wells helped determine how better to build lasting systems that would improve the insurance, maintenance, and other business processes around water pumps.

Programme highlight: the Tax Assistance Programme

Since its founding in 1972 by Mendoza, Ken Milani and a group of students, the University of Notre Dame's Tax Assistance Programme (TAP) has played a significant role in preparing accounting students for public accounting and tax practice. Through the programme, Mendoza accounting students volunteer to assist low-income and disabled taxpayers with preparation of their tax returns. The TAP, which involves both a domestic and international segment, offers students practical field experience while also responding to tax assistance needs in the community.

The TAP, with more than 90 student volunteers, offers 9 Michiana area service centres. Mendoza faculty members, as well as local accountants, volunteer their time to support these students. For those clients unable to travel, student volunteers visit disabled taxpayers in their homes and hospital rooms as an extension of the service.

Annual records highlighting details regarding the TAP season, available beginning 1992, reveal a tremendous growth in outreach. In 1992, 1,025 taxpayers sought assistance from the TAP, with 1,970 forms filed that year (974 federal and 996 state). By 2011, the number of taxpayers had more than doubled to 2,059 clients, with a total of 3,902 filed tax papers (2,016 federal and 1,886 state).

Internships highlight: Gigot Centre social internships

At Mendoza, social internships are a critical component to the Gigot Centre for Entrepreneurial Studies programme. Gigot Centre internships provide students with an eight-week experience in which they have the opportunity to apply their classroom learning in context and to make an impact in the community. Internships are located both domestically, such as in New York, and internationally, such as in Cape Town, Jamaica.

Through the internships, students are matched with partner organisations who present entrepreneurial challenges faced by local business ventures. While responding to these challenges, students implement the knowledge they have gained in the classroom. Students have been partnered with organisations such as Grassroots Soccer, Catholic Welfare and Development, Ikamva Labantu, the Catholic Parliamentary Liaison, and The Business Place.

Through the internships, student accomplishments have included:

- Researching and writing white papers on low-income housing, micro-enterprise development, and black empowerment, among other subjects.
- Composing business plans for a dialysis unit, an assisted-living facility, and a hydroponic farm.
- Developing and teaching community workshops to low-income local entrepreneurs and, in Kingston, Jamaica, to students at the University of West Indies.

HOW TO BUILD POWERFUL LEARNING ENVIRONMENTS THAT FOSTER RESPONSIBLE MANAGEMENT

Aston Business School, Birmingham, England, United Kingdom

RESPONSIBILITY, REFLEXIVITY AND TRANSDISCIPLINARITY: REFORMING THE BUSINESS MANAGEMENT CURRICULUM AND THE ORGANISATION

Introduction

As one of the largest and most successful business schools in Europe, Aston Business School is triple accredited by AACSB, EQUIS and AMBA and has over 4,000 students on various programmes. This includes an annual intake of over 800 undergraduate students on general and specialist undergraduate programmes, over 900 postgraduate students on a variety of general, specialist and professional master's and MBA programmes. Aston also offers executive development programmes. Aston is committed to influencing organisations and their leaders worldwide through world-leading research, inspirational learning and teaching, and business engagement. We aim to make a sustainable contribution to businesses, economies and societies worldwide and equip our students to become responsible business leaders.

Challenges

Integrating ethics, responsibility and sustainability started in 2003 when a review of the Aston MBA resulted in its inclusion in the programme (not all academics agreed, but the support of the dean helped). The challenges then became about the approach and philosophy, the content and disciplinary

focus. Would it be at the heart of the programme or on the periphery, and how could personal values and reflection be incorporated?

In 2007, the executive discussed ideas relating to social responsibility and sustainability (SR&S). This led to the formalisation of School roles (co-directors of SR&S) and the development of a strategy. At a School away day, staff contributed to sessions on SR&S. It was at this time that we became an early signatory to the Principles for Responsible Management Education (PRME) initiative and set out our plans under each of the Principles.

The challenges included: discipline-based resource allocation systems for teaching, research and recruitment. Introducing new modules met with conflicts about space in the curriculum. Most colleagues were broadly supportive of initiatives relating to responsible management education, but not all; one example being: "this has no relevance for teaching finance". In research, developing publications is restricted by the spectre of the UK Research Excellence Framework (REF) (dominated by discipline-based journals). As one colleague stated, "I'd love to publish in this area, but I have my career to think about".

When I started teaching business, ethics, responsibility and sustainability, 10 years ago, it was seen by many as quirky, not mainstream and even subversive! Times have changed and responsible management education is now accepted, but there has never been a more important time to ensure it is fully integrated into all we do. In the film, *The Age of Stupid*, people look back to today from 50 years in the future and cannot understand the way we treat the planet. Similarly, I believe people will look back at management education in the future (in maybe less than 50 years) and not understand why management education has not always been responsible. Be persistent, be passionate and believe in what you are doing.

Carole Parkes, Co-Director, Social Responsibility & Sustainability,
Aston Business School

Actions taken

The learning approach for ethics, responsibility and sustainability in the MBA is different to the conventional business programme; it involves emotion and not just rational thinking and promotes reflexivity. It adopts a transdisciplinary approach, taught by staff of different disciplines drawn from within and outside the Business School.

Experiential learning is used to make students aware of the ethical, social and environmental dimensions of managerial decision making. Students are supported in developing skills of critical thinking, analysis and reflection and teaching methods are highly interactive. Discussions of live case studies with business practitioners are also used. On a meta-cognitive level this invariably entails engaging with the intellectual and practical imperatives of transdisciplinarity and reflexive practice.

In 2008, a curriculum review of all undergraduate and post graduate programmes was undertaken aimed at creating "social responsibility and sustainability literate" graduates. This included an audit of all course documentation and discussions to provide an overview of the SR&S content in the existing curricula and to make recommendations for the future. The review highlighted that while there were some final year specialist electives, there was very little in the early years. One graduate commented: "during my time at Aston, I never had a lecture on any of this".

The recommendations included:

- At undergraduate level, the introduction of a new core module on SR&S in the early years for all business undergraduates to provide underpinning knowledge.
- During the placement year (80% of business students at Aston) students would report on the company's SR&S policies and practices (theory into practice).
- At postgraduate level, a review of MSc courses to identify inclusion of SR&S.

- The introduction of a new MSc in Social Responsibility and Sustainability.

Results

In 2010, over 300 reflections of MBA students (from 34 countries with different legal, cultural, philosophical traditions) were analysed using the following categories: origin of personal values, experience of ethics/responsibility in business, conflicts with personal values, perceived barriers and impact on future plans and decision making.

Common reflections included: a heightened sense of awareness about issues, "voice" and "legitimacy" (knowing the vocabulary or gaining confidence), making a difference to future policies and practices. For example:

- "We were taken out of the passive role and placed into an active, thinking mode".
- "I realised how easy it is to find yourself demonstrating behaviours in business that go against the basic moral judgement you apply to personal life".
- Some also said, "Without overstating the case – this has changed my life".

For further details see Parkes and Blewitt (2011).

Following careful negotiations, all the undergraduate recommendations of the curriculum report were implemented in 2009/2010, including undergraduate students having responsible management as core to their programmes. Students on placement are now required to investigate the organisation's policies on SR&S as part of their company report. At postgraduate level, all MSc degrees were reviewed to highlight SR&S content. Recruitment processes were amended to allow for appointment in SR&S. Finally, the new MSc in Social Responsibility and Sustainability started in 2011. This programme follows the philosophy of the MBA teaching, taking a transdisciplinary and reflexive approach.

Reference

Parkes, C. and Blewitt, J. (2011), "Ignorance was bliss, now I'm not ignorant and that is far more difficult: transdisciplinary learning and reflexivity in responsible management education", *Journal of Global Responsibility*, Vol. 2 No. 2, pp. 206-221.

Why PRME is/was important

- PRME plays a key role as a "strategic lever" to secure top management support and credibility within the organisation. Institutions value accreditation and association with validating bodies and institutions. While PRME is not an accrediting body, it provides a framework for engagement with the issues and places responsibility firmly on the agenda.
- PRME provides "legitimacy" for the issues, topics and subjects and the opportunity to place responsibility at the heart of business education.
- PRME facilitates a community of practice to share ideas and initiatives. Aston helped to organise, hosted and participated in UK and international events for PRME aimed at encouraging Universities to become signatory to the initiative by sharing benefits and strategies for implementation as well as ideas/practices in teaching, learning and research.

CENTRUM, Centro de Negocios, Pontificia Universidad Católica del Perú, Lima, Peru

TEACHING IN AN ELECTRONIC SOCIAL NETWORK

Introduction

CENTRUM Católica, the leading business school in Peru, was founded in 2000. Programmes offered are DBA, MBA (both in English and Spanish, part time and full time, in-campus and off-campus), executive education and in-company training programmes, in nine cities around the country and also outside Peru. CENTRUM Católica is the only business school in Peru and the seventh in Latin America to achieve the Triple Crown Award given to schools that have achieved business accreditation AACSB, EQUIS, and AMBA. The School is among the first signatories to the Principles for Responsible Management Education (PRME), an initiative supported by the United Nations Global Compact.

Challenges

The contemporary world is going through major transformations in the 21st century and is facing problems that highlight the necessity to find better solutions than those already existing. We have traditionally been taught that the first and basic responsibility of any organisation is to be profitable and that if we want more of something we are forced to take less of something else. Also, the modern world seems to have understood the importance of leadership in instilling meaning to the groups that are being led, and has, therefore, developed complex innumerable models that were incorporated in business schools, teaching us how to be good and responsible leaders. Yet, the truth is that we lack the necessary understanding of today's business world and the question is: why? Business schools have the responsibility to address this topic. We think, therefore, that we need to evaluate the following challenges that our business school is facing:

- The need to understand the effects of globalisation on business education and how to respond to this phenomenon, addressing social issues.
- The need to introduce softer skills into the curriculum without disregarding the more analytical and concept-based courses.
- The need to understand the effects of information and communication technologies on teaching and learning methods.

> Our advice in order to promote the inner and outer action learning is to create a virtual/ electronic learning platform that integrates the facilities of a social network (social media tools such as wikis and blogs), which would allow the interaction between all concerned stakeholders. This would promote an integrated learning process, creating therefore a continuous interaction among all the participants, which leads to the creation of knowledge through the transformation of experience.
>
> *Tatiana Gherman, Professor and Percy Marquina, Director, CENTRUM Future, CENTRUM Católica, Pontificia Universidad Católica del Perú*

Actions taken

We believe that one of the solutions to tackle the above challenges is the creation of powerful learning environments that foster responsible management. This could be enforced by developing multi-stakeholder learning-platforms in communities.

This new approach to multi-stakeholder platforms for community learning has its most immediate antecedents in the recent novel virtual collaborative learning experiences. The new business schools need to be more innovative. The "collaboratories" should be understood as laboratories of collaborators or action-learning platforms for multiple stakeholders that make up the social fabric, meaning for all citizens as a whole. In that sense, to successfully address the complex problems we face as a global society.

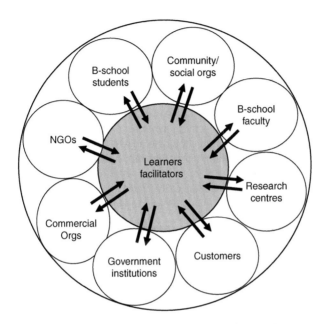

Figure 1. The actors involved in the collaboratories (own elaboration).

In Figure 1, we show the actors of these platforms.

In this sense, we need to seriously re-think the relationships that exist in this framework, given the fact that each of the actors of this platform would serve a dual role of facilitator and learner simultaneously to the extent that each has something to contribute to the solution of the global problems, i.e., regardless of whether it is a physical or virtual space between the multiple stakeholders, it is important to ensure the necessary dynamics to enable the decentralisation of the present learning process of the business school. This way, business schools could open themselves in a more realistic way to the complex reality they must face, learning at the same time from the other actors, and offering viable alternatives to the contemporary challenges.

Given the above statements, our Business School decided to study the possibility of developing a virtual platform in order to allow the interaction between our Business School and the multiple stakeholders who can contribute with their ideas to the vision of creating the responsible leader of the future.

> Students should also deepen and enrich their knowledge and understanding regarding the values promoted by PRME, and develop a set of competences that will allow them to transform their knowledge (which has a passive nature) into practice (which has an active, dynamic nature). We all should live according to what we preach and should be able to influence in others in order to satisfy their needs, in other words we talk about developing a spiritual leadership.
>
> *Tatiana Gherman, Professor, CENTRUM Future, CENTRUM Católica,*
> *Pontificia Universidad Católica del Perú*

Results

Transform learning into a dynamic experience. Learners become contributors, not passive recipients of information. Users in general become actively engaged. It enables communication within school and beyond, on a one-to-one, one-to-many, or many-to-many basis.

Create a powerful online community by bringing together different stakeholders. Students, professors, the community, among others, can participate in collaborative activities, each contributing with their own experiences and solutions to different global problems. Each will work at their own pace and with a wider choice of learning styles, through a more personalised curriculum. Students will communicate by email and participate in live discussions and forums with other stakeholders.

Create and share teaching materials that can be accessed online. Moreover, the content of learning materials can be customised for the exact needs of students and the society to which they belong to and desire to improve.

This virtual platform will allow different stakeholders to play a greater role in students' learning, and they will support students in any learning that takes place outside the Business School. They will also be able to communicate effectively with professors, school administrators and others supporting students' learning process. Basically, stakeholders will become active partners with the Business School.

HHL - Leipzig Graduate School of Management, Leipzig, Germany

TEACHING BUSINESS ETHICS: HOW TO CONVEY MEANINGFUL ETHICAL HEURISTICS TO STUDENTS OF BUSINESS ADMINISTRATION

Introduction

HHL – Leipzig Graduate School of Management was founded in 1898 as Germany's first business school. It was re-established in 1992 as a private institution with full university status granting dissertation and habilitation degrees and today it is considered one of the leading business schools. HHL offers full- and part-time master's degree programmes (MSc), full- and part-time programmes in general management (MBA) and a doctoral programme. Around 120 students are enrolled each year. In May of 2008, the School became signatory to the Principles for Responsible Management Education (PRME), an initiative supported by the United Nations Global Compact.

Challenges

Despite various scandals and economic crises, it is still a challenge to convince many students of business administration that the topic business ethics has serious relevance for (future) managers. That is, the challenge consists in the question of how to teach business ethics to students who are mainly interested in getting to know the relevant knowledge and instruments for effective management. This problem can also be traced back to the fact that the typical content of business ethics seems to be either rather trivial ("be honest"), idealistic, or abstract – that is, not connected to day-to-day conditions of business life. Making use of case studies is only partially helpful, as generally they do not provide conceptual knowledge.

> Invest in the conditions of social cooperation for mutual advantage!
> *Andreas Suchanek, Chair of Economic and Business Ethics, HHL – Leipzig Graduate School of Management*

Actions taken

Two examples are:

1. Applying an appropriate heuristic (possibly also two or three), which enables the introduction of theories of business ethics as well as being illustrated by case studies. The heuristic we have found to be rather helpful is the golden rule in an economically reformulated and expanded version: **Invest in the conditions of social cooperation for mutual advantage**. Another one (which can be seen as a specification, sort of, of this golden rule): **Keep your promises** – The task for the teacher is then to demonstrate the concrete implications of these heuristics, e.g., (with regard to the golden rule): What are common examples of social cooperation for mutual advantage (team production, division of labour, trade, etc.)? What are necessary conditions to realise these forms of cooperation (e.g., trustworthiness, institutions, etc.)? Which investments are needed? Which impediments exist for managers to do these investments? One should also use concrete examples, possibly in combination with cases, to demonstrate how the consideration of these ethical concepts might change business strategies or might enrich the considerations, which guide the use of tools students have learned in other courses.

2. The discussion of these heuristics, where possible in the classroom, with some colleagues (note: they have to be interested in such a discourse) on what their use might imply from a different subject perspective (e.g., marketing, human resources, accounting, etc.). In the last years we have implemented co-teaching sessions where specific topics such as customer relationship management were

discussed from a marketing perspective and ethical aspects were introduced, e.g., which measures to win new customers may possibly transgress the line to corruption, and which "investments" are necessary to maintain the company's integrity?

Results

Through combining heuristics with the discussion of ethical theories, as well as cases in the teaching context, we have experienced a higher than average degree of interest from students. They realise that ordinary day-to-day actions have ethical aspects, but that one can easily lose sight of them. Another benefit comes from the co-teaching sessions where we have learned to develop and apply ethical concepts more appropriately due to a deepened understanding of the (theoretically modelled) business context.

Why PRME is/was important

The Principles help to:

- support faculty commitment to responsible management education, and
- convince students that responsible management education is an important topic – not only for HHL.

Rotterdam School of Management, Erasmus University, Rotterdam, Netherlands

EMPOWERMENT OF WOMEN IN MANAGEMENT EDUCATION

Introduction

Rotterdam School of Management, Erasmus University (RSM) is one of the largest and most international European business schools, with more than 7,200 students and 350 active researchers. It offers BSc, MSc, MBA and executive education programmes, taught in English. There are 100 nationalities on campus and 20,000 alumni active around the world. RSM was placed seventh in the Financial Times 2011 meta-ranking of European Business Schools, and its MBA programme is in the European top 15. The School is among the first signatories to the Principles for Responsible Management Education (PRME), an initiative supported by the United Nations Global Compact.

Challenges

According to Soares, R., Carter, N. and Combopiano, J. (2009) career progression for women into senior management positions in business is still dismal, with women making up only 3% of Fortune 500 chief executive officers (CEOs), and less than 15% of top corporate executives worldwide McTiernan, S. and Flynn, P. (2011). Redressing this problem requires the active support and even leadership of the international management education industry. Curricula remain male dominated in innumerable respects. Faculties continue to be predominantly men, presentation of texts often present an implied gender bias, and there are far too few business cases that feature women and dominant characters in executive positions.

Class composition at graduate level needs to reach gender parity as soon as possible. The management education industry also needs to do far more to increase the number of women business faculty and deans as part of its programme of responsible management education development.

The MBA initiatives at RSM as outlined here demonstrate its commitment to PRME and, particularly, to supporting the acceleration of women into executive positions. There are a lot of great ideas that business schools discuss around women in management and my advice would be to implement these ideas, take some risk, think out of the box and be quick – we are losing such wonderful talent every single day.

Dianne Bevelander, Associate Dean of MBA programmes,
Rotterdam School of Management, Erasmus University

Actions taken

To address this challenge, RSM has made fundamental revisions to its full-time and executive MBA programme. Central to these efforts is a proactive process focusing on the empowerment of women through emphasising the importance of taking greater initiatives in helping one another. This has been supported by new courses and learning approaches that develop these capacities among women across the programmes and by using student social network surveys to graphically show all students the inherent gender biases that exist within and across their student professional networks. Men and women in the classes can observe how they build their networks of trust and are then supported to improve their approaches to engaging professional colleagues in small and large group settings. The School has also developed a women-only course as part of this initiative. The course is made available to female students across all the MBA programmes and involves a leadership experience climbing Mount Kilimanjaro – Africa's highest mountain.

In August 2011, 15 women from 3 MBA programmes joined the Mount Kilimanjaro Women Empowering Women Leadership Elective. The core of the design was oriented to supporting participants in developing a greater understanding of how to work with other women in high performance environments. Activities in the course were designed to address the specific challenges that women face when climbing the corporate ladder – a subject of great interest to the project initiator and RSM associate dean of MBA programmes, Dianne Bevelander, who has actively researched the subject.

In an article "Ms. Trust: gender, networks and trust – implications for management and education", forthcoming in *Academy of Management, Learning and Education*, Dianne Bevelander and her co-author Mike Page examined the hierarchies of trust among female students, and found that women tend to trust each other less in a risky professional environment compared with men. "Women socialise with each other, but when it comes to a matter of risk taking, women exclude each other and prefer to network with men," she said. "When I started the women only elective I was accused of discriminating against men," said Dianne. "I readily admit that this programme was designed specifically for women to the exclusion of men". However, once the project began, both female and male students joined together and expressed pride about the Kilimanjaro project. "If this happened in business, wouldn't it be wonderful?" she asks.

The Kilimanjaro elective was specifically designed to only have women participants because of the belief that this would best enhance their leadership and networking capabilities among women. Learning to mutually support one another is key to women's career progression in male dominated organisations. Dianne engaged the help of Rebecca Stephens, the first British woman to successfully conquer Mount Everest and a professional leadership and team coach, to head the team of RSM female students. Coursework before and following the expedition involved writing personal blogs, attending seminars and working together in order to gain a greater understanding of how women can and must support one another in high performance environments.

Results

The success of the elective and the publicity it received has had a major buying in impact. Individuals previously somewhat negative or neutral about the idea have become overwhelmingly enthusiastic. A number of companies have asked Dianne Bevelander to speak to their leadership teams about her research and the proof-points of the electives, and also expressed an interest in some of their women executives joining future courses of this type as participant observers – even if not registered for the full MBA. The opportunity for this type of "women only" elective to actively bring together women alumni, women in business and female participants across MBA programmes to help expand the network of and for women is phenomenal. The women who participated in the climb, whether or not they reached the summit, frequently expressed the benefits of the transformative experience and how it has helped them reflect on what they as individuals and as a group of women need to do to achieve all they hope for in their own careers. As one of the MBA students said after returning from Kili:

> But is everything still the same? Well, no. The world seems like a much easier place to live in since I am back from Kili. It is much less complicated, clear and simple. Apparently, all I needed was lack of oxygen to see things clearer in the mist of daily noise. My ears are more sensitive and my eyes are sharper but not to hear everything and to see every detail. They are better to judge what is worth and what I value the most. I see and hear less and I sense all those with great joy and energy. Life is simple and life is beautiful...
>
> *MBA student*

While this course evolved out of research into the career development of women, it has also provided fruitful ideas for future research. This pedagogical research is desperately needed and it offers the potential for alternative and respected outlets for academics seeking to build their scholarly careers. Although pedagogical journals continue to be less valued than discipline-based outlets, increased opportunities for research hold the promise for new reputable outlets being established.

References

McTiernan, S. and Flynn, P. (2011), "Perfect storm on the horizon for women business school deans?", *Academy of Management Learning and Education*, Vol. 10, No. 2, pp. 323-339.

Soares, R., Carter, N.M. and Combopiano, J. (2009), *Catalyst Census: Fortune 500 Women Executive Officers and Top Earners*, Catalyst, NY.

Kyung Hee University School of Management, Seoul, Korea

TOWARDS CONSCIOUS TEACHING IN THE AGE OF CONSCIOUS BUSINESS: A CASE OF STUDENT-CENTRED LEARNING IN RESPONSIBLE MANAGEMENT EDUCATION

Introduction

Kyung Hee University's School of Management has an ongoing commitment to innovative teaching and research, embedding the Six Principles of the Principles for Responsible Management Education (PRME) initiative throughout the curriculum and research agenda. Since its foundation in 1949, Kyung Hee University has been distinctly committed to its mission, **Creation of a New Civilised World**, and its philosophy is based on humanity, democracy, and world peace. The long history of international peace activities initiated by Kyung Hee University in collaboration with the world's leading universities and the United Nations (UN) has been the solid platform for the School's commitment to the PRME initiative. As of January 2011, the School has a student population of 2,047 in its undergraduate programme, with 60 full-time tenure track professors. In addition, 100 and 80 students are currently being enrolled in master's of science and PhD programmes, respectively.

Challenges

Over the past couple of decades, corporate social responsibility (CSR) has become a mainstream management paradigm, and CSR is no longer a question of **whether** but **how**. However, for many companies, CSR still means adding just another new tactic for a public relations effort, rather than a serious change in their relationships with society. In order to make the ongoing CSR movement authentic and strategically meaningful and effective, both researchers and practitioners of contemporary business should realise that business organisations need to be in harmony with their employees, customers, government, community and environment.

As such, management education in business schools around the world has been going through major change as have organisations in the post-modern era themselves as responsible providers of contemporary management education. Just as in the corporate world, management schools now need to adopt a newly emerging stakeholder perspective, which will easily become a serious challenge for them. Successfully managing the change is most important not just for management schools, but also for the sustainable corporate world with authentic and responsible leadership. However, 100 year old management education based on the industrial age paradigm will be difficult to change.

The new management education paradigm will require change in the vision and mission of the entire business school, and every corresponding functional area such as teaching, research, social service, as well as its own organisational administration. In particular, active communication with stakeholders and inviting them for genuine participation will be critical. Here, we present Kyung Hee University School of Management's recent experience with a student-centred pedagogy, PBL (problem-based learning), which turned out to be quite effective in dealing with the challenges associated with teaching the newly emerging responsible management paradigm.

My advice to teaching responsible management is to make the stakeholders of today's management education truly engage with the ultimate purpose of doing business (the question of why). As much as cotemporary business management needs a new paradigm for the stakeholder perspective, so too do the management schools. Traditional lecture- (or professor-) centred teaching methodology will not work in this post-industrial age where complex and interdependent problems dominate. In the age of conscious business, we must not cease from searching for conscious teaching methodology. This journey will become a significant and meaningful challenge for all of us, as business and management professors of our time. PRME provides a solid platform that will contribute to our journey onward.

Stephen Yong-Seung Park, Director, Institute for Peace through Commerce,
Kyung Hee University School of Management

Actions taken

Kyung Hee University's School of Management has offered an undergraduate elective business-major class (titled Business and Society) with a new teaching technology (called PBL: Problem-Based Learning) for the last three semesters (i.e., spring and fall semesters of 2010, and spring semester of 2011) with an average class size of 60 students. PBL is a student-centred pedagogy in which students learn about a subject in the context of complex, multifaceted, and realistic problems. Teaching the new management paradigm, which requires students to have non-linear and complex problem-solving capabilities, may be well suited with the goals of PBL, which are to help students develop flexible knowledge, effective problem-solving skills, self-directed learning, effective collaboration skills and intrinsic motivation.

Results

We believe that effective teaching in responsible management should incorporate the following four components; 1) professor engagement, 2) student participation, 3) flexibility and improvisation in teaching, and 4) intimate collaboration between the corporate world and academia in conjunction with business classes.

From our experience, adopting PBL as a teaching methodology for responsible management education quite successfully fulfilled all of these requirements. Post-semester, in-depth interviews with students suggest that the class has been highly regarded by students, and the impact on students in making them critically think about CSR and responsible management was significant. In addition, through the process of intimate collaboration with real world business in dealing with problems and developing CSR strategies, both academia and the corporate world have mutually benefited from each other in a meaningful way. Finally, our experience showed that professors' engagement and leadership in teaching PBL course was the most critical aspect of its success.

Why PRME is/was important

In particular, PRME is important in:

- providing management schools with the opportunity to reflect upon their own purpose in this new age of conscious capitalism (i.e., addressing the question of who we are);

- playing a role in sharing valuable information regarding development and implementation of strategic planning in the creation and actualisation of the new paradigm of responsible management education (i.e., addressing the questions of what and how);
- building a learning community that enables signatory universities to better keep in touch together and encourage each other along the journey, eventually building a critical mass for the responsible management education movement.

HOW TO FIND, PRODUCE AND INTEGRATE CASE STUDIES THAT PROMOTE PRME VALUES

Richard Ivey School of Business, Western University, London, Ontario, Canada

UTILISING CASE COLLECTIONS

Introduction

The Richard Ivey School of Business at Western University is Canada's oldest business school. It is a large institution, with degree programmes at the undergraduate, MBA, MSc, EMBA and PhD level. Its main campus is located in London, Ontario, with over 100 full-time faculty with PhD, and 200 staff. It also has campuses in downtown Toronto and in Hong Kong.

Challenges

As an early signatory to the United Nations Global Compact (GC) and the Principles for Responsible Management Education (PRME), a GC-supported initiative, an immediate question we faced was how Ivey might further the Ten Principles of the GC, internally, and especially externally. The most obvious solution seemed to be to somehow utilise the Ivey Publishing case collection. By way of background, Ivey Publishing is the world's second largest producer and distributor of comprehensive, decision-oriented business case studies. It markets cases produced by Ivey faculty as well as those from individual professors at other institutions.

> My advice to university and college professors who have been contemplating using GC-focused case content in their courses is to simply get on with it. The high-quality material already exists, in large quantity. New, relevant cases are being added to the collection each week. Full teaching notes are available for the cases. There is now even a new case and textbook commercially available.
>
> *Paul Beamish, Professor of International Business,*
> *Richard Ivey School of Business, Western University*

Actions taken

The first action that was taken was to determine how many of the cases in the overall collection could be matched to the GC's Ten Principles. In fact, there seemed to be a large and growing number. By mid-December 2011, there were already over 250 relevant cases in the collection. The next action was to make it easy to locate the cases, by category. The Ten Principles are organised under four main categories. The categories can be found on the Ivey Publishing website (www.iveycases.com) by clicking on Browse Catalogue (upper left) and then scrolling down to Cases By Theme to "Global Compact Initiative Themes" (subcategories = Anti-Corruption Practices (47), Environmental Sustainability (105), Human Rights (58), Labour Standards (45)).

A very large number of business professors worldwide prefer or are required by their institutions to use textbooks rather than compilations of cases and readings. Recognising this, as a next action the decision was taken to try and publish a GC-focused case and textbook. To that end, Ivey Professor Paul Beamish and Hult Professor Joanne Lawrence proposed such a book to Sage Publishers. Their proposal was accepted and the co-edited case and textbook was commercially published in March 2012 as part of the Ivey-Sage series.

The 550 page softcover book is entitled *Globally Responsible Leadership: Managing According to the UN Global Compact*. It is made up of 8 chapters and 21 Ivey case studies. The book is organised according to the Ten Principles. It is intended to serve as the basis for a standalone course in business schools.

All of the case studies have full teaching notes available at no cost to qualified faculty via Ivey Publishing. The 21 cases included in the book were selected after an exhaustive review of the entire case collection. The eight invited chapters were contributed by faculty members from around the world. A foreword to the book was provided by Georg Kell, Executive Director of the UN Global Compact.

Results

There will be a number of benefits from the aforementioned initiatives. First, university professors worldwide now have a very large and pre-sorted set of GC-focused case studies, which they can select from for use in their teaching programmes. Second, there is now a case and textbook available should professors wish to introduce a GC-focused integrated elective course. Third, should faculty members anywhere actually wish to engage in their own GC-focused case writing, they now have a large pool of relevant examples to draw from as potential prototypes.

Why the Global Compact is/was important

• The Ten Principles of the United Nations Global Compact provide a practical organising framework for a university level course.

Kozminski University, Warsaw, Poland

HOW TO CREATE A NEW MINDSET OF A TYPICAL MBA STUDENT IN CENTRAL AND EASTERN EUROPE

Introduction

KOZMINSKI UNIVERSITY

Kozminski University is a private and independent business school established in 1993 in Warsaw. It is now the only EQUIS, AACSB and AMBA accredited university in Poland and Central and Eastern Europe. Kozminski University offers recognised BBA, MA, MBA, and PhD programmes in business management and finance. The University has about 8,000 students overall; apart from students of Polish origin there are students from over 50 nationalities. The total number of the Kozminski staff is around 300. Kozminski University expressed its commitment to the Principles for Responsible Management Education (PRME) on 1 April 2008 in order to accelerate corporate responsibility issues into the knowledge, skills and mindsets of today's and tomorrow's leaders in Central and Eastern Europe.

Challenges

Corporate responsibility has become a hot topic in Central and Eastern Europe (CEE) because of the region's increasing "embeddedness" into the global political and economic system in recent decades. There is an emerging need for integration of corporate social responsibility (CSR) in the mainstream management education and executive education in CEE countries. Now an education in this field is dominated by an "import" of best practices and case studies from developed markets. But CSR is culturally-dependent not only in the process of implementation, but in the education as well.

My advice in order to have a better understanding of how business can at the same time create financial value and improve people's lives is to move beyond "CSR as usual" to innovative approaches with value for all. Case studies are always the best source of inspiration and can provide valuable insights into critical points at different stages of business decision taking. The role for business in coming years is to play a more active role in tackling the main social and environmental challenges through innovative and creative solutions. The main driver for CSR in Central and Eastern Europe (CEE) is business itself: not governments, not consumers, not civil society. Business could be the most mature player in the field of an inclusive and sustainable global economy, but the biggest barrier in CEE is the widespread narrow-minded model of free-market economy. Responsible management education is crucial.

Boleslaw Rok, Assistant Professor, Business Ethics Centre, Kozminski
University

Actions taken

It was decided by the rector of Kozminski University that there was a need to implement CSR modules into MBA programmes before EQUIS, AACSB and AMBA accreditation. But the question was: how to do it? The mindset of a typical MBA student is based on several stereotypes: in business there is no place for ethical behaviour and the main characteristic is a free, unimpeded pursuit of profits; the market knows better; the scope of legal regulations and voluntary self-regulations should be reduced, etc. MBA students are starting their programme with an expectation for a higher level of the narrowly understood professionalism, better risk management models and the assessment of shareholder value. For those students CSR meant discreet donations towards worthy causes, a soft issue or a nice-to-do activity on the fringe of business. In order to provide MBA students with practical solutions for the CEE market it was necessary to find real life examples of business dilemmas concerning visible opportunities to build bridges between business and society – creating value for all that can be captured.

CSR has appeared in CEE in the special circumstances of unfinished market reforms and opening up to the global economy from one side and a dynamic process of integration with the European Union (EU) from the other side. The biggest challenge in CEE from a business perspective is the ability of enterprises to meet the growing expectations of the global market and society, beyond basic consumer demands, and the ability to compete while investing in responsible management. Expectations from different stakeholders are growing but still, even among multinational companies, which are often the best CSR performers in the developed markets, there is a low level of knowledge concerning the local context of CSR. It is well known that CSR is culturally specific; it varies according to political traditions, the nature of social dialogue, and the degree to which certain social and environmental issues are regulated by law.

We decided that a collection of CEE educational case studies could be an important tool for this purpose. The project was financially supported in the frame of the Academy of Business in Society (EABIS) Corporate Founding Partner Programme on CR and Sustainability. It was led by the Business Ethics Centre at Kozminski University, in cooperation with the Centre for Business and Society of the CEU Business School, the Graduate School of Management St Petersburg State University and CSR Ukraine. Although each country is different, there is a common socialist heritage: a perception that tackling social and environmental issues is the government's role. Central planning and collective ownership were supposed to ensure that the needs of the entire community were recognised and its well-being safeguarded.

A special team consisting of practitioners and educators was established. The role of the team was important in the process of selection of the most inspiring business dilemmas concerning the role in society and the final form of case studies suitable for education. Eight detailed case studies were prepared in cooperation with local academics and the firms. In this project the academics/practitioners partnership was a vehicle for generating usable CSR knowledge. The intention was to provide companies and their future and present managers with a better understanding of the business dilemmas on CR in the reality of "New Europe".

Results

Eight case studies were prepared, two from each country, with additional teaching notes. Case studies were prepared in cooperation with selected companies, which in itself was an educational process for these companies.

All cases are used in MBA programmes already. The intention is to distribute them to selected business schools from CEE. There will be a special issue of the *Journal of Business Ethics Education* devoted to CEE markets with all cases presented there.

Why PRME is/was important

- PRME became a practical tool for Kozminski University to start a dialogue with representatives of academic and business community in Poland and CEE on ethical and responsible behaviour.
- PRME provides the opportunity to make connections with the most progressive part of the global academic community.
- Engagement with PRME encourages our University to undertake radical transition, because we are convinced that concern with social issues and a commitment based on the principles of fairness and justice will be defining characteristics of the near future.

SECTION 4. ALIGNING PRME AND RESEARCH

INTRODUCTION

Developing high quality research on corporate sustainability is a crucial and distinctive area of expertise for leading signatories to the Principles for Responsible Management Education (PRME) initiative. On the whole, signatories highlighted in this Guide agree that research is a key aspect of corporate sustainability and responsible management education, and plays an important role. Nevertheless, advancing conceptual and empirical research to better understand key dimensions of sustainable value creation and corporate sustainability is a challenging objective for management schools. The main challenges are:

- How to encourage and align faculty to develop research relating to corporate responsibility.
- How to embed sustainability related research on the broader framework of management research.
- How to publish sustainability research throughout the top ranked management research journals.
- How to design and fund groundbreaking research projects.
- How to build global research networks.

PRME signatories have undertaken a wide array of efforts to embed a sustainability research framework into their research policies. Leading signatories in the field of sustainability research have taken a medium-term approach based on three basic elements. The first concerns the commitment of the dean and the direction of the school. The second relates to various key strategic decisions adopted over the years that encourage faculty involvement in the development of research projects and the subsequent publication of their results. The third element involves the existence of a research centre that integrates all projects and expertise occurring in the field. Overall, PRME is seen as a coherent set of guiding principles that provide institutional legitimacy to a sustainability related research agenda. As some signatories show in their case stories, by aligning the school research policy with PRME, deans send a clear message to faculty about the strong institutional commitment to sustainability.

The main dilemma for management schools regarding the inclusion of sustainability research within the parameters of traditional academic research is whether or not to make the aspect of sustainability mandatory. During recent years, faculty members have been given rigid timelines and a list of journals in which they are expected to publish. Alignment with PRME redirects the main focus towards encouraging sustainability research without imposing a mandatory framework.

Some signatories have prioritised sustainability as a distinguishing area of expertise for their respective schools, building on the interdisciplinary character of corporate responsibility and sustainability research. Their faculties have been involved in defining the main areas of expertise as corporate responsibility, corporate sustainability, and sustainable business. Faculty members have been encouraged by the prospective benefits of interdisciplinary cooperation in promoting the overall recognition of their school in this particular field.

Management schools in Latin America and Africa have concentrated on research topics that, while of interest and relevance to the developed world, are firmly rooted in the cognitive expertise of the developing world. Consequently, schools in these regions have awarded priority to such topics as the Millennium Development Goals as their chosen framework for approaching sustainability.

Throughout their cases, signatories have highlighted how the identification of corporate sustainability research as a key priority affords the opportunity to distinguish their expertise from that of other management schools. As part of their main strategy to promote sustainability research, many schools have inaugurated leading research centres as well as research networks and chairs. Efforts have been made to acquire internal and external funding and other resources to better promote sustainability research. Obtaining funds from corporate and institutional partners for research projects has become an important priority. A further element has been the development of groundbreaking research projects and the setting-up of important research networks with external organisations and management schools.

To demonstrate their commitment to the importance of corporate sustainability research, some signatories have hired renowned scholars and other research-based faculty focusing on sustainability, incentivising excellent young scholars to work on sustainability research topics. Furthermore, bonuses have been established for researchers based on both the quality and quantity of corporate responsibility and sustainability research produced. Departments of corporate responsibility and sustainability have been created to integrate the foremost research groups across faculties, and executive and doctoral programmes dedicated to corporate responsibility have been established. Academic conferences and doctoral colloquia have been organised and doctoral research assistants have been contracted. As a consequence, recognition has been awarded by international ranking agencies that incorporate sustainability issues, notably the Aspen Institute's Beyond Grey Pinstripes review and ranking.

We also have seen how management schools have worked directly with companies to disseminate new findings in the field of sustainability. During recent years, these research results have been published in executive journals, and research papers have been published in A/B journals.

As highlighted in this section, PRME has been an important influence on research in management schools as a key element for motivating signatories to think outside of the traditional research framework and to promote sustainability as a research priority. It has given conceptual clarity to their sustainability research strategies. For some signatories, PRME has validated corporate responsibility and sustainability research as a core responsibility. Moreover, it has brought together a community of like-minded thinkers and inspirational schools. It has fostered the identification and establishment of research networks in areas of sustainability and helped to launch common research projects. And beyond that, the United Nations affiliation confers prestige on PRME, which encourages mainstream sceptics to consider integrating corporate responsibility and sustainability elements into their research agenda.

Among all the case stories in this section, we have seen how leading sustainability research policies are based on key strategic dimensions, such as:

1. Securing commitment and promotion, at the school/dean-level, of sustainability as an important research priority.
2. Hiring top scholars and motivating them to publish and promoting young scholars to become excellent researchers in the field.
3. Creating research groups and networks focused on corporate responsibility and sustainability.
4. Involving faculty members from different department in research projects.
5. Developing and funding of strategic research projects.
6. Obtaining funding for research from corporate and institutional partners and a convergence of interests between the researchers and their new partners.
7. Establishing local and global research networks.
8. Establishing research chairs on sustainability.
9. Organising international corporate sustainability research conferences.
10. Encouraging faculty to publish sustainability papers in A/B Journals.

HOW TO ENCOURAGE SUSTAINABILITY RESEARCH WITHIN THE PARAMETERS OF TRADITIONAL ACADEMIC CAREER EXPECTATIONS/ADVANCEMENT FRAMEWORKS

Audencia Nantes School of Management, Nantes, France

DEVELOPING CORPORATE RESPONSIBILITY AS *THE* DISTINCTIVE AREA OF EXPERTISE

Introduction

Over the last years, Audencia Nantes School of Management has implemented several initiatives aimed at encouraging a huge part of its faculty to develop research related to corporate responsibility. Rather than to make the integration of these issues mandatory, the School's management has decided to present this change as an opportunity for the faculty. Indeed, by focusing on corporate responsibility defined as the School's distinctive area of expertise, each member of the faculty benefits from the potential interdisciplinary cooperation with colleagues and academic partners as well as from the overall recognition of the School in this area. The School is among the first signatories to the Principles for Responsible Management Education (PRME), an initiative supported by the United Nations Global Compact.

Challenges

Building on the interdisciplinary character of corporate responsibility

Given the limited size of the Business School's faculty, it seems necessary to focus on a small number of areas of expertise in order to insure the visibility and the impact of their research. Audencia has used this context to progressively define corporate responsibility as the School's distinctive area

of expertise. This choice was possible because of the transversal character of corporate responsibility, but also because of the strong and constant support both from the School's management and a huge part of the faculty. Rather than to consider the integration of corporate responsibility issues in research as a constraint, it was used as an opportunity to favour cooperation beyond different academic disciplines, to obtain funding from companies and public authorities, and to strengthen the School's visibility in line with its culture and its commitment to the principles of corporate responsibility.

Actions taken

Advancing step by step

The definition of corporate responsibility as the School's distinctive area of expertise was an organisational learning process that took several years. Rather than impose this theme on faculty via a single decision from the School's management, several coherent decisions were made over the years to encourage the development of research projects in this area. This explains that a large part of the School's academic production is related to the area of corporate responsibility and led to a consensus among faculty that it should be considered as the distinctive area of expertise in which the School should continue to invest in the following years to further strengthen its visibility in this field.

Involving faculty members on a project base

One of the first actions was the creation of a Centre for Global Responsibility, which had the mission to develop research and teaching in the area of corporate responsibility at Audencia. In 2005, this Centre was just one research centre among many. To highlight the School's support for corporate responsibility issues, the Centre was initially funded by the School's budget, but it rapidly obtained contracts with companies and public entities at the regional, national and European level to develop its own budget. By 2008, the Centre had become one of the most active at Audencia. In order to encourage even more faculty members of the School to be involved in research projects on corporate responsibility, the Centre was transformed in 2008 into a transversal institute. This means that the members of the different research centres at Audencia may be involved on a project basis in the research activities managed by the Institute, which is thus not in competition with the other research centres. On the contrary, its mission is to help all research centres in the School to integrate corporate responsibility issues in their agenda.

> My advice in order to mainstream corporate responsibility in a School's research is to create incentives for the faculty to develop academic research in this area. The business school may for example offer special funding to research projects related to this subject. These funds can come from companies committed to these principles, encouraging thus the recognition of this research area as useful for companies and their stakeholders.
> *André Sobczak, Dean for Research, Audencia Nantes School of Management*

Funding research on corporate responsibility

In 2010, Audencia launched its own foundation, which has the aim of collecting funds from companies and individuals to ensure the development of the School. To be coherent with the School's strategy, it was decided to focus the first campaign for the Foundation on corporate responsibility. This enabled the funding of more ambitious research projects in this area and the recruitment of new faculty members specialised in this subject.

Involving the faculty in the definition of the main area of expertise

Finally, in 2011, when a new dean was appointed at Audencia, he decided to launch a consultation among the whole faculty to identify what differentiates the School from its main competitors. Within each discipline, the professors were invited to identify the areas where the School is in a leading position today and on which areas it should concentrate its efforts in the future. Corporate responsibility clearly appeared as the main area of differentiation for Audencia, be it among faculty members in marketing, management and even finance. This led to the appointment of the Institute's founding director as associate dean for research. His mission is to continue to develop research in this area, to mainstream it throughout all research centres and to launch a doctoral programme dedicated to corporate responsibility.

Results

One of the results of the School's decision to focus on corporate responsibility as the main area of expertise is Audencia's recognition by international rankings focusing on these issues, such as the Aspen Institute's Beyond Grey Pinstripes ranking, and also by companies that fund research. Such collective successes strengthen faculty's motivation to focus their research on corporate responsibility and to cooperate with colleagues who have already published in this area.

Why PRME is/was important

- PRME legitimises the School's strategy by clearly emphasising that the development of academic research in the area of corporate responsibility is one of the core responsibilities of business schools.
- PRME helps the School to identify other universities that want to develop research in this area and to launch common projects.
- Given its links with the United Nations, PRME offers a certain prestige that may convince sceptical researchers that it is in their interest to consider integrating corporate responsibility into their research agenda.

Euromed Management, Marseilles, France

TAILORING SUSTAINABILITY RESEARCH – HOW TO PROMOTE IN A PUBLISH OR PERISH WORLD

Introduction

Founded in 1872, Euromed Management is one of the largest and top ranked business schools in France. The main campus is located in the heart the Callanques National Park in Marseille, France with campuses and offices in Toulon, Avignon, Bastia (France), Marrakech (Morocco) and Suzhou (China). With over 5,700 students, the School offers an array of undergraduate, graduate and executive education programmes. Euromed Management is accredited by AACSB, AMBA and EQUIS. The School joined the United Nations Global Compact in 2005 and became signatory to the Principles for Responsible Management Education (PRME) in 2008.

Challenges

Promoting research on a specific topic is a challenge for any business school. Stimulating research on sustainability is one of the main challenges and opportunities a school must face in its efforts towards providing a responsible management education. By becoming a PRME signatory, the School also agreed to "engage in conceptual and empirical research that advances our understanding about the role, dynamics, and impact of corporations in the creation of sustainable social, environmental and economic value" (Principle 4). At Euromed Management, over 30% of academic activities and publications are linked to corporate social responsibility (CSR) or sustainability issues and the number of publications continues to rise. These increasingly satisfactory results are due to various initiatives including the creation of projects, networks and research chairs. However, the deciding factor lies in the School's decision to structure research into five priority groups, one of which is dedicated to CSR.

The reality of the situation is that researchers need resources, funding and contacts with companies. On the one hand, Euromed Management seeks to be effective in hiring top scholars and motivating them to publish. On the other hand, the CSR Department of the school works on creating ties with business and organisations. It is because both the researchers and the CSR Department share objectives and interests that things happen. The academics bring their knowledge to the companies, companies provide funding for research and the academics work on subjects of interest for the companies. By making sustainability a priority and by findings areas of interest that meet both corporate and academic needs, Euromed Management aims to produce both conceptual and empirical research as well as knowledge on sustainable business.

It takes more than money to encourage researchers to work on our projects. It takes a topic that corresponds to their research interests. When promoting sustainability-related research, I advise you to start by identifying the needs of your research team and your stakeholders. Once you understand the existing framework, your job is to find individual objectives that can be shared by a diverse and multifaceted team. Sustainable development is a transversal topic. If you adopt a transversal approach your researchers will take interest.

Jean-Christophe Carteron, Director of Corporate Social Responsibility,
Euromed Management

Actions taken

Structuring research to promote sustainability

One of the main ways Euromed Management has incited professors to carry out research on sustainability was by making it a School research priority. In other words, the School put resources behind each priority which allows for the development of publications and events, and guides the hiring of professors and research assistants. Although professors do not belong to a priority, they tend to orient their research around each of the five poles. The research priority "Environmental and ethical dimensions of business and organisations" is coordinated by Julien Hanoteau, associate professor of Sustainable Development Economics. This priority has produced a number of articles such as "Beyond the bounded instrumentality in current corporate sustainability research: towards an inclusive notion of profitability" by T. Hahn and F. Figge that was published in the *Journal of Business Ethics* (Vol. 104).

Scientific research stimulation

Euromed Management, like many other schools, places great importance on the production of scientific research. As an institution we use a number of resources to stimulate research in general and on sustainability topics in particular. For example, researchers receive bonuses based on the quality and quantity of research produced each year. The School also provides professors with resources for the organisation of conferences and doctoral colloquiums and hires doctoral research assistants. Another way to promote research is through finding funding for projects, either with corporate or institutional partners.

An example of this would be the work published with the International Research Network on Social and Environmental Aspects in Business and Management (SEABUS). SEABUS is an international academic network that has been funded by the German Federal Ministry for Education and Research since 2006. For three months in 2010, under the SEABUS umbrella, Euromed Management hosted a guest researcher from the Institute for Futures Studies and Technology Assessment (IZT Berlin). In addition, together with other network members, Dr. Tobias Hahn has published special issues of two academic journals on "Trade-offs in corporate sustainability" and "A new future for business".

In September 2010, the Corporate Responsibility Research Conference (CRRC) was hosted at Euromed Management in partnership with the University of Leeds and Queen's University in Belfast. The organising chair, Dr. Tobias Hahn, associate professor of Corporate Sustainability, welcomed approximately 100 participants from 25 nations, providing a platform for the exchange of ideas on "Sustainability management in a diverse world". The 2010 CRRC, which also hosted a PhD workshop, helped Euromed Management re-enforce its leadership position in CSR and sustainability research.

Working with companies and disseminating knowledge

The third way Euromed Management nourishes research on sustainability is by finding projects that converge with the interests of researchers and corporate partners. For the past few years, the School has gradually oriented corporate partnerships, projects and events around CSR themes. The CSR Department is particularly implicated in this process as it is integrated into the Corporate and Markets Directorate.

Results

To date, the CSR Department and committed professors have promoted CSR research activities through the creation of projects, think-tank activities, networks and research chairs. An example of this is the Responsible Management Network that was launched in 2007. With over 20 corporate members, the Network acts as think tank with a mission to contribute to the emergence of "responsible management" in order to reconnect business dynamics with those of society. Through a participative methodology, the Network encourages innovating, emulating, capitalising and co-creating knowledge, actions and a new "savoir faire".

Research chairs are another means used to promote sustainability research. Euromed Management's first chairs in sustainable performance and finance demonstrated that in order to effectively increase research on sustainability it is important to mix partner profiles that incite the faculty to work transversally. An example of this approach can be seen in the creation of the chair in sustainable purchasing in a network environment. In April 2010, the chair was launched with funding from three companies: L'Occitane, SNCF (French Rail), and Sodexo, together with three NGOs: WWF, Max Havelaar and Extra-Muros. These partners provide data and analysis regarding the economic, environmental and societal dimensions of responsible purchasing. A new partner, ERDF, joined the chair in August of 2011. The chairs financed by companies not only enable the development of research on sustainability and CSR issues from a theoretical perspective, but they are also guided by the practical questions the companies wish to tackle.

In conclusion, it is clear that the most efficient way to encourage sustainability research lies in the creation of strategic orientations and research structures that prioritise this vast and transversal field. However, structure and organisation are not enough; schools must use corporate partnerships to fund dynamic and pertinent research activity. Committed faculty and staff members have shaped Euromed Management's approach and the result speaks for itself. In this increasingly complex world, the importance of sustainability research is increasingly evident. Sustainability provides researchers and multifaceted teams with an opportunity to work together while enabling them to carry out research in their different fields. The question that every school can ask itself is simple, "If one must publish or perish, why not publish on sustainability?"

Why PRME is/was important

- Context and legitimacy enabling the promotion of CSR related research.
- Institutional motivation to go beyond traditional research frameworks and to make sustainability a research priority.
- Facilitation of a network of schools that share our interests and helped us effectively adapt our approach.

University of Stellenbosch Business School, Bellville, South Africa

RELEVANT RIGOUR: SUSTAINABILITY RESEARCH IN AN AFRICAN CONTEXT

Introduction

The University of Stellenbosch Business School (USB) has been a signatory to the Principles for Responsible Management Education (PRME) since 2008. The USB operates as a department within the Faculty of Economic Management Sciences of Stellenbosch University (SU), its parent university. Situated in Cape Town in South Africa, the USB offers an MBA (EQUIS and AMBA accredited), MPhil degrees in development finance, management coaching and futures studies, a PhD, and postgraduate diplomas in dispute settlement and leadership. The total number of students for 2011 was 1,041, with 37 full-time faculty members, 71 part-time faculty members and 105 administrative staff. The USB's programmes are characterised by the development of critical thinking abilities and leadership skills in a multicultural setting.

This brief case explains how the USB tries to encourage sustainability research within the constraints of a more traditional academic framework, and how its participation in PRME has been of assistance in this regard.

Challenges

As a relatively small school in an African context, the USB faces the traditional research output constraints with regards to capacity and funding, while private companies and public institutions also display a reticence to make data available to researchers or to grant interviews. As a PRME signatory, the USB is committed to produce research related to sustainability. However, faced by these constraints, the fundamental challenge is to determine the most appropriate format and frequency of such research.

Actions taken

To meet this challenge, there is a need to reframe the "publish or perish" position within an African framework (and the developing world) to ensure that all research on sustainability has both academic rigour and practical, relevant application. Recently, the SU has prioritised the Millennium Development Goals as preferred themes in the SU research strategy. Hence, the SU provides financial support for projects that advance the selected goals. This initiative, called the HOPE Project (www.thehopeproject.co.za), also drives the collective social engagement efforts of the USB and its stakeholders. Three of the USB's research centres have been singled out by the HOPE Project: the Africa Centre for Dispute Settlement, the Centre for Corporate Governance in Africa and the Security Institute for Governance and Leadership in Africa. (It is important to note that sustainability in a South African context leans more towards social development and not, as in Europe, towards environmental development).

> My advice is, at least in the developing world, to concentrate on research topics which, while they are of interest and relevance to the developed world, are strongly grounded in the cognitive expertise of the developing world. In other words, it is necessary to bring something to the intellectual party from Africa that is of interest to Washington and Paris.
> *John Powell, Director, University of Stellenbosch Business School*

The USB has attempted to find multiple ways of sharing research not only in academic journals, but also in practitioner publications and popular media pieces, as well as its own publications, such as *USB Agenda* and *USB Leaders' Lab*. The intention is not to discard traditional journal publication, but to try and find ways in which an academic article can be published and also transformed into a piece to be published in the popular media. The goal is to make the research more accessible to readers other than those of academic journals.

The most recent action taken to increase research capacity and encourage publication was the introduction of research fellowships whereby an acknowledged international researcher is invited to undertake joint research with a USB academic over a period of one year. The required output is at least one academic paper published in an accredited journal in the year to follow, one research seminar and one open lecture, which is also accessible to students.

Therefore, research related to sustainability within the parameters of traditional academic career expectations/advancement frameworks (i.e., "publish or perish" in A or B Journals) is encouraged while steps are taken to increase output in this regard by encouraging academics to form research partnerships (either individually or as part of a research centre or specific degree programme in the USB) to enable research to take place.

A few examples are:

- The Centre for Corporate Governance in Africa collaborated with the Global Reporting Initiative (GRI), the United Nations Environment Programme (UNEP) and KPMG on a document entitled *Carrots and Sticks: Promoting Transparency and Sustainability.* The publication provides an update on trends in voluntary and mandatory approaches to sustainability reporting and was launched at the GRI conference in Amsterdam in 2010. The document is available for download on the Centre's website (www.governance.usb.ac.za).
- The Centre for Corporate Governance in Africa was appointed by the South African Public Investment Corporation (PIC) to develop a Corporate Governance Rating Matrix to be applied to listed South African corporations. The PIC is a government-owned asset manager, one of the largest on the African continent. The project is currently in its fourth year and covers the top 100 companies listed on the Johannesburg Stock Exchange.
- The Base of the Pyramid (South Africa) Learning Lab at the USB strives to integrate initiatives started under this project into other "social and/or development engagement initiatives" at the USB. Thus, they can link up with initiatives around sustainability, corporate social investment, small-business development and local economic development (e.g., focused township development). The Learning Lab publishes fact sheets on sustainable social and environmental

initiatives as a way to disseminate information to students and other stakeholders (see www.bop.org.za).

- Sustainability has been incorporated into the MBA curriculum for 2012 as a core subject (previously an elective), which will encourage students to undertake research in this direction. This sustainability module, called Business in Society, unpacks ways in which corporates can invest in the betterment of society. Sustainability is also ingrained in the content of various other MBA modules and electives.

- The head of the MPhil in development finance programme initiated an African development finance stakeholder engagement workshop in 2011. The goal is to introduce a development finance forum with the objective of developing partnerships between academic institutions and the private sector to encourage research and enable access to relevant data. Going forward, this forum will meet four times a year to provide feedback to the USB's MPhil in development finance team, and to report on workshops with stakeholders and the dissemination of research. The USB and its students, development finance institutions and corporations will collaborate on this forum.

Results

The USB's view is that responsible management education should be underpinned by responsible research. This responsibility points to the traditional academic community (including its journals) as well as the broader society. In conclusion, the USB believes that the most comprehensive contribution will be made by focusing on relevant topics and making research results available in multiple formats to different audiences.

Why PRME is/was important

The USB's participation in PRME has certainly benefited its thinking in this area. The USB believes that PRME provides the following benefits:

- Conceptual clarity.
- A community of like-minded and inspirational schools.
- Procedural structure.

SECTION 5. FOSTERING PRME PARTNERSHIPS AND CONSTANT DIALOGUE

INTRODUCTION

Pleading the case for sustainability issues to the business and management community has been an important part of the strategy for advancement in the area of responsible management education for signatories of the Principles for Responsible Management Education (PRME) initiative. Most signatories are strongly promoting responsible management education through partnerships and dialogue on critical issues related to global social responsibility and sustainability with businesses and other stakeholders, such as local communities, civil society organisations and other interested groups.

PRME signatories are clearly committed to share their knowledge with companies of how to meet social and environmental responsibilities. The case stories in this Guide demonstrate that advocating the case for sustainability issues has not been an easy task. The work of developing corporate partnerships on sustainability demands a new collaborative approach. Time must be spent on clarifying objectives and expectations, and both faculty and companies must make a strong commitment to ensure excellence and a strong commitment from both sides to the partnership itself.

PRME signatories have recognised the key role played by the business community in helping to promote responsible management education and to raise the awareness of courses about sustainability and sustainable business. PRME signatories are asking businesses to be involved in courses in which professional resources are shared, and input and recommendations are offered from industry, partnering organisations and individuals. Faculty engagement with the business community has generated various initiatives such as the launching of business advisory councils, MBA courses, project-based learning programmes and internships, and helped to create and develop new business opportunities.

In addition to partnering with the business community, one of the main challenges facing PRME signatories is how to engage with the wider community – for example, NGOs, governments, and the media – to create partnerships that advance responsible management education. The case stories in this Guide provide some indications of the work done by leading schools, namely the objective to work in partnership with all stakeholders, promoting research projects, developing new courses, launching new publications, organising events and exchanging professors and participants.

Finally, a key dimension for establishing/enhancing partnerships and dialogue is how to engage with students and inspire them to participate in activities related to PRME. During recent years, PRME signatories have organised a wide range of activities, such as international competitions, open debates and student fora, to raise the awareness of programme offerings related to responsible management education and corporate sustainability. These activities enhance the awareness and value of responsible management education. Students, faculty and social institutions collaborate to solve specific community needs, employing and sharing their knowledge to develop projects for the common good. MBA participants learn about different social realities and thus gain a better understanding of the meaning of professional responsibility working in sustainable business and community projects and partnerships.

In the area of partnership and dialogue, PRME has been important because it has encouraged management schools to organise debates with companies and other stakeholders on how best to implement corporate responsibility and sustainability principles and values. PRME gives signatories a holistic approach, bringing together researchers, scholars, students and managers on shared projects, providing a common vision. It emphasises the need to broaden applied research, which is useful not only for academic peers and networks, but also for the business community and society in general.

In this section, PRME signatories detail how the initiative has provided a framework and an opportunity to structure change and redirect the learning process towards corporate responsibility, sustainability and responsible management education. PRME has helped to integrate the concepts of responsible management in business education through supporting partnerships. And beyond that, it has provided a framework and an opportunity to enhance student and alumni engagement.

Schools that are signatories of PRME have been awarded a new credibility. It has pleaded the case for involving the business community in business education and helps them to design the framework for advocating a management school/company partnership approach to facilitate the transfer of knowledge, and ensure the values of corporate sustainability are embedded in the learning process.

PRME signatories have adopted various strategies to further their case for sustainability within the business and management education community, such as:

1. Creating business advisory councils and recruiting corporate members to their advisory boards.
2. Building concrete partnerships with industry and individual companies.
3. Organising business conferences in order to present new research findings.
4. Organising seminars addressing corporate responsibility.
5. Promoting responsible practices via the publication of reports, websites, and case studies.
6. Designing courses, service learning programmes and internship programmes with corporate partners.
7. Promoting the case for corporate responsibility with the media and raising public awareness of sustainability issues.
8. Participating in industry fora and business meetings in order to explain the issues of corporate responsibility and sustainability.
9. Sharing professional resources in order to advance corporate responsibility and sustainability.
10. Involving companies in programmes and courses.

HOW TO INCREASE ADVOCACY FOR PRME/SUSTAINABILITY ISSUES WITHIN THE MANAGEMENT COMMUNITY

Audencia Nantes School of Management, Nantes, France

FROM CORPORATE RESPONSIBILITY AWARDS TO CORPORATE RESPONSIBILITY BOOKLETS

Introduction

Audencia Nantes
School of Management

In order to increase the relevance of the research conducted by its faculty, Audencia Nantes School of Management involves researchers, students and partner companies in launching a series of booklets aimed at analysing and disseminating innovative responsible business practices, in particular those developed by local small- and medium-sized companies. The School is among the first signatories to the Principles for Responsible Management Education (PRME), an initiative supported by the United Nations Global Compact.

Challenges

Training today's and tomorrow's leaders, business schools have a huge responsibility in advocating and disseminating responsible management practices. Publishing in top academic journals is not enough to influence corporate strategies and to favour the integration of social and environmental issues. Business school's faculty has to develop new tools in order to advocate for responsible business practices among managers and guide them in their implementation.

> My advice in order to spread responsible business practices among managers is to highlight the economic advantages of taking into account social and environmental issues. Moreover, it is important to explain the organisational context and the role of individuals in the development of responsible business practices in order to facilitate their translation to other contexts. Finally, it is difficult, but very useful to highlight also experiences that failed rather than to concentrate only on success studies.
> *André Sobczak, Dean for Research, Audencia Nantes School of Management*

Actions taken

Identifying and valuating responsible companies via the Global Responsibility Awards

Since 2006, Audencia, with the support of the regional government, has been responsible for organising the annual Global Responsibility Awards. The aim is to identify and to award companies that have adopted innovative practices in the area of corporate responsibility. To do this, the School relies on company audits and interviews conducted by students with different stakeholders. The Global Responsibility Awards are thus also a learning experience for the students who have the opportunity to discover innovative practices. Trained by faculty members and coached by corporate responsibility consultants from Grant Thornton, the students use an auditing grid to evaluate the economic, social and environmental performance of the participating companies. These evaluations are presented to a jury made up of different stakeholders. Every year, this jury awards companies in three categories defined by the size of the company. With the support of the regional government, Audencia decided to integrate also social economy institutions, which allows the students to discover a broader range of business models.

Disseminating responsible practices via the Global Responsibility booklets

In 2008, based on the experiences discovered via the Global Responsibility Awards, Audencia decided to edit a series of booklets dedicated to corporate responsibility. The booklets are based on case studies of regional companies that have implemented innovative practices in the area. Each booklet deals with one specific aspect of corporate responsibility, such as responsible purchasing, diversity management or partnerships with NGOs. Students actively contribute to the global responsibility booklets. In cooperation with faculty, they identify innovative practices and the relevant actors that managers who want to implement a corporate responsibility strategy should enter into contact with. The students then learn more about these practices by conducting interviews with all major stakeholders and comparing them to actions developed in other contexts. Together with faculty, they select the most innovative actions as well as those that may help managers in other companies. Finally, in cooperation with a journalist, they learn how to present their ideas. The booklets also constitute an innovative learning opportunity for the managers who are involved in the process. They have to work with the faculty member and the students to analyse the strategies and actions they have implemented and to present their results, communicating openly on both the managers to improve their strategy for the future and to learn how to share it with stakeholders and other companies. The 5,000 booklets are disseminated to managers in the region as well as to participants in executive education programmes. They are also sold via Amazon.

Results

Developing research on responsible management in SMEs

Building on the experience of the Global Responsibility Awards and booklets that have highlighted innovations in small- and medium-sized companies, in 2011, Audencia launched a chair on corporate responsibility in SMEs. This chair will allow the recruitment of a new faculty member and doctoral students who will continue to identify, analyse and spread innovative practices and develop comparisons with practices in other countries.

The School's activities aimed at advocating global responsibility within the management community are closely linked to its core activities, i.e., research and teaching. This seems important to justify the time and energy invested in these projects by faculty members and students.

Why PRME is/was important

- PRME encourages the School to organise debates with companies and other stakeholders on the principles of corporate responsibility and their concrete implementation.
- By covering the different activities of business schools, PRME favours a holistic approach, bringing together researchers, students and managers on common projects.
- PRME emphasises the need to develop research that is useful not only to academic peers, but also to the broader society.

La Trobe Business School, La Trobe University, Melbourne, Australia

STAFF AS KEY ENABLERS OF CHANGE

Introduction

 La Trobe Business School offers a full suite of business courses across five campuses in Victoria, Australia. The flagship MBA programme taught at the main Melbourne Campus has been completely redesigned in line with Principles for Responsible Management Education (PRME) and received the EFDM EPAS accreditation in 2011 as well as Beyond Grey Pinstripes recognition. The Business School is part of the La Trobe Faculty of Business, Economics and Law, which has more than 9,000 students and 500 staff. Postgraduate course offerings include the MBA, as well as courses in international business, marketing and information technology, accounting and finance. In regard to the MBA, the student body profile comprises around 800 students from over 40 countries.

Challenges

Increasing advocacy for PRME and sustainability is an important challenge that will bring about change and should cover engagement across many aspects, both within the university and business sectors and across the wider community. La Trobe University has been involved in many actions that build partnerships and networks in these communities and is an advocate for responsible management education and business practices: from organising joint conferences, speaking at business seminars, using media to get the responsibility message to wider communities, being engaged in service-learning activities to link education to other sectors, and increasing internal engagement.

> My advice in order to increase advocacy for PRME and sustainability issues within management community is to use key staff as change agents and to encourage them to move out of their offices and into broader communities – whether academic, industry or community. This provides benefits at many different levels: the individual, the organisation and the community.
> *Suzanne Young, Associate Professor, Faculty of Business, Economics and Law, Department of Management, La Trobe Business School*

Actions taken

Building partnerships with industry, other PRME participant institutions, and academics in the ethics and responsibility fields through international and local networks are all important. Joint academic conferences and student and staff exchange with other PRME universities have been used to promote the initiative. La Trobe University became the fourth member of the CR^{3+} conference, together with Hanken School of Economics (Finland, host 2011), Audencia Nantes School of Management (France, host 2012), and ISAE/FGV (Brazil, host 2013). La Trobe University has agreed to host the CR^{3+} conference in 2014. (For more information on the conference see Section 6: "The International Corporate Responsibility Conference (CR^{3+})"). In addition, La Trobe University was one of the driving powers in establishing the Australasian Business Ethics Network (ABEN) after actively being a part of the European Business Ethics Network (EBEN UK).

Hosting and attending **business conferences** and presenting papers on responsibility at these events also raises the profile of the field and this has occurred with partners such as the Australian Centre for Corporate Social Responsibility. Moreover, La Trobe University, through its Institute for Sustainability, hosts a yearly business forum with business and government partners.

Media attention is also important in advocating for the PRME initiative and raising the profile of sustainability issues. This has been achieved through opinion pieces written for newspapers and universities, and speaking at industry forums.

As part of this development a **corporate responsibility seminar series** was also developed where industry speakers presented to staff, students and alumni on their activities and the context of business.

In 2011 using a **service-learning pedagogy**, internships were offered, matching indigenous leaders and students with a particular area of expertise. Such community-learning activities are an ideal way to supplement the course content and embed learning. Students are also offered study abroad opportunities working in businesses for a short period of time.

In addition **internal momentum** is important and has been gained by presenting seminars to internal staff on events attended, and asking students to speak on their learning and extra curriculum PRME-related activities to staff at student seminars. Having an ongoing agenda item at school meetings on PRME has also been used to raise the profile of the initiative internally. In addition, the School under the umbrella term **Responsible Management in Action** offered tailored staff-development activities in areas of responsible behaviour and anti-discrimination. All research students and staff were also offered the opportunity to attend subjects in responsible management as professional development.

Results

Conferences

Sharing work on PRME and sustainability issues at both academic and business conferences, seminars and workshops has demonstrated the ideas that are being generated in the education sector, testing their application with business leaders while contributing to the sharing of ideas on how to progress even further. Increasingly, staff have been asked to speak at these events and are considered experts in sustainability and responsibility.

The CR^{3+} and ABEN conferences have provided an opportunity to present and develop ideas and interact with people in the space of responsibility. They have created a network for people working with the PRME initiative and advocating for change.

Media

Writing opinion pieces has raised the profile of the need for responsible management practices and demonstrated the watchful eye that academics have over these practices and their willingness to speak out. It has also created a wider discourse across social media spaces.

Service learning

Service learning activities have been successful in broadening students' experiences and providing them with context and complexity where they can question their own cultural values. In particular the indigenous programme contributes to students' understanding of their own values and learning about different cultural contexts, stakeholder groups, communication styles, and leadership. The liaison and promotion of such programmes under the PRME banner increases the profile of PRME across industry and community groups.

Internal momentum

Gaining internal buy in has meant that the PRME initiative has now been adopted as a platform for all new programmes and has been increasingly seen as relevant by all staff. This case demonstrates the importance of faculty staff in their role as champions in overcoming barriers to organisational learning and as advocates for change in business practices.

Actions to increase advocacy across the whole of the management community – both within and external to the university sector – has raised the profile of responsibility in both education and business practice. The discourse around this provides legitimacy for all involved and challenges established ways of working. It has created a movement that is relevant to all.

Why PRME is/was important

- The use of a framework, such as the Principles of PRME, has provided an opportunity to structure the change process.
- The PRME is a framework that provides support for the integration of responsible management into education through partnerships.
- PRME provides an opportunity to build student and alumni engagement.
- Signing up to PRME aligned with the wider La Trobe University agenda of creating a sustainability-conscious, social and environmentally responsible tertiary institution.
- PRME provides the opportunity to embed graduate capabilities into new course offerings – capabilities that make students more employable and graduating with wider and diverse skills required by stakeholders, while providing them with a more holistic education.

HOW TO ENGAGE WITH THE BUSINESS COMMUNITY TO CREATE PARTNERSHIPS

Mendoza College of Business, University of Notre Dame, Notre Dame, Indiana, United States

ENGAGING WITH THE BUSINESS COMMUNITY TO CREATE PARTNERSHIPS

Introduction

 Mendoza College of Business at University of Notre Dame in Notre Dame, Indiana is a premier Catholic business school that seeks to foster academic excellence, professional effectiveness, and personal accountability in a context that strives to be faithful to the ideals of community, human development, and individual integrity. Mendoza, home to 2,535 students and 155 faculty members, offers programmes including: undergraduate Studies, MBA, executive MBA, executive education, MS in Accountancy, Master of Nonprofit Administration, non-profit professional development, and associated programmes, such as ESTEEM, joint MBA/JD, joint BS/MA, and joint BS in Engineering/MBA.

Under the leadership of former Mendoza College of Business Dean, Carolyn Woo, Mendoza began its long history as an advocate of the United Nations Global Compact. In 2007, Mendoza advanced the Global Compact cause further when Carolyn Woo represented AACSB to engage an international task force of 60 deans, university presidents and official representatives of leading business schools to develop the Principles for Responsible Management Education (PRME), which was officially launched in July 2007.

In January 2008, Mendoza College of Business became signatory to PRME. In doing so, Mendoza joined business schools and academic associations worldwide in committing to align its mission and strategy, as well as its core competencies – education, research and thought leadership – with UN values embodied by the Six Principles of PRME.

Challenges

In its new "Ask More of Business" platform, Mendoza College of Business presents the challenge of asking more of the individual, more of business, and more of the world to bring greater emphasis on, and awareness of, business for good (http://business.nd.edu/ask_more/). As part of this campaign, Mendoza recognises the immense value and resources its corporate partners and alumni offer to deepen the College's effectiveness in teaching about and acting on ethics. From getting involved in courses to sharing professional resources to offering industry recommendations, partnering organisations and individuals are invaluable to the achievements and efforts of the School.

> I think that successful corporate partnerships can be achieved by attention to the following:
>
> - Corporate partnerships reside generally within the community, the alumni network and recruiters. As such, it is beneficial to cultivate these relationships on a regular basis that includes frequent interactions (networking), communication (informing), and engagement (building affiliation).
> - Faculty are generally insufficiently aware of such relationships, and yet the richest form of collaboration comes from joint course development and research assistance. Efforts to draw faculty into or inform them of such relationships and opportunities should be moved from ad hoc to systematic.

- Corporate partnerships succeed when there are mutual benefits to both parties: the university and the company. To do so, there are three requirements: (1) time spent to achieve clear objectives and deliverables when the collaboration is project-based; (2) commitment of school resources (faculty time, attention) to assure a high level of performance; and (3) sessions to debrief, learn and improve so as to set the thinking for the next collaboration.

Carolyn Woo, former Dean, Mendoza College of Business,
University of Notre Dame

Actions taken and results

Inter-term intensives

Inter-term intensives, held twice per academic year, at Mendoza provide its MBA students with learning opportunities that fulfil several objectives. These objectives include focusing on building specific capabilities that students can add to their business "tool kits", expanding their learning beyond the classroom by assisting not-for-profit organisations, and engaging in deep-dive corporate cases to hone their problem-solving and decision-making skills. Inter-term intensives involve four types of courses: live cases, critical skills courses, social impact courses, and international immersions.

In the social impact courses, students help a non-profit organisation address an issue that is critical to success. Students have a significant social impact as their solutions are often implemented by the organisation. Past organisations have included the International Rett Syndrome and The Fig Tree Foundation. In addition, first-year MBA students take on a current corporate social responsibility case facing a major corporation. They work closely with company executives, analysing the issue, and present their findings to a panel of judges. Past corporations participating in inter-term intensives include Coca-Cola, General Electric, Green Mountain Coffee Roasters, IBM, McDonald's, and Whirlpool Corporation.

Through inter-term intensives, Mendoza continues to strengthen its relationship with corporate partners, who are often connected to the School through alumni. Examples of past projects include:

- **Business research, decision making, and communication fundamentals** – First-year MBA students worked in teams to participate in a case competition involving a corporate social responsibility issue faced by General Electric.

- **Positioning corporate social responsibility** – Students participated in a live case that addressed CSR as a potential strategic differentiator for Green Mountain Coffee Roasters, Inc. (GMCR), a leader in the specialty coffee industry, and its brands.
- **Creating an experiential marketing campaign** – Students teamed up to function as independent marketing agencies who receive a request for proposal from the Trisomy 18 Foundation, a not-for-profit for a devastating genetic disease that results in high rates of mortality in the first month of life.

Business Advisory Council

The Business Advisory Council (BAC) of Mendoza strives to advance the College's mission by involving alumni, organisations, and friends of the College in its work. Council members commit to supporting Mendoza financially, while also serving as ambassadors of the College. BAC members also engage in the internal operations of the College, by offering counsel to the deans and directors and by assisting in targeted initiatives as appropriate.

The Business Advisory Council meets annually on campus to discuss College updates, financial budget reviews, and curriculum changes. In addition, council members also make personal contributions to the School, such as through financial donations or through involvement in student activities or courses. Examples of past involvement by BAC members include:

- Dan Hesse, president and CEO of Sprint Nextel, presenting a Foresight in Business and Society lecture on why business leaders must think about future trends, and the qualities he values in employees.
- Frank Belatti, managing partner at Equipcorp Partners, serving as adjunct instructor to a micro-venturing course in the Management Department
- José Rafael Fernández, vice chairman, president, and CEO of Oriental Financial Group, sending members of his organisation to receive leadership and executive training at Mendoza's executive education.

IrishAngels®

The Gigot Centre for Entrepreneurial Studies houses the *IrishAngels*®, a select network of Notre Dame alumni and friends who possess entrepreneurial experience and a passion for supporting new venture development. The mission of the *IrishAngels*® is: "to serve as a focal point for entrepreneurially-minded members of the Notre Dame family worldwide who are seeking information and assistance related to the creation and development of new business opportunities". In addition, *IrishAngels*® seek "to support the work of the Mendoza and the Gigot Centre for Entrepreneurial Studies by advising and mentoring Notre Dame students, and by helping these students to tap into the personal and professional networks that are essential for building successful new businesses" (https://www.business.nd.edu/gigot/irishangels/).

IrishAngels® members include individuals from a variety of industries, such as health care, technology, and finance, and with an array of professional titles, including senior executives, educators, scientists, engineers, lawyers, venture capitalists, and small-business owners among others. Despite these diverse backgrounds, these individuals all share a common tie: Notre Dame. Their commitment to the University, and to its mission, propels *IrishAngels*® to generously contribute their time, energy, expertise, and resources to Mendoza's development of future entrepreneurs.

IrishAngels® members and their contributions are instrumental to the thriving entrepreneurial programmes offered at Mendoza. *IrishAngels*® have supported Mendoza through services such as mentoring Notre Dame students, sponsoring internships, and sharing in classroom lectures or special events. Annually, members also participate in the New Venture Competitions by serving as a significant and valuable source of feedback and mentoring to aspiring Notre Dame students and alumni entrepreneurs.

Why PRME is/was important

The Six Principles of PRME play an important role in Mendoza's relationship with the business and alumni community by:

- Providing a common vision for Mendoza and its business and alumni partners as they collaborate on business for good initiatives.

- Serving as benchmarks for assessment to provide a means of accountability in the partnerships and to move away from self-serving objectives and towards the greater good.
- Providing credibility to Mendoza as a signatory institution with PRME – business partners and alumni understand the commitment Mendoza makes when allying itself with the PRME initiative and its Principles.

Nottingham University Business School, Nottingham, England, United Kingdom

SUSTAINABLE DECISIONS AND ORGANISATIONS

Introduction

Nottingham University Business School (NUBS) has campuses in the United Kingdom, China, and Malaysia and is among a select group of AMBA and EQUIS accredited business schools. The School has global reach and a reputation as a leading research institution and offers undergraduate, master's, MBA, executive MBA, PhD, and executive education programmes – with a particular emphasis on responsible and sustainable business practice. In 2002, the International Centre for Corporate Social Responsibility (ICCSR) was founded at NUBS to lead CSR teaching and research. Its teaching activities have grown in scope and scale and two postgraduate programmes in CSR – an MSc in CSR and an MBA in CSR – have become highly regarded specialist programmes. The School is among the first signatories to the Principles for Responsible Management Education (PRME), an initiative supported by the United Nations Global Compact.

Challenges

The School's strategic aim is for students in all its programmes to understand the difficulties that businesses face in meeting social and environmental responsibilities and to develop capabilities to respond to these challenges in their professional lives. So that the concepts of business responsibility and sustainability are not confined to students studying on specialist programmes, the ICCSR introduced "Sustainable Decisions and

Organisations" in 2009 as a core module for all MBA students. The module enables students to appreciate the challenges of making long-term decisions and understand the broader societal and environmental impacts of those decisions. Collaboration with NUBS's partners from the business community underpins this module, in which students confront the challenge of developing a sustainable business strategy for a failing business. Commended by our external examiners for its realistic treatment of sustainability, the module has been expanded; it was initially introduced onto the full time MBA programmes in Nottingham and Singapore but it is now also delivered on the executive programmes and to students in Malaysia.

A key challenge for NUBS in running this module has been to engage the business community and the media. A wide range of practitioners feature in this module and our business partners are usually engaged because of their previous collaboration in an advisory or teaching role. As the module has proceeded, they have become so positive about it that they now contribute to refining and updating the content. By working together, our faculty and practitioner partners are educating a generation of MBA students who are sustainability literate and can apply their understanding as they move into influential roles across sectors and around the world.

My advice to engage business in the teaching of sustainable business is to design a course that takes business contributions to learning seriously, rather than either being tokenistic or reducing everything to the business case. The course that business representatives contribute to should include issues of clear relevance to business. It should creatively combine academic and practitioner knowledge. The rationale for business contributions should be clear to the students and the business representatives (e.g., a business briefing pertinent to the class challenge; a board meeting to evaluate student strategies). Business representatives should be invited to reflect on the module and their experience of it. This not only brings useful insights, but also a greater sense of a partnership approach rather than contractual relationship.
Jeremy Moon, Professor and Convenor of the MBA Sustainable Decisions and Organisations, Nottingham University Business School

Actions taken: Combining practitioner and academic knowledge to enhance learning about sustainability

The purpose

The Sustainable Decisions and Organisations module takes place in the second semester of our full- time MBA students' one-year programme. It was developed to provide a platform to integrate learning from across all the MBA modules and to afford students the opportunity to apply this multidisciplinary perspective to a business scenario. Given the complexity of interactions between business, the economy, the environment and society and the considerable scope for tensions to arise, the School considered it essential that the module include a strong real life element so that students have the opportunity to engage with and learn from the experiences of practitioners who face these challenges every day. Accordingly, the module is built around a large-scale fictitious case study of a failing retail business. Students work in groups on the development of a new strategy aimed at restoring the fortunes of this failing business. The groups are specifically asked to address how a strategy for sustainability would contribute to business success.

The format

The course is delivered through lectures and group work. Lectures are complemented with workshops on:

- Sustainable scenario planning (led by Forum for the Future).
- Crisis management and media training (led by a media consultancy).
- The retail sector (led by a retail sector expert).
- The economy (an economic briefing provided by the Bank of England).

For the duration of the module, students work in groups with specific operational roles: CEO, marketing director, financial director, etc. As each group develops their strategy, they face a series of crises that threaten the operation and reputation of the business. The module culminates with each group presenting their strategy at a media conference and to the executive board of the business, during which they are questioned on the crises that they have encountered and their responses to them. The press conference includes an array of experienced journalists who have written for the *Financial Times*, *The Times*, *The Independent*, and the *Guardian* and has included the chief BBC East Midlands news presenter. The executive board is populated with senior business people briefed to really test the groups. Board members are experienced members of executive boards and have included the former chief executive of Boots. Extensive business engagement is key to the learning experience afforded by this module and this innovation made it the subject of a BBC Radio 4 documentary *The New MBAs* in November 2010.

Results

The students

Around 140 MBA students now graduate from Nottingham each year having studied Sustainable Decisions and Organisations. Feedback from students consistently affirms that the module helps them to develop both an integrated understanding of business and the importance of sustainability to strategy. A former student admits:

> I was sceptical that you could marry the fundamentals of the programme with sustainability without short-changing one or the other, but this module managed to do it very well.
>
> *Glen Robinson, 45 year old Chartered Accountant*

Personal reflections submitted by the students also indicate that working on this business problem prompts deep reflection on their ideas about leadership and management style.

The Business School

Around 12 members of the business community contribute to the module, which runs up to 4 times a year. Over the last three years, more than 30 business and media organisations have been actively involved in the module. The School benefits from closer relationships with this array of business partners. Faculty that teach each core subject on the MBA contribute to the module, which improves the integration of student learning across the MBA programme.

Why PRME is/was important

The PRME initiative has added considerable momentum to the expansion of responsible management education. In particular, it is important for the development of learning experiences that involve engagement with business and the broader community because it:

- clearly sets out the core tenets of teaching and learning for responsible and sustainable business management,
- advocates the need for a partnership approach to facilitate knowledge transfer and ensure that learning is useful,
- provides an influential mandate for involving practitioners from various social institutions in business education.

San Francisco State University College of Business, San Francisco, California, United States

ENGAGING WITH THE BUSINESS COMMUNITY

Introduction

For more than 60 years, the College of Business (CoB) at San Francisco State University has served as a regional catalyst for educating and inspiring future business leaders. As part of the University's long-standing commitment to equity and social justice, the CoB created a regional Center for Ethical and Sustainable Business to leverage the growing momentum among conventional businesses to implement socially and environmentally responsible business practices. The CoB has 4,000 undergraduate students and 400 full and part-time MBAs. In June of 2008, the CoB became signatory to the Principles for Responsible Management Education (PRME), an initiative supported by the United Nations Global Compact.

Challenges

Our MBA with an Emphasis in Sustainable Business and our Center for Ethical and Sustainable Business were relatively new and not widely known in the business community. As a result, we were faced with a need to create awareness and establish credibility.

Actions taken

Ethics Week

Every fall semester, the CoB focuses a full week on topics related to social, ethical and environmental issues. This Business Ethics Week supports the efforts of the Center for Ethical and Sustainable Business to integrate ethics and sustainability across the curriculum. Business Ethics Week, in its sixth year, is a major event that showcases the CoB's commitment to educating

students on the importance of ethical and sustainable thinking and action. During Ethics Week, all faculty members in the CoB are asked to focus at least one class session on ethical, social or environmental topics related to their discipline (accounting, finance, marketing, etc.). In addition, speaker and panel sessions are scheduled that are open to the college community and the public.

For the fall semester of 2011, the overall theme of Business Ethics Week was "Ethics across the disciplines". Speakers and class discussions focused on best practices in ethics and sustainability in functional areas such as accounting, marketing, finance, and management and concluded with a dinner at which community service awards were presented to students and Bay Area business leaders who have demonstrated leadership in ethical and sustainable business practices. Past speakers and panellists have included:

- Roger Gray (former) CIO of PG&E
- Jon Hoak, chief ethics and compliance officer, Hewlett-Packard
- Kim Winston, director CSR – 2Civic and Community Affairs, Starbucks Coffee Co.
- Katie Excoffier, sustainability specialist, Genentech
- Ben Packard, VP Global Responsibility, Starbucks Coffee Co.,
- Deanna Robinson, VP Social Responsibility/Monitoring & Vendor Development, Gap Inc.
- Bonnie Nixon, (former) director Environmental Sustainability & Ethical Sourcing, Hewlett-Packard
- Suzanne DiBianca, executive director, Salesforce.com Foundation.

Annual speakers series

Each month during the academic year, the Center, Net Impact and other student organisations bring executive speakers to the San Francisco State downtown campus from Bay Area businesses, non-profits and government to speak about their experiences on topics relating to business ethics and sustainability. Recent speakers have included:

- Kevin Danaher, co-founder, Global Exchange and Green Festivals
- Larry Chang, (former) VP Finance, Hewlett-Packard
- Chris Benjamin, manager of Environmental Leadership, PG&E
- Matt Flannery, co-founder and CEO, Kiva
- Randy Hayes, founder, Rainforest Action Network
- Marcus Chung, director of corporate Citizenship, McKesson
- Michael Pace, general manager, W San Francisco Hotel
- Fiona Ma, California State assemblywoman on California High Speed Rail, Infrastructure & Jobs
- Network of Executive Women Panel on Sustainability & Opportunity in the Marketplace (Clorox, Clif Bar, Sunset Magazine, CauseConnect executives).

Sustainability consulting projects

Each year, Center and CoB faculty develop project-based learning opportunities for students to apply what they are learning in the classroom to real world situations. Student teams work with local business and non-profit organisations to address specific ethical or sustainability issues. As a product of the projects, the student teams make recommendations to the client organisation and assist in the implementation of known best practices in ethical and sustainable management. Some examples of recent student consulting project clients include the following:

- W San Francisco Hotel
- Whirlwind Wheelchair International
- Premier Organics
- Genentech
- Cohn & Wolfe
- New Leaf Paper

- Nestle Dreyer's Ice Cream
- Pacific Gas & Electric
- Union Bank

> I think that it is critical to support faculty in bringing in speakers. Many individuals in the business community like to engage students, and relationships with speakers provide an opportunity to deepen relationships with their organisation. Also, organising a speaker series is another avenue for engaging the business community.
>
> We found that creating the Ethics Week event gave us a straightforward way to approach the business community for speakers and panel participants. Ethics Week also provided a vehicle to engage many in our faculty, both in terms of involving them in planning and in asking them to build ethics or other sustainability topics into their courses that week.
> *Murray Silverman, Professor of Management, College of Business,*
> *San Francisco State University*

Results

Over the past five years, we have gone from being fairly insular in relation to the business community to being on a steady path of engagement. We have found that there are many businesses and individuals who are interested in engaging with us. Our students value the outside projects and speakers for both the exposure to real world experience and for the contacts they make. As a state university, fundraising is new to us. Our engagement efforts have established a platform for fund-raising that is reaping benefits.

Why PRME is/was important

- The opportunity to sign on to PRME a number of years ago created an opportunity for us to have our faculty think about the College of Business's commitment to social, environmental and ethical issues in business. It allowed us to show our faculty that there is a movement among business schools to address these issues. Our faculty voted 85% "yes" to becoming a PRME signatory.

- Developing the PRME Sharing Information on Progress (SIP) report after two years gave us a platform to create a cross-disciplinary committee to gather relevant information, and this deepened the commitment of the committee members and further engaged faculty who were contacted for information.
- The SIP reports institutionalise our process of periodically evaluating progress.

HOW TO ENGAGE WITH THE BROADER COMMUNITY TO CREATE PARTNERSHIPS

ISAE/FGV, Curitiba, Parana, Brazil

CREATING MEANINGFUL PARTNERSHIPS THROUGH THE INTERNATIONAL EDUCATION AND SUSTAINABILITY FORUM AND THE PRME CHAPTER BRAZIL

Introduction

 Located in the south of Brazil, on Curitiba City, the Advanced Institute of Administration and Economy (ISAE) has provided, since 1996, a high quality executive education for more than 3,200 professionals each year from all over Paraná State. Having the sustainable development of Brazil as a mission, the Business School has around 100 staff members and offers several MBA programmes, medium- and short-period courses beyond the main issues of management, in a partnership with one of the most recognised academic institutions in Brazil, the Getulio Vargas Foundation/ Fundação Getulio Varga (FGV). ISAE has 146 part time faculty and more than 400 professors from the FGV network.

One of the main business schools in the state of Paraná, ISAE won the Paraná Price of Quality in Management in 2011. ISAE has good relations with the local business community, and several partnerships, which include customised management programmes, research and large scale events involving public and private companies.

Challenges

In order to engage more actors with the Principle for Responsible Management Education (PRME) initiative, gain in scale and consolidate a new role for management education in Brazil, ISAE works with several stakeholders besides students and teachers, such as government, business

community, media, NGOs, and supporting organisations. This arrangement has the fostering of partnerships as a goal, providing advantages to both sides, and reinforces the market perception of the value of organisations with this kind of position. Through effective communication and networking, ISAE tries to show these partners the advantages of being a PRME participant, giving examples and information about the importance of adopting sustainable behaviour, and spreading sustainability values to every stakeholder, developing a new model of thinking and doing business. Through the International Education and Sustainability Forum and the creation of a PRME Chapter Brazil, ISAE is engaging the broader community.

Actions taken

International Education and Sustainability Forum

The International Education and Sustainability Forum, held on 13-14 September 2011, is a great example of how to engage several institutions in PRME. Developed by ISAE, and the Latin America Management Schools Council – CLADEA, the event brought together the academy, business, NGOs, and civil society to discuss how the educational process can help to build a better future embedded in sustainable values. More than 300 people attended over the two-days of lectures and activities, bringing to the table a great diversity of opinions and experiences.

The outcomes of the event were the consolidation of PRME in Brazil, and alignment and mobilisation of stakeholders in the discussion of responsible education. The PRME initiative also gained 32 new signatories, tripling the formal number of signatories in Brazil to further consolidate the Principles and the Global Compact in our country.

PRME Chapter Brazil

Despite the great challenges of participating in the task force that created PRME and integrating the Principles with ISAE's vision, strategy, processes and actions, our main mission beyond this initiative has been to disseminate and fortify a PRME Chapter Brazil. As ISAE was one of the first PRME signatories in Brazil and has now fulfilled most of the aspects of implementation, we believe that now is the time to engage more organisations in this process to gain in scale and strength.

The PRME Chapter Brazil reflects the importance of local networks' contribution to global initiatives, such as PRME. In order to help the group of new signatories who joined in September at the International Education and Sustainability Forum, an agenda of meetings and activities concerning this initial phase of implementation are being put together, which will contribute to the success of these new organisations beyond PRME application and understanding. The idea is to help other schools, companies and supporting organisations, and, on the other hand, ensure that the PRME initiative will have strong signatories in Brazil.

As soon as this first goal is achieved, the PRME Chapter Brazil will be a space for the exchange of best practice, information and experience sharing, uniting a group with different views and ideas. In spite of this rich sharing process, the idea for future is to work on partnerships for research, large-scale events, exchange of teachers and students, courses, publications and other activities.

> Given these examples, my advice on how to engage with the broader community to create partnerships is by reinforcing the real value that rises in sustainable organisations, among the market, consumers, partners and society perception. This position ensures that these partnerships will bring advantages for both sides, showing strategic vision and certifying a gain of scale. Involving as many actors as possible, and working with them by providing knowledge and emphasising the need of engaging all stakeholders in the process, is a strategy that has been working. In conclusion, I advise to not forget the internal groups, in order to have coherence between actions and speech. You cannot teach what you don't practise.
>
> *Norman Arruda Filho, CEO,*
> *Advanced Institute of Administration and Economy (ISAE),*
> *Fundação Getulio Varga (FGV)*

Results

With this group of initiatives, ISAE aims to enlarge the number of PRME signatories and fortify the initiative while supporting these new participants. With these actions, we believe that a phenomenon of growth will occur and that the values of sustainability will bring spread throughout the Brazilian education system to involve teachers, students, and the wider public.

Why PRME is/was important

- PRME has helped to awaken academia for its new role in facing the future.
- PRME, as an initiative of the UN Global Compact, creates in the business community a true good will around sustainability, rather than actions motivated only by financial reasons, thereby increasing value to companies, governments and societies.

Nottingham University Business School, Nottingham, England, United Kingdom

THE COMMUNITY ENGAGEMENT PROGRAMME

Introduction

Nottingham University Business School

UNITED KINGDOM · CHINA · MALAYSIA

Nottingham University Business School (NUBS) has campuses in the UK, China, and Malaysia and is among a select group of AMBA and EQUIS accredited business schools. The School has global reach and a reputation as a leading research institution and offers undergraduate, master's, MBA, executive MBA, PhD, and executive education programmes – with a particular emphasis on responsible and sustainable business practice. In 2007, NUBS launched the Community Engagement Programme (CEP) to expand the opportunities for its Business School students to work with community stakeholders. The School is among the first signatories to the Principles for Responsible Management Education (PRME), an initiative supported by the United Nations Global Compact.

Challenges

When the University of Nottingham was founded in 1881, service to the community was central to its vision as it aimed to provide for the distinct higher educational needs of the working men and women of Nottingham. The University remains committed to the City of Nottingham and engagement with our local communities. Staff and students at the Business School have worked with community stakeholders over many years but in 2007, the School harnessed the potential of community engagement activities by launching a formal

Community Engagement Programme. This is a joint initiative between NUBS, Community Partnerships (the University of Nottingham's community engagement initiative), local businesses, and community organisations. It is open to both undergraduate and postgraduate students in all years of study.

Actions taken

Our community engagement projects focus on either business or cultural projects and the Programme aims to:

- Develop students' understanding of what it is to be a social citizen.
- Help students to integrate with their local community and improve the reputation of the School and University within the local community.
- Support learning within the various academic disciplines of the undergraduate and postgraduate degrees with relevant practical experience within a community setting and additional training where appropriate, thereby enriching the overall student experience.
- Support local communities and business organisations with volunteer input particularly relevant to their business needs and practice.
- Promote global perspectives and diversity by sharing information on different cultures.
- Develop students' knowledge and skills to improve employability after graduation.
- Promote the potential for careers within the third sector.
- Provide a platform for integration of undergraduate and postgraduate students.
- Provide a platform for the integration of the international, EU, and UK students.

Managing engagement

Key challenges for NUBS in running the programme have centred on preparing and supporting students to work effectively with the community organisations, whose resources are typically stretched, and managing expectations of both students and organisations as to what is achievable in a restricted time period. To address the challenge of supporting students,

NUBS has developed a portfolio of training opportunities. The Business School, Community Partnerships, other University departments and external business partners who are part of the Business School's Employer Programme deliver these through workshops. Training includes subjects as diverse as communication and teamwork, project management, health and safety and specific academic related subjects such as running a focus group. Support is provided throughout projects by the Business School's skills and development manager, Community Partnerships and academics from the Business School. To smooth the process of working with the various organisations the School works closely with the Community Partnerships office, which has successfully established enduring relationships with the wider Nottingham community.

> In order for all parties to get the best out of the community projects we have learnt that it is important to be realistic and manage people's expectations from the start. Organisations need to be realistic about the abilities of undergraduates and the timescales available. Students have approximately 10 weeks each semester and will only be able to work on the projects a few hours a week. Students need to be aware that organisations often come to us because they lack the necessary resources and, sometimes, they are unable to spend much time with the students. The key is to be able to identify a project that the students can work on and complete within the given timescale so that both parties see a tangible benefit from the collaboration.
>
> *Jackie Andrews, Skills and Development Manager,*
> *Nottingham University Business School*

Students who participate in the CEP complete the training and produce a presentation on their projects receive the Community Engagement Programme Certificate. Our students' work with community engagement projects also counts towards the requirements for the Nottingham Advantage Award, a university-wide scheme that develops students' employability skills.

Examples of recent projects

CEP projects have been carried out in partnership with Oxfam, the YMCA, the Nottinghamshire Domestic Violence Forum, community social enterprises and schools. Below is a brief description of two current examples.

The Sharing Culture programme
The Sharing Culture programme aims to forge closer links between international, EU and UK students and the local community in Nottingham. The University attracts students from all over the world, many of whom are keen to share their culture and language with local school children. Students develop and deliver practical sessions relating to either Asian or European culture in local primary schools. UK and EU students link with exchange students from Nottingham's campuses in China and Malaysia to build understanding of different cultures within the partner primary schools.

Groups of five or six students work with one school to deliver a number of cultural sessions over the semester. The sessions might involve interactive activities such as dance, music, food and language and can be tailored to match the needs of the school and complement teaching that is already taking place.

Hadden Highlights – a community business project
This new project aims to develop Hadden Highlights, which is a school hairdressing and beauty salon. This initiative is part of a project run by Nottingham City and a local NGO that aims to raise standards in education and improve outcomes for children, young people, and their families.

Presently, the salon is used for student training and has a small number of local clients, but it has much greater potential and is underutilised. The plan is to develop it into a sustainable hair and beauty salon business that will bring the wider community onto the School's campus to use the salon.

Eight students are working on the project, undertaking research and competitor analysis for Hadden Highlights and writing a new business plan. They are also producing a marketing strategy to increase the number of customers and to promote other opportunities on the School's campus.

Results

Over 100 students participate in the CEP each year. In the past year, the Sharing Culture programme alone has provided the opportunity for 42 Chinese students on exchange from Nottingham's China campus, 4 Spanish-speaking students, and several UK students to work with schools in and around Nottingham. CEP projects give students the chance to put business theory into practice, with positive impacts on their academic performance and employability. The programme also develops students' transferable skills and allows them to gain new cultural experiences and an understanding of diversity.

Feedback from our students consistently affirms that they recognise the value of these learning experiences:

> One of the things that I do is teach about Spanish culture at a local primary school... You benefit a lot from skills you gain, so presentation skills, teamwork skills, leadership, just really strong interpersonal skills learning to work with people from different areas, cultures, and backgrounds.
>
> *Ameya Shah, BA Management with French, working on the*
> *Community Engagement Programme, 2010*

The CEP has enabled the School to work with a wide variety of community stakeholders. It is an important means for embedding the Business School within the community and has served to develop the sustainability literacy of all our constituents, although it goes without saying, this work goes on ...

Why PRME is/was important

- PRME has provided an important steer for engagement of the broader community in management education. The Community Engagement Partnership provides just one illustration of NUBS's commitment to Principle 1: Purpose to prepare students to generate a more inclusive and sustainable society.

Kozminski University, Warsaw, Poland

HOW TO CREATE A LEARNING COMMUNITY WORKING ON CSR DEVELOPMENT

Introduction

KOZMINSKI UNIVERSITY

Kozminski University is a private and independent business school established in 1993 in Warsaw. It is now the only EQUIS, AACSB and AMBA accredited university in Poland and Central and Eastern Europe. Kozminski University offers recognised BBA, MA, MBA, and PhD programmes in business management and finance. The University has approximately 300 staff and 8,000 students overall; apart from students of Polish origin, there are students from over 50 nationalities. Kozminski University expressed its commitment to the Principles for Responsible Management Education (PRME) on 1 April 2008 in order to accelerate corporate responsibility issues into the knowledge, skills and mindsets of today's and tomorrow's leaders in Central and Eastern Europe.

Challenges

Corporate responsibility and sustainability management are not well-known areas of practice in companies operating on the Polish market. If there is no demand from the market there is no supply from academic institutions. The biggest challenge was how to create a market for competencies and skills on sustainable value creation.

Actions taken

In 2001, faculties from the Business Ethics Centre (BEC) at Kozminski University were instrumental in organising the launch of one of the first local networks of the United Nations Global Compact in Warsaw in partnership with the United Nations Development Programme (UNDP). The second significant event at that time was cooperation in the process of establishing the first Polish NGO working in the area of CSR – Responsible Business Forum. Both organisations were based on partnerships with businesses. But it became clear that companies operating in Poland, even those owned by multinationals, were not ready for the implementation of social and environmental responsibilities. The first initiative guided by academics from BEC was to create a very simple tool "20 steps to implement CSR". It was prepared in the form of survey for new business partners in order to start a process of internal learning inside those companies. After a few years the membership base has reached over 20 companies, mostly multinationals operating in Poland.

The next step was to establish a partnership between BEC and the main economic newspaper to launch a national yearly ranking for responsible companies. The set of questions has been expanded every year, according to new challenges on the market and the level of implementation among participating companies. The ranking was prepared by BEC in cooperation with the Responsible Business Forum, economic journalists from the newspaper, and was verified by PwC. For many companies it has served as a benchmark for maturity in CSR, but the lack of knowledge concerning different instruments to manage properly a growing area of CSR was widely expressed by managers working in this field.

My advice in order to have effective programmes for future CSR leaders is to overcome the unnatural divide between students and experts. It is worth remembering that in the beginner's mind there are many possibilities and in the expert's mind there are only few. The main question here is about the ultimate driving force for CSR in a particular country. Is it the pull from the market demand or the push from the academia programmes? We need both of them. Corporate responsibility is such an area that we all are desperately looking for the unusual solutions because we are facing unusual challenges.

> We are all part of the problem and together can be part of the solution. Everyone can be and should be the change maker.
> *Boleslaw Rok, Assistant Professor, Business Ethics Centre, Kozminski University*

So, the next step was quite natural, it was demanded by the market itself. Three years ago we started at Kozminski University a full programme of executive study on CSR under the name "The strategy for responsible companies". It is a joint programme with PwC – they have 40 hours of a formal training in CSR strategy – some academics and several CSR managers from the first group of 20 companies. The whole programme is based on practical knowledge sharing during weekends. From the first edition we were trying to have a kind of multi-stakeholder group of students. Some of them were already employed by companies that were beginners in CSR, but always we had students from NGOs working with businesses, journalists, local governments and some people wishing to start their career in CSR. In fact, the process of knowledge sharing is not in one direction only – we are convinced that, according to the tradition of Zen Buddhism, in the beginner's mind, there are many possibilities and in the expert's mind there are only few. The process of learning is both ways.

Results

Over 100 students have participated in our programme, with a group of 30 trainers over the last 3 years. The ranking for responsible companies is published every year – it has become an educational tool for a growing group of responsible leaders. Almost 140 companies have already taken part. The questions in the survey (66 in the last edition) are in the process of continuous improvement; changes are discussed in a group of best graduates from Kozminski's programme learning community. Several partnerships were created between NGOs and businesses based on relations started during our programme. Some beginners from the first edition are now experts for the next edition.

Why PRME is/was important

- PRME became a guiding tool in our programme. We have recognised that every successful programme should be based on understanding of the real challenges on a particular market in meeting social and environmental responsibilities.
- Instead of dualism, "we-academics" and "they-managers" we decided not only to explore jointly-effective approaches, but also to be jointly involved in practical learning and sharing.
- We started to facilitate a dialogue among academics, business consultants, managers, civil society organisations and journalists on a practical level. It will help to create an educational platform to meet growing concerns of the market in responsible leadership. And – through ranking – it will help to involve more companies in this journey.

HOW TO ENGAGE STUDENTS WITH PRME

Hong Kong Baptist University (HKBU), Hong Kong, China

ENGAGING STUDENTS IN ACTIVE LEARNING

Introduction

The School of Business of Hong Kong Baptist University (HKBU), accredited by the AACSB International in 2010, has been nurturing future business leaders since 1956. The School is composed of 85 academic faculty members and offers BBA, BCom, MBA, MSc, DBA, MPhil and PhD programmes to around 2,000 students. The School is among the first signatories to the Principles for Responsible Management Education (PRME), an initiative supported by the United Nations Global Compact.

Challenges

To better equip our students to face the challenges of today's fast-changing global business environment, the School of Business of HKBU strives to prepare our graduates with the essential business knowledge and management skills such as leadership, critical and analytical thinking, decision making, problem solving, negotiation, conflict resolution and crisis management. We adopt the active teaching and learning pedagogical approach and motivate students to learn beyond the classroom by participating in open debates and international competitions to engage them in research on current issues and develop their talents and public speaking skills.

Our curriculum incorporates the essential business values for corporate sustainability: business ethics, corporate governance, corporate social responsibility, civic responsibility and good citizenship. These important business values and concepts are integrated into our syllabi and extra-curricular activities to prepare students for their future careers.

Actions taken

The School organises a wide range of activities which include international competitions and open debates, such as the Wing Lung Bank International Institute for Business Development (IIBD) Case Competition and the "mindXchange" Student Forum to encourage and engage our students in active learning and research on issues relating to responsible leadership, global social responsibility and sustainability.

> In order to effectively instil the principles of responsible management in students, academic institutions should explore new initiatives and organise extra-curricular activities that require active participation from students with guidance from faculty and the administrative staff.
>
> Based on our experience, the student-centred activities such as organising and hosting international inter-university competitions and intra-university open debates are effective in raising students' awareness of the importance of PRME. We motivate our students and engage them in research on topics related to responsible management. This is also in line with the education philosophy of our School of Business – "Whole-Person Business Education" as we prepare our students to become all-rounded, value-conscious business graduates and future leaders.
>
> *Stephen Y. L. Cheung, Dean, School of Business and Professor (Chair) of Finance, Hong Kong Baptist University*

IIBD Case Competition

In order to allow our students, tomorrow's business leaders, to be better prepared to meet the challenges of a rapidly changing global business environment, the Wing Lung Bank International Institute for Business Development (IIBD) of the School of Business, HKBU has organised and hosted the IIBD Case Competition for student teams from universities worldwide since 2008. During the competition, students have to work under pressure to solve a real world business problem, using cases to simulate business conditions such as time-critical deadlines and incomplete information, to formulate workable, action-oriented recommendations. Each student team has six hours to work on the case before presentation to a panel of judges. This annual competition attracts an average of 33 student teams from 15 countries every year. To enhance students' awareness of responsible management strategies, cases related to corporate sustainability are chosen, as follows:

- **Year 2009**
  - Theme: Corporate social responsibility.
  - Champion: Hong Kong Baptist University, Hong Kong SAR.

- **Year 2010**
  - Theme: Corporate sustainability.
  - Champion: Fudan University, Shanghai, Mainland China.

- **Year 2011**
  - Theme: Value creation through branding.
  - Champion: University of Prince Edward Island, Canada.

"mindXchange" Student Forum – a student debate on business ethics and corporate sustainability

Since 2010, the School of Business has organised two student debate forums entitled "mindXchange" every academic year to encourage students' active participation in free exchange of ideas on current issues especially connect to timely topics of sustainability, corporate conscience and business ethics. For each debate, two teams composed of undergraduates, postgraduates and/or alumni from the School and other faculty debate "for" and "against" a motion focused on corporate sustainability. The audience voted to decide the winning team after the debate that lasted for an hour. The following motions were used for the debates:

- "Despite the Rise of Shanghai as a Financial centre, Hong Kong's Ethical Business Environment will Safeguard its Regional Competitiveness beyond 2020" (November 2010).
- "CSR Practice is a Luxury that Only Large Corporations can Afford" (April 2011).

- "NGOs/NPOs are the Main Drivers of CSR Advancement Today" (November 2011).
- "Islamic Banking as a Model for Ethical and Sustainable Banking Tomorrow" (March 2012).

The "mindXchange" student debate provides a very good platform to stimulate their interest in the important value of business ethnics and corporate social responsibility, and further enhance student involvement in contemporary issues and active research on corporate sustainability, which is the strategic theme of the School of Business.

Results

With concerted effort from the School, students and alumni, both events have received favourable feedback and support from our University while the IIBD Case Competition is gaining its reputation worldwide. These extracurricular activities effectively engage students to conduct research on current issues relating to ethical behaviour, moral standards, social and civic responsibility, both at the personal and corporate levels. Through active participation and coaching by faculty members, our students are able to understand these essential concepts, which are the cornerstones of their career success in future.

Why PRME is/was important

- It provides very good frameworks for us to integrate into our curriculum the key concepts of sustainable value for business and society.
- It enables us to learn from PRME participant institutions and corporations the best practices of sustainable social, environmental and economic value.
- It facilitates dialogue and debate among educators, business, government, consumers, civil social organisations, interest groups and other stakeholders on important issues relating to global social responsibility and sustainability.

ESADE, Ramon Llull University, Barcelona, Spain

SOLIDARITY INTERNSHIPS: UNIVERSITY SERVICE FOR DEVELOPMENT

Introduction

ESADE is an independent, non-profit business and law school, founded in Barcelona in 1958 by a group of business leaders and the Society of Jesus (Jesuits). The School aims to be a global reference that inspires and empowers people and organisations to develop innovative and socially responsible leadership for the construction of a better future. For this reason, the motto of the School is "Inspiring Futures".

Challenges

ESADE's mission is to educate and produce research on management and law in addition to creating and contributing to social debate. More specifically, the School aims to provide integral training for the development of competent and responsible future leaders, to create knowledge to help improve organisations and society and to participate in social debate on building a free, prosperous and fair society. In order to achieve these aims, the School must grapple with the challenge of going beyond the development of professional, effective managers and lawyers to instilling them with a keen sense of ethical behaviour (justice, social, civil and political values), human values and an awareness of spiritual values (be they religious or secular).

To achieve this, the School aims to encourage students to explore beyond their own (often privileged) social backgrounds, helping them to experience a more complex and sometimes disturbing reality, in such a way that they learn to constructively engage in transforming society by thinking critically and responding to problems and suffering. The goal being that our students graduate as informed, compassionate professionals, committed to justice and human development.

ESADE contributed to the creation of the Principles of Responsible Management Education (PRME), an initiative sponsored by the United Nations Global Compact, in 2007 and was among its first signatories. Since 2007, ESADE, has firmly upheld the first three Principles of the initiative (purpose, values, and method), and views solidarity internships as an essential element for a socially responsible business and law school.

> ESADE's accession to the Six Principles of the PRME initiative has helped enrich our educational vision and practice, as well as enhancing our focus as a business and law school with a serious commitment to social responsibility and sustainability. The development of the Progress Report has been a highly valuable tool in taking stock of our progress and has helped us to take into account new challenges and initiatives in our strategic plan.
>
> *Eugenia Bieto, Director General, ESADE*

Actions taken

For many years, ESADE has helped encourage social responsibility by initiating and backing social initiatives, volunteer schemes and charitable cooperation, involving the School's current students, alumni, professors and staff.

In 2003, ESADE created the University Service for Development, known by its Spanish initials as SUD. This service encourages education and social awareness in the academic community, supports the strengthening of other university organisations and encourages cooperation for training in values.

Among other initiatives, SUD provides a summer internship programme for undergraduate Business Administration and Law students. These internships take place in Latin American countries and consist of a minimum of 8 weeks and a maximum of 12 weeks, during which teams of 2 or 3 students work with various organisations or partners to help them realise their social goals. These internships require the application of knowledge and skills acquired during the degree course and the taking on of considerable personal and professional responsibility.

Internships use service provision and learning as an educational methodology. Students, professors, and institutions work and learn together to solve specific community needs, using and transferring knowledge to develop projects for the common good. Furthermore, these internships provide an experience of solidarity in action that implies involvement and compassion. Participants discover the different social realities and thus better understand the meaning of professional responsibility.

The internship programme has been in operation for 8 years and a total of 298 Business Administration, and Law students have participated in 25 different organisations (companies, cooperatives, NGOs, and public and private universities) located in Bolivia, Costa Rica, El Salvador, Guatemala, Honduras, and Nicaragua.

In total, 169 different projects have been developed, including: marketing plans (51), business plans (35), strategic analysis (22), field work in legal aid for the poor (22), financial and cost studies (15), legal research (12), information and operations systems (9), and human resource plans (3).

The internship is divided into four phases:

1. **Training**: ESADE's undergraduate degree curriculum includes a course entitled "Cooperation in Latin America", which introduces students to the region from economic, geographic, demographic, historical, and cultural points of view. Interested students apply for a place on the SUD programme and their motivation and maturity is then assessed through interviews. Once selected and before the internship begins, a weekend training course is organised to further develop participants' personal and professional skills and help them to work as a team.

2. **Action**: During the time on the ground in Latin America, a SUD team composed of ESADE professors and staff monitors progress of the internships and the participants, and is on-hand if difficulties arise.

3. **Reflection**: This process guides students to individually examine critical issues relating to their project and encourages them to develop skills and values, giving a personal relevance to their tasks.

4. **Evaluation**: Students prepare a report on the internship that includes an assessment of lessons learnt, results, personal experiences, and the role played by the host partner. This report is then assessed by ESADE professors, who focus particularly on team performance, the value and impact of projects, and presentation.

Results

The programme helps students develop the qualities that define our graduates: competence, conscientiousness, commitment and compassion – individuals who can offer the best of themselves for the common good.

The programme reinforces the knowledge and skills that are acquired in the classroom and also develops areas such as teamwork, critical thinking, awareness of personal limitations, entrepreneurship, communication, leadership, sense of civic responsibility and distributive justice, empathy, respect, solidarity, and global awareness.

Why PRME is/was important

- ESADE has supported the PRME initiative since its inception in 2007, because the initiative so fully reflects our aspiration and commitment to being a socially responsible academic institution. ESADE, since its foundation in 1958, has had and continues to articulate a mission that, in its own terms, closely aligns with the Six Principles.
- The Principles provide a very valid frame of reference to orient, in a collective manner, our intention to be a socially responsible institution in our teaching, research and social debate. In addition, they allow us to establish progress indicators to monitor how this intention becomes a reality and the levels of satisfaction it generates.
- The PRME initiative offers us the opportunity to create spaces for reflection about our mission aims and our institutional policies. Some examples: What does it mean to be a socially responsible business school? How do we put into practice a culture of social responsibility? What practices must we implement for the management of our School to be socially responsible?

INTRODUCTION

"What gets measured gets done", claims the popular saying. Challenges faced by signatories of the Principles for Responsible Management Education (PRME) in order to translate PRME integration/adoption into indicators to monitor and foster progress, or to outline future directions, have been many. However, the success stories outlined in this section show a common feature: taking a very practical approach has been top priority. As one school puts it, indicators may be blunt, measuring efforts may just be incipient, but it is important to start the measuring follow up processes, to find a way to quantitatively track the extent to which sustainability initiatives are isolated efforts – or start to become the norm.

Most of these efforts have revolved around the use of the PRME Sharing Information on Progress (SIP) reports. The elaboration of SIPs has been central to assembling dedicated teams of faculty who are critically involved in the reporting task, to develop key performance indicators, and to evaluate and communicate progress on the implementation of the Principles to multiple stakeholders. Measurement efforts have targeted multiple dimensions and served to open dialogue around pedagogy (are we using learning methodologies that foster sustainability?), on education programmes (how many of our programmes clearly contain sustainability offerings?), on research (are we publishing significantly in this area?), institutional and operations management (do we walk the talk in our own institution?), at student and relationship levels (to what extent do we make sustainability a reality when we interact with these and other stakeholders?). That is, measurement initiatives have been used to evaluate undergraduate courses, executive programmes, MBA courses, consulting assignments, etc. For research, leading schools have quantified the proportion of the faculty engaged in research projects related to sustainability and examined in detail the kind of research in place or the existing competencies among the faculty. For the schools' own operations management, key performance indicators have aimed to quantify sustainability-on-campus initiatives (leading signatories have used different methodologies such as the Carbon Disclosure Project, the report on metrics around waste to landfill, water use, volume of paper sourced, recycling or Forest Stewardship Council® (FSC) certification, etc.).

Some signatories have used the Global Reporting Initiative (GRI) guidelines as a source for inspiration, which has provided a useful framework for both curriculum development and integration of relevant industry practices. One signatory has created a process to prepare its sustainability report to show PRME, United Nations Global Compact and GRI principles in an integrated way. Charts of the principles and other visuals have been used as "scorecards" to provide an overview of the main sustainability projects, ensure collaboration and progress and engage a variety of stakeholders.

Inspiringly, one school published an externally assured sustainability report – which won the Association of Chartered Certified Accountants Sustainability Reporting Award – demonstrating a robust commitment to build external transparency and internal accountability. Overall, signatories have used a "whole school/university approach" to foster the adoption/ integration of sustainability efforts at multiple levels and by all faculty members. Thus, beyond merely using reporting as a "bureaucratic" mandate, measurement and reporting efforts have been creatively used to generate synergies among dedicated faculty – whose efforts in this quest have been acknowledged as particularly relevant to their schools – as well as to help AACSB, EQUIS and other accreditation processes, to benchmark efforts with other organisations, to create guidelines and, ultimately, to help translate strategic plans into concrete courses of action.

At the same time, initiatives aiming to consolidate PRME efforts have included the organisation of events, often at a regional level. This last section of the Guide highlights several examples of multi-stakeholder engagement, "out-of the box" thinking, and fruitful initiatives advocating the value of corporate sustainability to diverse stakeholders. Here, management schools become global communities that transform them-selves into active agents of change – rather than passive objects of conformity – impacting on not only young entrepreneurs and executives, but the broader society.

Signatories are establishing/developing alliances between themselves to better create synergies, networks and more efficient learning. This has included organising events, facilitating exchanges and partnerships, creating internships in diverse countries, etc.

The cases portrayed in this section also show a growing tendency towards PRME transitioning from a global learning community to an action community, working actively to transform the management school paradigm. Without doubt, much more needs to be done. The seriousness of the current challenges that we face (environmental threats, social inequality, etc.) makes corporate sustainability an urgent, as well as fascinating educational task. This last section of the Guide provides a relevant, accessible signpost for further implementation of these endeavours.

In order to manage and consolidate PRME efforts to meet the needs of the sustainability agenda, PRME signatories have undertaken initiatives, such as:

1. Using indicators to quantify sustainability efforts.
2. Using the writing of Sharing Information on Progress (SIP) reports as an opportunity to bring together faculty and staff, raise awareness and foster sustainability efforts at multiple levels.
3. Using and integrating guidelines to expand efforts and find inspiration for reporting.
4. Using reports and scorecards as marketing and awareness-raising tools to engage a variety of stakeholders.
5. Exploring non-traditional options including, such as having reports externally assured as a way to demonstrate robust commitment by building external transparency and internal accountability.
6. Exploring a range of additional benefits, such as benchmarking efforts that help to translate strategic plans into concrete courses of action and others that aid in formal accreditation processes.
7. Working to quantify the proportion of the faculty engaged in research related to sustainability.
8. Establishing key performance indicators with the aim to quantify sustainability-on-campus initiatives for the schools' own operations management.
9. Engaging a wide range of stakeholders and building dynamic global communities.
10. Developing alliances between schools to create synergies, networks and learnings.

HOW TO TRANSLATE PRME INTEGRATION/ ADOPTION ACHIEVEMENTS INTO INDICATORS AND OTHER MEASURES FOR THE PURPOSE OF EVALUATING PROGRESS

Ashridge Business School, Berkhamsted, England, United Kingdom

IMPLEMENTING MEASURES TO CREATE AWARENESS OF SUSTAINABILITY CONCEPTS

Introduction

Based in England, Ashridge Business School is consistently ranked as one of the world's leading business schools and works with over 100 organisations and 9,000 managers in over 40 countries every year. It enables individuals and organisations from around the world to build management capability and to address individual and organisation development challenges. Clients span the private, public and not-for-profit sectors.

Its activities include open and customised executive education programmes, organisation consulting, MBA, MSc, doctoral and diploma qualifications, applied research and virtual learning. It is one of the very few schools worldwide to achieve triple accreditation from AMBA, EQUIS and AACSB; the UK, European and American accreditation bodies for qualification programmes.

Challenges

Ashridge has attempted to develop indicators to evaluate progress on the integration of sustainability principles in each of the following areas: education, research, operations management. The following sets out what we did and what we learnt from it.

It is important and relatively easy to share and promote individual case stories of innovation within a particular business school: it can be valuable inspiration, a source of learning, and an indication of how things are starting to change. But if the goal is to embed this kind of change across the whole of an institution's programme of educational and research activity, then it is really important to try to find a way to quantitatively track the extent to which these case stories of innovation are just isolated examples, or whether they are starting to become the norm.

> The indicators we've managed to come up with so far for education and research are inevitably blunt, but nevertheless we think it's important to try to get some sense of the proportion of faculty that are engaging in research and new thinking in this area, and the proportion of educational programmes that have some focus on themes to do with sustainable business.
> *Matthew Gitsham, Director, Ashridge Centre for Business and Sustainability,*
> *Ashridge Business School*

Actions taken

The kinds of changes we are trying to promote with the Principles for Responsible Management Education (PRME) in education and research do not easily lend themselves to measurement. We accept that what we have tried to do is blunt and has as many weaknesses as strengths, but the initial approach we have adopted is as follows.

Education

For education, we have attempted to measure whether any kind of focus on sustainable business appears at all in a programme. The value of this is that it gives some sense of the proportion of programmes including some focus on sustainability. When we did this exercise for our first PRME Sharing Information on Progress (SIP) report in June 2010, we found that five of our seven qualification programmes included a focus on sustainability, 24% of our open enrolment executive programmes, 8% of our tailored executive programmes, and 7% of our organisation development consulting assignments. While it is useful to have this sense of proportion, the downside is that it gives no indication of the quality or extent to which sustainability is discussed, or indeed, how much of the rest of the programme might be focusing on what some might call unsustainable business.

Research

For research, we wanted to understand the proportion of faculty engaged in research that related in some way to sustainability, our thinking being that if a member of faculty was researching around how sustainability related to their core area of expertise, then that could be a good indicator as to whether new thinking on sustainable business might also be coming into their educational work. As a result, we decided to measure over an 18 month period (the original PRME SIP reporting period, which was extended to 24 months in January 2011) the proportion of our faculty who had either published some kind of research or thought leadership, or spoken or played a facilitative role in an event, where there was a connection with the theme of sustainable business. In our June 2010 PRME SIP report, 25% of our faculty had either spoken at an event or published on a subject relating to sustainability in the previous 18 months.

Operations management

Finally, alongside education and research, the third area of focus for Ashridge has been how we manage our own organisation. Metrics here were perhaps easier, both because the issues are more easily quantifiable, and also because so much has already been standardised in other sectors. We report on our carbon footprint across scope 1, 2 and 3, using the methodology of the Carbon Disclosure Project, and also report on metrics around waste to landfill, water use, volume of paper sourced, and the proportion of which is recycled or Forest Stewardship Council® certified. We also publish our score in the International Association of Conference Centres' Code of Sustainability, which we found to be a good external benchmarking tool for many of the issues we have at an operational level.

Results

Our learning from this is that although these quantitative measures have many weaknesses, they are valuable in provoking awareness and conversation around the extent to which sustainability concepts are permeating across the School's education, research and campus management activities. We have also found that the process of generating the relevant data has also created many opportunities to raise awareness about the PRME initiative and have more in-depth conversations about the nature of the organisational change entailed in embedding PRME.

Why PRME is/was important

- A drive to stimulate change across all these areas at Ashridge was already under way before the PRME initiative was launched, but the specific requirement to publish a SIP report pushed us into thinking about public reporting and appropriate metrics sooner than we would have otherwise done.
- Once we started considering this because of PRME, it quickly became obvious that we needed to put some thought into what kind of quantifiable indicators might help us in understanding our progress.

La Trobe Business School, La Trobe University, Melbourne, Australia

RESPONSIBLE FUTURES: DEMONSTRATING SUSTAINABLE DEVELOPMENT AS A CORE BUSINESS STRATEGY

Introduction

 La Trobe Business School offers a full suite of business courses across five campuses in Victoria, Australia. The flagship MBA programme taught at the main Melbourne Campus has been completely redesigned in line with the Principles for Responsible Management Education (PRME) and received the EFDM EPAS accreditation in 2011 as well as Beyond Grey Pinstripes recognition. The Business School is part of the La Trobe Faculty of Business, Economics and Law, which has more than 9,000 students and 500 staff.

Postgraduate course offerings include: MBA, as well as courses in international business, marketing and information technology, accounting and finance. In regard to the MBA, the student body profile comprises around 800 students from over 40 countries.

Challenges

Signing up to the PRME initiative aligned with the wider La Trobe University agenda of creating a sustainability-conscious, social and environmentally responsible tertiary institution as well as providing the opportunity to embed graduate capabilities into new course offerings – capabilities that make students more employable and graduating with wider and diverse skills required by stakeholders, while providing them with a more holistic education.

Actions taken

The first PRME Sharing Information on Progress (SIP) report was written in 2010 and currently the second SIP report is being written. Measures being used are in the areas of the Six Principles. The report will integrate what is occurring across the whole faculty while incorporating University sustainability measures as reported in the University sustainability report.

The University's sustainability report called the *Responsible Futures* report is externally assured following the Global Reporting Initiative's sustainability reporting guidelines. External assurance demonstrates the University's honest and transparent appraisal of the impact the University has on its community and the environment. This report includes educational and research measures as well as those related to environment, social (students and staff) and supply chain.

> My advice in integrating indicators to evaluate progress is to use a whole of school/ university approach to ensure measures reflect actions at many levels. This also enables staff who are working in different areas with varying priorities to engage in the process and feel a sense of achievement when their work is recognised. Moreover using each of the Principles, and measuring against each ensures both processes and outcomes are used together to drive PRME.
> *Suzanne Young, Associate Professor, Faculty of Business, Economics and Law, Department of Management, La Trobe Business School*

Results

Responsible Futures, La Trobe University's first sustainability report won the award for best first-time report at the Association of Chartered Certified Accountants Sustainability Reporting Awards in August 2011. Released in April 2011, La Trobe University was the first university in the world to publish an externally assured sustainability report on the University's social, environmental and economic footprint that strictly follows the Global Reporting Initiative's sustainability reporting guidelines.

La Trobe University pro vice-chancellor, Professor Carol Adams said the award recognised the role sustainability plays in connecting different parts of the University under a common goal.

"*Responsible Futures* was a collaborative effort that highlighted University staff working across sustainability at all levels, from the University Council to the La Trobe Wildlife Sanctuary volunteers," she said.

Responsible Futures provides an honest and transparent look at the University's performance and nominates targets the University is required to meet in the future. Along with the appointment in 2010 of Australia's first pro vice-chancellor (sustainability), the report is a major response to the University's 'Vision 2015' strategic plan, which has outlined to "operate sustainably and ethically", as one of its four main pillars. The report was said by the judges to "clearly demonstrate that sustainable development is a core business strategy" and "gives specific targets for the short term, medium term and long term" as well as "identifies areas of poor performance".

The PRME SIP report focuses on the educational and research components, but by including actions against each of the PRME initiative's Principles it adds in detail processes used as well as outcomes achieved. For instance, inclusion of measures against "dialogue" and "partnerships" demonstrates how networks can be used to achieve more integrated and industry-relevant responsible management education. Reporting against "method" provides a framework for curriculum development and integration of relevant industry practice. Adding measures against "values" provides a forum for academics to discuss what are the values that underpin their courses and how these are to be integrated into courses – whether implicitly or explicitly – and to use this to link more closely with the values of the University.

By adding measures at the course, pedagogy, institutional, student and relationship levels, students can leave the University with the best possible business education to cope with the changing nature of the environment, an understanding of complexity and an ability to make connections with actors through new types of partnerships and relationships.

It is important that measures reflect actual achievements, otherwise insiders will view the report as simply "greenwashing". The actions have to drive the change rather than the reporting.

Why PRME is/was important

- PRME is important as a framework for continual improvement.
- PRME provides a forum for discussion of educational values.

- PRME provides an important link to integrate processes to outcomes of responsible management.
- PRME provides a framework to drill down into how responsible management can be achieved.

HOW TO SUCCESSFULLY REPORT ON PRME INTEGRATION/ADOPTION

Fundação Dom Cabral (FDC), Nova Lima, Minas Gerais, Brazil

CONTRIBUTING TO SUSTAINABLE DEVELOPMENT BY BEING RELEVANT TO SOCIETY

Introduction

FUNDAÇÃO DOM CABRAL

DEVELOPING EXECUTIVES AND COMPANIES

Fundação Dom Cabral (FDC) is a Brazilian business school that has been practising dialogue and committed listening for 35 years, serving annually more than 30,000 public and private managers in its programmes.

FDC offers organisations the Aloysio Faria Campus, located in Nova Lima in the state of Minas Gerais, part of the Greater Belo Horizonte area, a complete infrastructure in 3 buildings with classrooms, amphitheatres, ample space for events for up to 600 people, restaurant, convenience stores and services, and the Cæsar Business Hotel, a flat with more than 100 rooms and leisure facilities.

FDC's Belo Horizonte Branch is located in the Belo Horizonte city centre, and it offers participants specialised programmes, fully equipped classrooms, meeting and breakout rooms, IT labs, and an auditorium. And the São Paulo Office, in a prime location in the new business pole of the capital: Vila Olímpia.

In 2011, FDC was ranked as the fifth best business school in the world, according to the executive education ranking of the *Financial Times*. In the customised programmes category FDC ranked in third place, and in open enrolment programmes the School is currently in the 10th position.

Challenges

Being relevant to society is one of the objectives that guide Fundação Dom Cabral, whose mission is to contribute to the sustainable development of society by educating, developing and building the skills of executives, entrepreneurs and public managers. As a signatory of the Principles for Responsible Management Education (PRME) initiative, the School seeks, through the organisation's daily processes and activities, to fulfil its role to educate for sustainability.

FDC recognises how important it is to share, in a detailed and transparent way, initiatives, efforts and results in its quest for more sustainable attitudes in executive education. However, it is not an easy task to organise and report on so many actions. The major challenge that FDC faced was to create a structure to coordinate sustainability issues and create synergy between all efforts and projects for social innovation and responsible management.

> My advice in order to report PRME adoption is to engage all the institution in this challenge. The task of preparing the report demands a deep quest into the institution's practices to find out both what it is that has collaborated to insert sustainability and what have been the main barriers and difficulties. That is why it is important that the report should be built collaboratively and involves a significant sampling of collaborators, while at the same time listening to external stakeholders' perceptions. Besides leading to a diversity of visions and activities, such a choice for this collaborative attitude is also a way to mobilise the whole institution to assess its part in this process.
>
> *Poliana Abreu, Coordinator, Sustainability Committee, FDC*

Actions taken

FDC created its Sustainability Committee in 2008 to enable it to respond to PRME and Global Compact principles and to coordinate sustainability actions. The committee's objective is to promote synergy and integrate the diverse strategic actions related to the several action programmes and projects in this field. FDC also has created a process to prepare its sustainability report to show PRME, UN Global Compact and Globally Responsible Leadership Initiative (GRLI) principles in an integrated way. Several issues must be taken into account while preparing the PRME Sharing Information on Progress (SIP) report. Taking into account the experience FDC has in the matter, we would like to highlight some points:

1. Make a list of the relevant initiatives that will be reported.
2. Follow up and systematically measure the projects that meet the undertaken commitments.

   FDC has created a simple, but highly practical way to list and follow-up projects linked to the Principles. It is a spreadsheet that lists the projects and the PRME, Global Compact, GRLI and FDC shared challenges for sustainability. This chart of compared principles allows us to have an overview of the main sustainability projects and their current status.

   To keep information safe throughout the year we have set up a monthly "Sustainability Committee Information Report" that reports on the highlights of the activities carried out by each work group linked to the Sustainability Committee. Furthermore, there is a space on the intranet that is dedicated to updating the news about all that happens at the Institution as regards the theme.
3. Engage and raise the awareness of a significant group of stakeholders so they will collaborate to build the report.

   The FDC Sustainability Committee's structure, made up by work groups linked to shared challenges, allows the information reported in it to come from various areas and collaborators, as the work groups are made up by FDC collaborators from several positions and functions.
4. Communicate, transparently, if there is coherence between corporate sustainability policy and the actions undertaken in the period.
5. Use clear language and be as clear and objective as possible to make the report easily understandable by all of the institution's audience.

   The report need not have a complex format, but it is extremely important that it clearly shares the main objectives, happenings and results while implementing the principles within the selected period.

Setting out indicators that will be measured and followed up helps the report's organisation and objectivity. Tools, such as the Global Reporting Initiative (GRI), can be very helpful to this process. Even though the institution may not yet be ready and organised to fully use GRI, it could start off on the right foot by inspiring itself and adopting some of its indicators to structure the report and to guarantee data transparency and organisation.

Special attention must be paid to chapter content and division, as they must be coherent with the priorities and the positioning that the institution adopts with regards to sustainability. The dean's letter at the opening of the document is essential to introduce the reader to what is relevant to the institution and to how the report will be presented.

6. Take the information gathered to the largest possible number of people.

It is important that the institution uses several communications processes to disseminate and multiply the principles. These include meetings with collaborators, professors, students and suppliers, and also material that will be prepared to be delivered to a specific audience. FDC has adopted the practice of launching the sustainability report during its annual lunch with the community that happens immediately after the board of trustees meeting.

The Internet is also a great ally that allows an enormous number of people from various sectors of society to receive the report. That is why FDC has made a digital version of the sustainability report available through social networks at the FDC portal home page and via the Global Compact and PRME sites. FDC has also emailed the launching of the report to all its participants and partner base.

Results

As it involves and engages the institution as a whole, the SIP report allowed us to develop internal management systems and tools to track, monitor and measure all of the educational efforts that our teachers and project directors have made towards sustainability. The report also helps us to share with all stakeholders the progress that FDC has made in implementing the principles of corporate sustainability and responsible leadership.

Why PRME is/was important

- To spread the new values and new ideas of responsible business.
- To mobilise academia to develop frameworks for sustainable practices.
- To create a culture of sustainability among business schools worldwide.

Hanken School of Economics, Helsinki and Vaasa, Finland

BEYOND BUREAUCRACY: REPORTING AS A STRATEGIC TOOL

Introduction

Hanken School of Economics is a leading, internationally accredited (EQUIS and AMBA) university in the field of economics and business administration. It has approximately 230 members of staff, including 120 members of faculty, operating in 5 departments: Accounting and Commercial Law, Economics, Finance and Statistics, Management and Organisation, and Marketing. Hanken has about 1,900 students studying for the BSc or MSc degrees and around 160 students studying for the PhD degree. The School offers seven international master's degree programmes in English. It has campuses in Helsinki and Vaasa.

Challenges

The first year that Hanken produced a Principles for Responsible Management Education (PRME) Sharing Information on Progress (SIP) report there were several hard questions that we had to address. Foremost were:

- The scope of the SIP report – should we settle for the minimum or aim higher and report on all of the Six Principles of PRME?
- Who should collect the necessary information across the departments? A comprehensive report would need to include data in terms of research, teaching and business relations in relation to responsibility – a term, which in and of itself, is open for interpretation.

In my role of managing the production of Hanken's PRME SIP reports, my advice to signatories who are preparing their first report is the following: 1) Do not approach this as another bureaucratic exercise – think creatively and positively in terms of how the reporting can be linked to other activities. 2) Have faculty centrally involved in the production of the report rather than outsourcing it to administrative support. 3) From the get-go, try to be comprehensive rather than minimalist – it will save a lot of effort in the coming years. 4) Use the report as a tool not only for affirming existing practice, but also for questioning your normalised practices. 5) Do not assume that a comprehensive and usable report requires significant financial support – we have been working on a shoestring budget to produce a report that has become an excellent tool both for internal improvement and external communication.

Nikodemus Solitander, Lecturer in Supply Chain Management and Corporate Geography, Hanken School of Economics

Actions taken

At an early stage, we decided to report on all Six Principles, and that we needed a thorough understanding of how the different departments interpreted the concept and how it manifested itself in their activities. For the task we hired a part-time assistant who interviewed all heads of departments and subject representatives, as well as collected the necessary data about relevant courses and publications. At the same time some faculty members, inspired by the task at hand, initiated a research project about responsible management education, thus the data collection also became related to a research project that led to fruitful synergies beyond a simplistic bureaucratic exercise. We also linked the data collection for the SIP report to the data collection for accreditations such as AACSB and EQUIS, further ensuring that everything we collected would be of value outside of the report itself. There was also a decision to spend some effort on the layout, which would make it more accessible and inviting for external stakeholders. In addition, we have used other PRME reports as benchmarks, and more particularly for the first report we used the PRME SIP report from our partner school, Audencia Nantes School of Management (France), as a benchmark.

Results

The decision to immediately start collecting data related to Six Principles was by far the best decision taken. It ensured that we had a base of data to build on for future reports, and gave us an understanding of the challenges related to getting the data for each Principle. It saved us immense work in our successive reports, which were even more comprehensive, but required much fewer resources to produce. Collecting the data also revealed activities related to responsible management education, of which the PRME team itself was not aware. The other great benefit has been that we have been able to use the data collected for other purposes, both for research and accreditation purposes. The final report itself is a good tool for the kind of transformation needed if we are to achieve something we could call "responsible management education", especially in terms of aiming for continuous improvement, by making us ask where we still need to improve, how to act on that, etc. As an example, Hanken adopted the WWF's Green Office Certificate as a direct result of trying to address how and what to report on the addendum Principle.

Why PRME is/was important

- PRME provides the structure for the report, as we follow the Six Principles in building up the report.
- We have used other PRME reports as benchmarks, for the first year we benchmarked against Audencia's PRME report.
- PRME gave us the impetus to use the reporting as a tool to look at the familiar as new, making us ask ourselves not only **what** we have done, but also questioning **why** we had done certain things the way we did, and if this was in fact contributing to a serious reading of the Principles.

Babson College, Babson Park, Massachusetts, United States

TELLING THE STORY OF PRME'S INFLUENCE

Introduction

Babson College is widely recognised as the educator, convener and thought leader for "Entrepreneurship of All Kinds". Located just outside Boston, Massachusetts, Babson has a strong global focus and is one of the few US schools to hold both AACSB and EQUIS accreditation. The College's innovative curriculum combines integrated and applied business and liberal arts programmes with unique, linked curricular and co-curricular learning experiences to prepare its 2,000 undergraduates and 1,300 graduate students to be entrepreneurial and responsible leaders.

Challenges

While the Principles for Responsible Management Education (PRME) initiative is a voluntary engagement platform, signatories are expected to regularly share information on the influence of the Six Principles at their institution. The formal mechanism of submitting a Sharing Information on Progress (SIP) report once every 24 months has two stated goals, according to the PRME Secretariat: ensuring the credibility of the initiative and facilitating the exchange of good practices across the community.

Preparation of a SIP report could be viewed simply as a requirement for being part of the network, but at Babson we view it as much more than that. Meeting the stated goals of the secretariat is important, but we believe that the reporting process can achieve more. First, we believe that the actual preparation of the report itself can serve as a powerful catalyst for continued change and further recognition of the influence of PRME on campus. The more that people on campus know about how PRME relates to our mission, the more likely they are to take steps to shape activities and programmes that will be aligned with and driven by the Principles. Second, we believe that we can engage more people, both on and off-campus, in our work related to PRME if we go beyond the minimum reporting requirements of the SIP report and think of creative ways to increase the visibility of what we are doing and how PRME influences that. Thus, the challenge at Babson was twofold: create a process that engaged many constituents in the actual preparation of the SIP report while providing ways to make the document itself become more than words on paper prepared simply to meet a minimum reporting standard.

> Babson's experience in sharing its progress, both on and off campus, offers clear advice to others on how to leverage this important process. Our experience indicates that sharing information on progress can itself be a catalyst for change, and that creating innovative ways to highlight PRME's role can create a campus culture that is even more focused on corporate sustainability and responsible leadership.
>
> *Dennis Hanno, Dean, Undergraduate School, Babson College*

Actions taken

To meet these challenges, we established a process for our first SIP report that went beyond tasking one person with simply chronicling our accomplishments. Perhaps the most important step in the process was asking a faculty member who is deeply involved in a variety of PRME initiatives to take the lead on preparation of the report. This ensured that someone was totally invested in making a strong case for the influence of the Principles at Babson. To signal the importance of this process to the Institution, the lead faculty member was rewarded at a level commensurate with other major administrative assignments. Rather than gleaning our activities related to PRME from already available sources, the next step in our process was to create forums for any constituent to share what they were doing that might relate to the Principles. With visible support from the administration and using multiple ways of reaching out to constituents on campus, many people came forward at these forums with activities that had not previously been identified. The frequent calls for participation also served as reminders to the community about PRME and its influence on campus.

The process at Babson also ensures that the report becomes much more than a document archived in the PRME SIP report database. Involving many people in the process of identifying PRME-related activities does create the issue of having too much to share with others, but this is a good problem to have and one that stimulates further discussion and debate about all the things we are doing and what should be in the report. Once prepared, the report is distributed broadly across campus and is a frequent reference source used at all levels of the Institution to recognise what we have achieved and, more importantly, to drive discussions about what we still need to do. We believe in the importance of this process to such an extent that we are committed to preparing a report on an annual basis rather than only every 24 months as suggested by the PRME Secretariat.

Results

Gathering information for the SIP report helped us to recognise that we needed other ways to share our progress beyond the preparation of the actual report. With so many positive things happening in so many different areas on campus, we needed to call more attention to them. We also realised that we needed a vehicle to attract more people to use PRME in their work since some parts of campus were still uninformed about our involvement in the network. To address these desires, a month-long celebration called "Thirty Days of PRME" was developed. During the first month of this academic year, an announcement was made every day about an innovative programme or activity that related to PRME. A Facebook Page was established and updated each day with a video that provided a short introduction to that day's highlighted activities. Events and activities took place throughout the month to ensure that our PRME-related work received high visibility across all parts of campus. The celebration as a whole was very effective in demonstrating the pervasive impact of the Principles on Babson and also received strong external recognition, further advancing our goal of sharing information on our progress.

Why PRME is/was important

The SIP reporting process is important to Babson, since it serves as a powerful vehicle for engaging all of the community in talking about the importance of the Principles to what we do.

- With our mission of "educating leaders to create great economic and social value", PRME serves as a valuable framework for what we do and the more it is known on campus, the more progress we can make.
- The SIP reporting process also enhances the value of belonging to the PRME community. Without a framework and incentive for sharing with others what we do and learning what they do, the opportunities to focus on action and innovation would be limited.

MOVING FORWARD – WHAT IS THE ROLE OF BUSINESS IN SOCIETY?

The American University in Cairo School of Business, Cairo, Egypt

SEIZING OPPORTUNITIES IN CHALLENGING TIMES: THE STORY OF THE 1ST PRME MENA REGIONAL FORUM

Introduction

 SCHOOL OF **BUSINESS** The American University in Cairo (AUC) School of Business (BUS), established in 1993, is the top business school in Egypt and one of the top business schools in the Arab and Africa regions. Its mission is to create an environment that fosters the development of principled and innovative business leaders and entrepreneurs who can make a difference. BUS offers a range of undergraduate and graduate programmes in economics, accounting and business administration including an extensive executive education programme. The School currently has 1,194 students and over 8,873 alumni to date. The AUC School of Business has been AACSB accredited since 2006.

 Although BUS was already engaged in various activities that fell within the realm of the Principles for Responsible Management Education (PRME), the School officially became a signatory to the initiative in late February 2011. At that time there was only 1 PRME signatory from Egypt, a total of 3 signatories in the Arab world and 10 across the MENA (Middle East and North Africa) region. As an educational pioneer in the region and a strong believer in the role of business schools in society, the School committed itself to two main quests. First, spreading the awareness of PRME and its importance; second, organising the 1st PRME MENA Regional Forum in early October 2011 to serve as a stepping stone towards establishing a

regional PRME network. Under normal circumstances such a plan would seem ambitious, however Egypt and the region at large were going through a phase that was far from normal.

Challenges

The wave of Arab uprisings quickly hit Egypt with a peaceful demonstration on 25 January 2011 that rapidly evolved into a full-fledged revolution. After peaceful protests, sit-ins, violent confrontations with police, military intervention, curfews and a complete telecommunication shutdown, the regime was overthrown in early February. The lingering question in the minds of Egyptians and many observers was, "What's next in terms of the political, economic, and social landscapes of Egypt?" The following seven months witnessed political unrest, weekly demonstrations, security concerns (which were sometimes unduly amplified by the media), and adverse travel advisories. Such uncertainties and problems were our main challenge. The School faced the risk of being unable to attract participants, especially international ones, or even cancellation of this important event.

We teach our students to be proactive, seize opportunities and make a difference, but we, as schools of business, should practise what we preach. If schools are to be considered effective members of their local, regional, and global communities, then they should be active agents of change, rather than passive objects of adaptation. Today, the traditional business education paradigm is not enough. The notions of corporate social responsibility, business ethics, corporate governance, and sustainability should be integral parts of the educational and research cultures of schools. PRME provides an excellent framework for implementing these values. Through responsible management education, the impact of young entrepreneurs and executives on the community, and even the world at large, would be magnified. I advise any business school, regardless of size, resource availability, or background to adopt PRME and to join the quest of making a difference.

Sherif Kamel, Dean, School of Business, American University in Cairo

Actions taken

Where there is a will there is a way

"I see an opportunity in any challenge; the key is planning, flexibility, and teamwork", comments Ahmed Abdel-Meguid, Assistant Professor of

Accounting and PRME contact person for BUS. With the executive support of Sherif Kamel, Dean of the School of Business, Professor Abdel-Meguid led a very committed team that had one main objective: to deliver an event that matched the gravity of the local and regional transformations. This was achieved by:

- Extensive correspondence with regional schools of business to increase the awareness of PRME among academic institutions and how PRME extends their roles vis-à-vis communities beyond providing education and research.
- Engaging different stakeholders, including faculty, deans, students, executives, NGOs, representatives and others as a build-up for an inclusive dialogue during the forum.
- Recruiting many international speakers from various regions and backgrounds including those associated with PRME signatories to showcase their experiences with potential signatories.

The 1st PRME MENA Regional Forum: "Entrepreneurship – Sustainability – Transparency: Promoting Responsible Management in a Changing Region"

The forum was attended by various stakeholders including deans of business schools, academic faculty, students, entrepreneurs, NGO representatives, and corporate executives. Presentations were delivered by more than 40 speakers from 10 different countries: Egypt, Germany, the Netherlands, Jordan, Lebanon, Nigeria, Qatar, Spain, Turkey, and the United States during 6 sessions. Such numbers and geographical and technical diversity were unprecedented in prior PRME regional meetings worldwide. Throughout the two days of the forum, timely topics such as responsible entrepreneurship, integrating responsible management in executive education, effective student engagement, matching academic efforts with corporate demands, and means of deterring corruption were discussed.

The forum also generated awareness of PRME, as evidenced by the increase in the number of schools that expressed interest in becoming signatories, including two from the United Arab Emirates, five from Egypt, and one from Morocco. In addition, as per a proposal of the School, the PRME Secretariat has agreed that BUS take the lead to establish a PRME Chapter MENA.

It is worth mentioning that the forum was supported by the Arab African International Bank, as the platinum sponsor, and The Bakery Shop, as the entrepreneurial sponsor. The forum was held in partnership with the PRME Secretariat, the Arab Society of Faculties of Business, Economics and Political Sciences (BEPS), the Holy Spirit University of Kaslik (USEK), and the John D. Gerhart Centre for Philanthropy and Civic Engagement at AUC. In addition, Endeavour Egypt recruited several of its mentors as speakers at the forum.

Why PRME is/was important

The AUC School of Business believes that PRME is important, because it is:

- **inclusive**, encouraging various stakeholders to engage in constructive dialogue that aims at creating more sustainable communities;
- **timely**, highlighting the adverse effects of today's less tolerable incidents of corporate malfeasance, while providing a framework for sharing solutions;
- **flexible**, being implementable, in one form or another and on any scale, by any institution that is committed to having a positive impact on its community.

The International Corporate Responsibility Conference (CR^{3+})

THE POWER OF RESPONSIBILITY: MAKING A POSITIVE DIFFERENCE

Introduction and Challenges

 Having been among the first business schools in their countries to sign up to PRME, Audencia Nantes School of Management (France), Hanken School of Economics in Helsinki (Finland) and ISAE/FGV in Curitiba (Brazil) decided to cooperate in their implementation of the Principles for Responsible Management Education (PRME). Several concrete projects in research and teaching between members of the faculty have been conducted, leading to publications in several academic journals. Faculty members from the three schools have taught in corporate responsibility (CR) classes at the other schools, focusing on the comparative dimension. Furthermore, students from Audencia have spent a semester at ISAE/FGV to follow courses and get involved in a local social economy project. These activities in particular led to the joint organisation of an international conference on Corporate Responsibility, named (CR^3), held at Hanken School of Economics in April 2011. With the contributions of additional PRME signatories, including La Trobe University (Australia), the group has become an extended CR^{3+} network.

Actions taken

The theme of the first CR^3 conference was "the power of responsibility". Its purpose was to generate thought leadership in terms of powerful CR actions that contribute to make a positive difference, as well as aspects of CR practice that are problematic, including in terms of power relations and power effects. This conference was conceived of as a meeting space where it was possible to exchange scholarly views from different geographical locations, academic disciplines, and ideological positions.

Most contributions were aimed specifically at one of eight streams:

1. Articulating the political role of business through CR: paradigm shift or business as usual?
2. Responsible management education: beyond complacency and contestation.
3. Business NGO relations: power, challenges and opportunities.
4. CR and the BOP (base/bottom of the pyramid): empowering the poor while exploiting new markets?
5. CR in the supply chain.
6. Differences within and/or outside organisations: diversity as corporate social responsibility.
7. Great expectations: stakeholder engagement for global responsibility.
8. Social responsibility investors: How do they use their power? How can corporate responsibility respond to SRI power?

One stream was specifically devoted to responsible management education, and most other streams addressed the role of different stakeholders of businesses and management schools. The streams were co-convened by faculty members from the three schools and from other universities – notably La Trobe University, now involved in the extended CR^{3+} network. The organisation of the streams was thus a further opportunity for faculty members to cooperate and learn about each other's research.

The thought leader who kicked off the event with a memorable keynote speech was Professor Guido Palazzo (himself very much involved in PRME implementation at HEC Lausanne (Switzerland). This event was open to all the key stakeholders of Hanken School of Economics, notably students and alumni, but also partner organisations, such as companies, NGOs and the media. At the end of the conference, after all the sessions of the academic streams had been completed, there was another plenary session with a panel discussion on art and global responsibility, involving academics from the partner schools as well as a Finnish company that provides facilitation through art, and a dance artist and choreographer. This provided the opportunity to broaden the discussion to a societal level.

The CR^{3+} has led to enhanced awareness of responsibility across subjects within each School, as conveners from four different subjects (management and organisation, marketing, supply chain management and corporate geography, and politics and business) were involved, and streams related to finance and law were convened by faculty members from partner schools.

Results

The importance of the CR^{3+} conferences lies in scholars having the chance of coming together to share their knowledge and experience. It has also developed a deeper relationship between Hanken and La Trobe University, as one of Hanken's master's students travelled to La Trobe from July to December 2011, to learn more about their PRME practices and participate in the first community development project at the School. The idea was to pilot this exchange and build up a partnership between the universities where students can, as a part of their exchange studies, participate in an internship in the field of CR. In turn, Hanken has been inspired to develop an internship for students interested in CR.

In addition to this, Hanken recruited a variety of students interested in participating in the stream sessions and conference activities to assist with conference operations. Further, the keynote speech was open for attendance by all students at Hanken. The students have subsequently done a great job of informing their networks about both the CR^3 event and PRME activity at Hanken. Since the conference, they have been actively involved in transforming the Net Impact club into Hanken Social Impact to support PRME activities at Hanken and students interested in the field.

Within Hanken, the conference has not only raised awareness around the work, research and activities around CR, but it has further strengthened the partner universities' leadership, not only within the CR field, but also as inspirational role models for the implementation of PRME.

Future CR^{3+} conferences

Future CR^{3+} conferences will be arranged by Audencia Nantes School of Management (France) in 2012 as a part of the RIODD (Le Réseau international de recherche sur les Organisations et le Développement Durable/Research on Organisations and Sustainable Development) Conference. In addition, plans are made to arrange CR^{3+} conferences at ISAE/ FGV in Curitiba, Brazil in 2013 and La Trobe University in Melbourne, Australia in 2014. The conference facilitates networking processes within the PRME learning community as well as the exchange of ideas based upon the principles of corporate sustainability and responsibility in general.

APPENDIX 1: THE SIX PRINCIPLES OF THE PRINCIPLES FOR RESPONSIBLE MANAGEMENT EDUCATION

As institutions of higher education involved in the development of current and future managers we declare our willingness to progress in the implementation, within our institution, of the following Principles, starting with those that are more relevant to our capacities and mission. We will report on progress to all our stakeholders and exchange effective practices related to these principles with other academic institutions:

Principle 1

Purpose: We will develop the capabilities of students to be future generators of sustainable value for business and society at large and to work for an inclusive and sustainable global economy.

Principle 2

Values: We will incorporate into our academic activities and curricula the values of global social responsibility as portrayed in international initiatives such as the United Nations Global Compact.

Principle 3

Method: We will create educational frameworks, materials, processes and environments that enable effective learning experiences for responsible leadership.

Principle 4

Research: We will engage in conceptual and empirical research that advances our understanding about the role, dynamics, and impact of corporations in the creation of sustainable social, environmental and economic value.

Principle 5

Partnership: We will interact with managers of business corporations to extend our knowledge of their challenges in meeting social and environmental responsibilities and to explore jointly effective approaches to meeting these challenges.

Principle 6

Dialogue: We will facilitate and support dialogue and debate among educators, students, business, government, consumers, media, civil society organisations and other interested groups and stakeholders on critical issues related to global social responsibility and sustainability.

We understand that our own organisational practices should serve as an example of the values and attitudes we convey to our students.

APPENDIX 2: THE TEN PRINCIPLES OF THE UNITED NATIONS GLOBAL COMPACT

The United Nations Global Compact's Ten Principles in the areas of human rights, labour, the environment and anti-corruption enjoy universal consensus and are derived from:

- The Universal Declaration of Human Rights
- The International Labour Organization's Declaration on Fundamental Principles and Rights at Work
- The Rio Declaration on Environment and Development
- The United Nations Convention Against Corruption

The UN Global Compact asks companies to embrace, support and enact, within their sphere of influence, a set of core values in the areas of human rights, labour standards, the environment and anti-corruption:

Human Rights
- **Principle 1:** Businesses should support and respect the protection of internationally proclaimed human rights; and
- **Principle 2:** make sure that they are not complicit in human rights abuses.

Labour
- **Principle 3:** Businesses should uphold the freedom of association and the effective recognition of the right to collective bargaining;
- **Principle 4:** the elimination of all forms of forced and compulsory labour;
- **Principle 5:** the effective abolition of child labour; and
- **Principle 6:** the elimination of discrimination in respect of employment and occupation.

Environment
- **Principle 7:** Businesses should support a precautionary approach to environmental challenges;

- **Principle 8:** undertake initiatives to promote greater environmental responsibility; and
- **Principle 9:** encourage the development and diffusion of environmentally friendly technologies.

Anti-Corruption
- **Principle 10:** Businesses should work against corruption in all its forms, including extortion and bribery.

APPENDIX 3: CO-EDITOR BIOGRAPHIES

The PRME Secretariat would like to extend special thanks to the co-editors and their institutions.

Manuel Escudero (Chair) is Director-General of Deusto Business School, University of Deusto, and Special Adviser to the PRME Secretariat. Previously, he served as Head of the PRME Secretariat from its inception in 2007 until June 2010.

Laura Albareda is Assistant Professor of Sustainability Strategy at Deusto Business School, University of Deusto, and Lead Researcher of the Deusto Global Center for Sustainable Business. She has been Postdoctoral Fellow at the Carroll School of Management of Boston College and Visiting Researcher at Boston College Center for Corporate Citizenship. From 2000 to 2008, she held the post of Research Fellow at the Institute for Social Innovation at ESADE.

Jose M. Alcaraz is the Research Director of Barna Business School (part of the IESE Business School network in Latin America). He currently holds the Vicini Chair of Sustainability and also researches for the UN-supported initiative PRME.

Giselle Weybrecht is author of The Sustainable MBA: The Manager's Guide to Green Business and a writer, speaker, lecturer and consultant on sustainability issues within management education. She also writes the PRiMEtime blog, a joint initiative with the PRME Secretariat.

Merrill Csuri is Coordinator at the PRME Secretariat and served as project manager for the Guide.

APPENDIX 4: CASE STORY CONTRIBUTORS

The PRME Secretariat would like to thank all contributors of the case stories included in this Guide who, through their work, make PRME a thriving learning community:

- **Ahmed Abdel-Meguid**, Assistant Professor of Accounting, American University in Cairo (AUC) School of Business, Egypt
- **Poliana Reis Abreu**, Coordinator of Sustainability, Fundação Dom Cabral (FDC), Brazil
- **Laura Albareda**, Assistant Professor of Sustainability Strategy, Deusto Business School, University of Deusto, Spain
- **Felipe Alfonso**, former President, Asian Institute of Management, Philippines
- **G. "Anand" Anandalingam**, Dean, Robert H. Smith School, University of Maryland, United States
- **Jacqueline Andrews**, Skills and Development Manager, Nottingham University Business School, United Kingdom
- **Osmar Arandia**, Research Assistant, EGADE Business School, Mexico
- **Melsa Ararat**, Director, Carbon Disclosure Project (CDP), Director, Corporate Governance Forum (CGFT), Coordinator, IFC-GCGF Emerging Markets Research Network, Sabanci University, School of Management, Turkey
- **Norman Arruda Filho**, CEO, ISAE/FGV, Brazil
- **Serap Atakan**, Associate Professor, Faculty of Economics and Administrative Sciences, Istanbul Bilgi University, Turkey
- **Walter Baets**, Director of the Graduate School of Business, University of Cape Town, South Africa
- **Tina Bailey**, Associate Director, Centre for Responsible Leadership, Queen's School of Business, Canada
- **Maya Baltazar Herrera**, Research Director, RVR Center for Corporate Social Responsibility, Asian Institute of Management, Philippines

- **Viva Bartkus**, Associate Professor of Management, Mendoza College of Business, University of Notre Dame, United States
- **Paul Beamish**, Canada Research Chair in International Management, Donald L. Triggs Chair in International Business, Director, Ivey Publishing, Director, Centre for Engaging Emerging Markets Research, Richard Ivey School of Business, The University of Western Ontario, Canada
- **Jan Bentzen**, Professor, Department of Economics, Aarhus University, Business and Social Sciences, Denmark
- **Dianne Bevelander**, Associate Dean MBA Programmes, Rotterdam School of Management, Erasmus University, Netherlands
- **Eugenia Bieto**, Professor and General Director, ESADE Business School, Spain
- **Anthony F. Buono**, Professor of Management and Sociology, Coordinator, Bentley Alliance for Ethics and Social Responsibility, Bentley University, United States
- **Horacio Borromeo**, Associate Dean, Graduate School of Business, Asian Institute of Management, Philippines
- **Melissa Carrier**, Executive Director, Center for Social Value Creation, Robert H. Smith School, University of Maryland, United States
- **Jean-Christophe Carteron**, Director for Corporate Social Responsibility, Deputy Director for Corporate and Markets Directorate, Euromed Management, France
- **Gabriel Cecchini**, Coordinator Center for Governance and Transparency, IAE Business School, Universidad Austral, Argentina
- **Stephen Y. L. Cheung**, Dean, School of Business and Professor (Chair) of Finance, Hong Kong Baptist University, China
- **Marc Cohen**, Assistant Professor Business Ethics, Albers School of Business and Economics, Seattle University, United States
- **Michael Crooke**, Assistant Professor of Strategy, The Graziadio School of Business, Pepperdine University, United States
- **Fernando D'Alessio**, Director General, CENTRUM Cató31lica del Perú, Peru
- **Tina Dacin**, E. Marie Shantz Chair of Strategy & Organizational Behavior and Director, Centre for Responsible Leadership, Queen's School of Business, Canada
- **Margarita Ducci**, Dean, Communications Faculty, Universidad Andrés Bello, Chile

- **Barbara Dunin**, PRME Liaison, ISAE/FGV, Brazil
- **Manuel Escudero**, Special Adviser to the PRME Secretariat and Director-General, Deusto Business School, University of Deusto, Spain
- **Martin Fougère**, Assistant Professor in Politics and Business, Hanken School of Economics, Finland
- **Jesus Gallegos**, former Dean, Asian Institute of Management, Philippines
- **Consuelo García de La Torre**, Chair of Humanism and Management, EGADE Business School, Mexico
- **Tatiana Gherman**, Professor and Researcher, Center of Leadership, Innovation and Strategy, CENTRUM Católica del Perú, Peru
- **Rebecca Giese**, Coordinator, Sustainability Center, ISAE/FGV, Brazil
- **Tashina Giraud**, Sustainable Development Manager, Department of Corporate Social Responsibility, Euromed Management, France
- **Matthew Gitsham**, Director, Ashridge Centre for Business and Sustainability, Ashridge Business School
- **David Grayson**, Director, The Doughty Centre for Corporate Responsibility, Cranfield School of Management, Cranfield University, United Kingdom
- **Milenko Gudić**, IMTA Managing Director, CEEMAN –Central and East European Management Development Association, Slovenia
- **Dennis Hanno**, Dean, Undergraduate School, Babson College, United States
- **Christian Hauser**, Professor of Business Economics and International Management, Swiss Institute for Entrepreneurship (SIFE), University of Applied Sciences HTW Chur, Switzerland
- **Kai Hockerts**, Professor and Academic Director of Responsible Management Education, Copenhagen Business School, Denmark
- **Frank Horwitz**, Director, Cranfield School of Management, Cranfield University, United Kingdom
- **Pernille Kallehave**, Head of Development, Interdisciplinary Center for Organizational Architecture (ICOA) Consultant to the Dean (Sustainability), Aarhus University, Business and Social Sciences, Denmark
- **Sherif Kamel**, Dean, American University in Cairo (AUC) School of Business, Egypt

- **Tina Karme**, Project Coordinator, PRME and Study Module in Corporate Responsibility, Project Assistant, Department of Management and Organisation, Hanken School of Economics, Finland
- **Soo Jin Kim**, Project Manager, Office of the Dean and Executive Education, Mendoza College of Business, University of Notre Dame, United States
- **Matthias Kleinhempel**, Professor, IAE Business School, Universidad Austral, Argentina
- **Janek Kobylinski**, Professor and Researcher, Center of Leadership, Innovation and Strategy, CENTRUM Católica del Perú, Peru
- **Marcus B. Kreikebaum**, Service Learning Program Coordinator, European Business School (EBS), Germany
- **Harald Löhndorf**, Professor, Head Foreign Languages, Intercultural Trainer and Coach, University of Applied Sciences HTW Chur, Switzerland
- **Ricardo Lim**, Dean, Asian Institute of Management, Philippines
- **Vivienne Luk**, Director of Wing Lung Bank International Institute for Business Development (IIBD), School of Business, Hong Kong Baptist University, China
- **Ivo Macek**, General Secretary, University of Applied Sciences HTW Chur
- **Daniel Malan**, Senior Lecturer in Business Ethics and Corporate Governance, University of Stellenbosch Business School, South Africa
- **Mark Mallinger**, Professor of Applied Behavioral Science, The Graziadio School of Business, Pepperdine University, United States
- **Percy Marquina**, Academic Director, CENTRUM Católica del Perú, Peru
- **Ligia Coelho Martins**, Researcher, PRME Secretariat and Advisor, ISAE/FGV, Brazil
- **Malcolm McIntosh**, Professor and Director, Asia Pacific Centre for Sustainable Enterprise (APCSE), Griffith Business School, Griffith University, Australia
- **Jeremy Moon**, Professor and Director, International Centre for Corporate Social Responsibility, Nottingham University Business School, United Kingdom
- **Jorge Vinicio Murillo**, Project Manager, Latin American Center for Competitiveness and Sustainable Development (CLACDS), INCAE Business School, Costa Rica

- **F. Byron (Ron) Nahser**, Senior Wicklander Fellow, Institute for Business and Professional Ethics, DePaul University, Managing Director, CORPORANTES, Inc., United States
- **Loretta O'Donnell**, Associate Dean, Education, Australian School of Business, University of New South Wales, Australia
- **Carl Obermiller**, Professor of Marketing, Albers School of Business and Economics, Seattle University, United States
- **Stephen Yong-Seung Park**, Professor and Director, Institute for Peace through Commerce, Kyung Hee University School of Management, Korea
- **Carole Parkes**, Co Director Social Responsibility & Sustainability Aston Business School, Aston University, United Kingdom
- **Kai Peters**, Chief Executive, Ashridge Business School, United Kingdom
- **John Powell**, Director, University of Stellenbosch Business School, South Africa
- **Lawrence Pratt**, Director, Latin American Center for Competitiveness and Sustainable Development (CLACDS), INCAE Business School, Costa Rica
- **Lorenzo Preve**, Professor, IAE Business School, Universidad Austral, Argentina
- **Lydia J. Price**, Associate Dean, MBA Director, China Europe International Business School (CEIBS), China
- **Danica Purg**, President and Dean, IEDC-Bled School of Management, Slovenia
- **Donna Rapaccioli**, University Professor, Dean of Business Faculty and Dean of the College of Business Administration, Fordham University, United States
- **Bolesław Rok**, Assistant Professor, Business Ethics Centre, Kozminski University, Poland
- **Francisco Roman**, Executive Director, RVR CSR Center, Asian Institute of Management, Philippines
- **David M. Saunders**, Dean, Queen's School of Business, Canada
- **Lutz E. Schlange**, Professor of Entrepreneurial Marketing, PRME coordinator, University of Applied Sciences HTW Chur, Switzerland
- **Murray Silverman**, Professor of Management and Sustainable Business, Co-Director, Center for Ethical and Sustainable Business, College of Business, San Francisco State University, United States

- **André Sobczak**, Associate Dean for Research, Audencia Nantes School of Management, France
- **Nikodemus Solitander**, Lecturer in Supply Chain Management and Corporate Geography, Hanken School of Economics, Finland
- **Lene Mette Sørensen**, PRME Manager, CBS Centre for Corporate Social Responsibility (cbsCSR), Copenhagen Business School, Denmark
- **Ross Stewart**, Professor of Accounting, School of Business and Economics, Seattle Pacific University, United States
- **Andreas Suchanek**, Professor and Dr. Werner Jackstädt Chair of Economic and Business Ethics, HHL – Leipzig Graduate School of Management, Germany
- **Eappen Thiruvattal**, Assistant Professor, College of Business Administration, University of Dubai, United Arab Emirates
- **Mike J. Thompson**, Professor of Management Practice, Director of the Centre for Leadership and Responsibility (ECCLAR), China Europe International Business School (CEIBS), China
- **Gregory Unruh**, Director, Lincoln Center for Ethics, Thunderbird School of Global Management, United States
- **Antonino (Nino) Vaccaro**, Assistant Professor of Business Ethics, IESE Business School, University of Navarra
- **Carey Weiss**, Sustainability Initiatives Coordinator, Fordham University Schools of Business, United States
- **Patricia H. Werhane**, Wicklander Chair of Business Ethics and Director, Managing Director of the Institute for Business and Professional Ethics, DePaul University, Professor Emeritus at the University of Virginia, United States
- **Gregory Whitwell**, Deputy Dean, Programs and Students, Australian School of Business, University of New South Wales, Australia
- **Carolyn Woo**, former Martin J. Gillen Dean and Ray & Milann Siegfried Professor of Management, Mendoza College of Business, University of Notre Dame, United States
- **Suzanne Young**, Associate Professor, Department of Management, La Trobe Business School, La Trobe University, Australia
- **Nadya Zhexembayeva**, Coca-Cola Chair of Sustainable Development, IEDC-Bled School of Management, Slovenia

For Product Safety Concerns and Information please contact our EU
representative GPSR@taylorandfrancis.com Taylor & Francis Verlag GmbH,
Kaufingerstraße 24, 80331 München, Germany

Printed and bound by CPI Group (UK) Ltd, Croydon, CR0 4YY
08/05/2025
01864333-0001